Recent Developments in Post-Keynesian Economics

THE POST-KEYNESIAN ECONOMICS STUDY GROUP

The Post-Keynesian Economics Study Group was established in October 1988 with a grant from the Economic and Social Research Council to cover the travel expenses of participants. We have a meeting at least once a term, at which normally three papers are presented and discussed. The purpose of the Group is to provide a forum for the presentation and active criticism of research along post-Keynesian lines, to promote contact among those of similar views, and thereby to encourage still further research and dissemination of results amongst interested specialists.

Post-Keynesian economics has passed an important turning point in its maturity: its phase of critique of mainstream theory and of exegesis has established its foundation for a forward-looking development of the methods and insights of Keynes, Kalecki, Joan Robinson, Sraffa and Kaldor, for application to the understanding of modern economic processes. This development is now well underway and gathering strength, as the range of work available for presentation to the Group, the numbers attending and the liveliness of discussion attests.

In the first three years of the Group's existence, 45 papers have been presented. Ten of the papers are published in this volume, and all the others are published or forthcoming in journals or other volumes. We intend this volume to be the first of many. The Group continues in 1992 with renewed funding from the ESRC. We are also grateful for support from the Royal Economic Society and Edward Elgar Publishing.

E·S·R·C
ECONOMIC
& SOCIAL
RESEARCH
COUNCIL

Recent Developments in Post-Keynesian Economics

Edited by
Philip Arestis
Professor of Economics
Polytechnic of East London

and

Victoria Chick
Reader in Economics
University College London

for the Post-Keynesian Economics Study Group

Edward Elgar

Published by
Edward Elgar Publishing Limited
Gower House
Croft Road
Aldershot
Hants GU11 3HR
England

Edward Elgar Publishing Company
Old Post Road
Brookfield
Vermont 05036
USA

A CIP catalogue record for this book is available from the British Library

Library of Congress Cataloging-in-Publication Data
Recent developments in post-Keynesian economics/edited by Philip Arestis and Victoria Chick.
p. cm. — (Post-Keynesian Economics Study Group; 1)
Includes index.
1. Keynesian economics. I. Arestis, Philip, 1941– . II. Chick, Victoria. III. Series: Post-Keynesian Economics Study Group (Series); 1.
HB99.7.R43 1992
330.15′6—dc20 91–41165
CIP

ISBN 1 85278 412 1

Printed and bound in Great Britain by
Billing and Sons Ltd, Worcester

Contents

Notes on the Contributors

Philip Arestis is Professor of Economics and Head of Department of Applied Economics at the Polytechnic of East London. His research and publications are principally in the area of post-Keynesian economics. He has also researched and published in the areas of macroeconomics in general and monetary economics in particular, and applied econometrics. He is the author of *The Post-Keynesian Approach to Economics: An Alternative Analysis of Economic Theory and Policy* (forthcoming, Edward Elgar 1992), and the co-author of *Introducing Macroeconomic Modelling: An Econometric Study of the United Kingdom* (Macmillan 1982). He is currently serving as a member on a number of various editorial boards of economic journals.

Paul Auerbach is Reader in Economics at Kingston Polytechnic. He is the author of *Competition: The Economics of Industrial Change* (Blackwell 1988) and has published widely on the structure and functioning of both capitalist and planned economies.

Victoria Chick is Reader in Economics, University College London. She has taught at McGill University and the Universities of Southampton, Aarhus, Louvain, and California at Berkeley and Santa Cruz; and she has worked in research at the Reserve Bank of Australia and the Federal Reserve Bank of New York. She has published two books, *The Theory of Monetary Policy* (Blackwell 1973) and *Macroeconomics After Keynes: A Reconsideration of the General Theory* (MIT Press 1983), and numerous articles on monetary theory and Keynesian economics; a selection of these is soon to be published by Macmillan, edited by Philip Arestis and Sheila Dow. She is on the editorial board of two economic journals and the Council of the Royal Economic Society.

Richard Damania went to a lectureship in economics at Flinders University, South Australia, after taking his MA and PhD at the University of Glasgow. He and Douglas Mair have published together on the post-Keynesian theory of tax incidence in various journals.

Amitava Krishna Dutt is Professor of Economics at the University of

Notre Dame in Indiana. He is the author of *Growth, Distribution and Uneven Development* (CUP 1990) and co-author (with E.J. Amadeo) of *Keynes's Third Alternative? The Neo-Ricardian Keynesians and the Post Keynesians* (Edward Elgar 1990) and many scholarly articles. His current research is on macro-models of growth and distribution, post-Keynesian economics, classical political economy and North–South trade and uneven development.

Athol Fitzgibbons is Associate Professor of Economics at Griffith University, Queensland. After teaching economics at the University of Newcastle (NSW), the University of New South Wales and the University of Queensland, he joined the Commonwealth Public Service in Canberra as the head of a branch concerned with microeconomic reform. After some years there, Athol resigned from the public service to run a farm and read poetry, political philosophy and Plato. He has written a book and several papers on Australian economic policy and a book on Keynes's philosophy, *Keynes's Vision* (OUP 1988).

Bill Gerrard is Lecturer in Economics at the University of York. He was an industrial economist at Unilever and has also taught at the Universities of Leeds and Manitoba. His research and publications are principally in the areas of methodology, industrial economics, macroeconomics and applied econometrics. He has published *Theory of the Capitalist Economy: Towards a Post-Classical Synthesis* (Blackwell 1989) and two edited volumes, *The Philosophy and Economics of J.M. Keynes* (with John Hillard) (Edward Elgar 1992) and *The Economics of Rationality* (Routledge 1992).

Suzanne Helburn is Professor of Economics at the University of Colorado, Denver. Her work on Keynes includes 'Keynes's Research Program' in Helburn and Bramhall, eds, *Marx, Schumpeter, Keynes: A Centenary Celebration of Dissent* (M.E. Sharpe 1986) and 'Burke and Keynes' in Bateman and Davis, eds, *Keynes and Philosophy: Essays on the Origin of Keynes's Thought* (Edward Elgar 1991). She has also published extensively in the fields of economics education and the economics of child care.

Douglas Mair is Reader in Economics at Heriot-Watt University, Edinburgh. He co-authored *The Structure and Growth of the Scottish Economy* (Collins 1971) and has recently edited *The Scottish Contribution to Modern Economic Thought* (Aberdeen University Press 1990) and (with A.G. Miller) *A Modern Guide to Economic Thought* (Edward

Elgar 1991). He has written a number of papers on post-Keynesian theory of tax incidence with Richard Damania.

Jerzy Osiatyński is Professor of Economics at the Polish Academy of Sciences. He studied under Michał Kalecki in the 1960s. He has published a complete edition of Kalecki's works in Polish and prepared the English edition now being published by Oxford University Press. He has also published two books, *Capital, Distribution and Value: The Crisis of neo-Marginalist Economics* (Warsaw 1978, in Polish) and *Michał Kalecki on a Socialist Economy* (Macmillan 1988). He was Minister of Planning in the Mazowiecki government and remains a prominent member of the Polish Democratic Union party.

Peter Reynolds is Principal Lecturer in Economics at Staffordshire Polytechnic. He has published on various aspects of Kaleckian and post-Keynesian economics, particularly theories of pricing and income distribution. He has written a textbook in this area, *Political Economy: A Synthesis of Kaleckian and Post Keynesian Economics* (Wheatsheaf 1987). He is currently writing (with Peter Phelan) a book entitled *Argument and Evidence*.

Malcolm Sawyer is Professor of Economics at the University of Leeds. One of his areas of research is industrial economics, with particular emphasis on policy; his books in that area include *Theories of the Firm* (Weidenfeld and Nicolson 1979) and *Economics of Industries and Firms* (Croom Helm 1985). His major area of interest lies in the development of post-Keynesian economics, and in this area he has published *The Challenge of Radical Political Economy* (Harvester 1989), *The Economics of Michał Kalecki* (Macmillan 1985) and *Macro-economics in Question* (Wheatsheaf 1982). He has recently edited (with Philip Arestis) *A Biographical Dictionary of Dissenting Economists* (Edward Elgar 1992) and is the managing editor of *International Review of Applied Economics*.

Jan Toporowski is a former City economist who currently teaches industrial and financial economics at the Polytechnic of the South Bank. He wrote the introduction to Kalecki's *Essays on Economic Planning* (Cambridge University Press 1970) and is currently writing a biography of Kalecki.

Adrian Winnett is Lecturer in Economics at the University of Bath. He previously taught at the University of Bristol. Apart from his research interest in post-Keynesian monetary economics, he is writing a book (with Cathy Winnett) on the Romantic, especially Ruskinian, critique of political economy, which brings together his interest in the history of economic thought and his enthusiasm for Victorian architecture.

Introduction

Philip Arestis and Victoria Chick

This volume, the first of what we hope will be a long succession of volumes, presents a selection of papers delivered to meetings of the Post-Keynesian Economics Study Group (PKSG) in the first eighteen months of its existence. The PKSG is the most recent addition to the programme of Study Groups funded by the Economic and Social Research Council (ESRC), which began over twenty years ago with the Money Study Group. These groups bring together, from all over Britain, academics and others with similar research interests, their travelling expenses being paid by the ESRC. We acknowledge with gratitude the support both of the ESRC and of the Royal Economic Society.

It is often said of post-Keynesian economics that it is more easily identified by its opposition to neo-classical, mainstream economics than by its own distinctive alternative approach. The chapters in this book reflect the newer phase of its development, in which the alternative approach takes precedence over critique. This forward impetus is balanced by a concern for the history of economics. One of the distinctive features of post-Keynesian economics is its understanding that economic theory is rooted in history and institutions – that the historical conjuncture influences the formulation of theory even as economic theory and the policies which flow from it create new institutions and modes of economic behaviour. Thus we have included in the volume studies whose themes closely reflect recent changes in the economic scene: the rise of rentiers in a period of high real interest rates, the effect of a change in the basis of taxation on relative income shares, the interplay between market and plan, and relations between the first and third worlds.

Post-Keynesian economists do not reduce all economic behaviour to that of 'agents', the economists' equivalent of atoms. They are concerned with group interests and power and recognise that individual actions have, in aggregate, unexpected and unintended consequences. Hence importance is accorded to monopoly, the power to create credit and money, the macroeconomic and distributive effects of pricing, taxation and market structure, to name only those elements which are the concerns of a number of chapters in the volume.

In shaping the post-Keynesian alternative, fundamental questions of how one *ought* to proceed – that is, interpretative and methodological questions – remain high on the agenda. More recently, examination of the philosophical and ethical well-springs of economics is perhaps the area of most striking advance in post-Keynesian economics. These matters are the subject of the first three chapters in this volume.

In Chapter 1, Bill Gerrard seeks to establish the origins and draw the implications of Keynes's transcendence of the Cartesian mode of thought. The chapter is a contribution to the important recent research which seeks to ground Keynes's economics and politics in his early philosophical writings. But Gerrard argues that much work in this area, which he characterises as the 'new Keynesian fundamentalism', has become excessively scholastic, a style of analysis which Keynes himself repudiated.

Keynes's revolt against formalism is described as an escape from what could be called the Cartesian Vice. Keynes laid much stress on the vagueness of knowledge caused by uncertainty, complexity and the organic nature of the world. This is illustrated by reference to Keynes's adoption of Ramsey's distinction between formal logic and human logic. The implications for the new fundamentalist interpretation of Keynes are explored.

Keynes's own changing views on his early beliefs reveal that his escape is best interpreted within the general context of the revolt against formalism that characterised Cambridge thought in the first half of the twentieth century. The writings of Whitehead, Ramsey and Wittgenstein also show a movement away from the rationalist modes of thought which characterised their own earlier work.

The chapter concludes with a discussion of the methodological implications of Keynes's transcendence of Cartesianism. In particular it is argued that Keynes rejected excessive reliance on deductivism. In contrast to Friedman's methodological views, Keynes argued for the need to choose realistic assumptions, a method of analysis similar to that argued for by the behavioural school (for example, Herbert Simon's notion of bounded rationality). Keynes's methodology is considered with particular reference to his attitude to classical theory and his critique of the use of the mathematical method. Thus Keynes's thought is seen to be suggestive of an attitude of mind which embraces an awareness of the fallibility of human knowledge, the need for pluralism and a tolerance of differences. Such an attitude of mind provides a middle way between dogmatism and scepticism and overcomes the 'paralysis of uncertainty'.

In Chapter 2, Athol Fitzgibbons continues the theme of Keynes's economic philosophy. He argues that many of the supposed defects of what passes for 'Keynesian economics' arise out of a failure to appreciate Keynes's philosophy and analytical method.

This chapter briefly outlines some of the problems of Keynesianism, which are political as well as theoretical, and then describes the philosophy on which Keynes based his economics. The virtual disappearance of that philosophy from the modern world has cut Keynes off, but when his wider system is reconstructed, there is a more satisfying logic in his economic theory than when his theory is described in scientific and politically neutral terms.

The evolution of Keynes's philosophy is traced through the early writings to the *Treatise on Probability* and the *Economic Consequences of the Peace*, and from there to the methodological consequences of his later work. The advantage of an historical development is that it gives a good insight into Keynes's theory of uncertainty and his monetary economics. It is also the best way to understand how he reconciled his belief in the principle of change with his long-run Utopian ideals. In his Bloomsbury youth and under the apprenticeship of the Cambridge philosopher G.E. Moore, Keynes analysed the duality of probabilistic knowledge and higher Ideals, and these still operate in the background in his later work. Both his theory of probability and his idealism have generally been ignored, but they deeply inform the theoretical method of his economics.

In methodological terms Keynes did not regard economics as a science in the usual sense but as an aspect of practical political life. The economy did not possess invariant mechanical regularities; rather, understanding it required practical wisdom and judgement guided by more general values, as the context allowed. That was the method the *General Theory* was based upon, but the 'Keynesians' could not understand the *General Theory* without turning it into a mechanical system. There is, therefore, a theoretical paradox at the heart of 'Keynesian' economics.

Suzanne Helburn's 'On Keynes's Ethics' is a step towards restoring the conception of economics as a moral science. She addresses two questions raised in recent interpretations of Keynes's ethics: the extent and form of egoism present in his ethics, and the adequacy of categorising him as a utilitarian, or as an act-consequentialist. Like Fitzgibbons, she argues for the primacy of the influence of the ancient Greek philosophers, Plato and Aristotle, over the nineteenth-century

Cambridge utilitarians, Henry Sidgwick and G.E. Moore, on the development of Keynes's moral philosophy. Helburn examines the hypothesis that Keynes was deeply critical of the utilitarian approach to ethics, which reduces ethical considerations to a single principle to permit comparisons. She finds evidence that Keynes gravitated to an ethic which emphasised individual character development, which legitimises a form of egoism.

Helburn traces Keynes's criticisms of *Principia Ethica*, beginning with his early observation that Moore's analysis had 'reduced us to moral impotence'. She knows how Keynes set about re-establishing our moral powers in a series of arguments which legitimise egoism by moving towards an ethics of virtue. In another, undated but still early, essay he argues that dispositions of character are desirable for their own sake, and that restricting judgements of intrinsic value to states of mind (as he argues Moore does) drives us, 'more than we actually are, to egotism'. There is a consistent development over three or four years of Keynes's position about what ends we are obligated to pursue. Starting from Moore's ideal utilitarian position that the greatest goods are certain states of consciousness related to appreciation of beauty and the pleasure of friendship, Keynes moves to a fuller description of character traits and states of affairs which are just and harmonious. One's obligation is to develop ethical dispositions; ends and means are not so clearly distinguished as they are in utilitarian morality.

An examination of Chapter 26 of the *Treatise on Probability* is then brought to bear to dispute O'Donnell's designation of Keynes's ethics as a form of probabilistic act-consequentialism. Keynes held that rational decisions about future actions depend on intuition at each crucial point of the decision-making process so that mere technical, that is mathematical, comparison of alternatives is usually not justified. The quality of judgement depends on the quality of intuition. Rational (and moral) action involves a continuous process of trying to achieve the best result (a moving target) under the circumstances. Thus it is motives rather than outcomes which are important. Getting the best solution requires both intellectual powers and the will to see a project through to the most successful conclusion possible. Categorising Keynes as an act-consequentialist detracts from this central feature of his ethics.

Finally, Helburn shows consistency in Keynes's early and later ethical position as stated in 'My Early Beliefs'. Keynes's sense of duty was governed by inner dispositions rather than by external moral expectations. This interpretation makes sense of his statement that he and his fellow-Apostles were immoralists.

In Chapter 4, Adrian Winnett opposes the reductionist approach to monetary theory. An assumption of money supply endogeneity has become almost an article of faith in much post-Keynesian monetary theory. Winnett criticises some versions of this assumption, particularly those which attempt to attribute special significance to the shape of money supply functions as a distinguishing feature of post-Keynesian as against neo-classical monetary theory. Money is a complex social institution, and understanding of this complexity is ill-served by such reductionist assumptions.

The origins and role of the endogeneity assumption in, first, the critique of the quantity theoretic foundations of monetarism, and, secondly, non-neo-classical models of the pricing process, are considered. It is pointed out that, in both cases, analytical reliance is placed on the parametrisation of the money interest rate, and endogeneity is really a justificatory assumption for this.

Winnett then focuses on three questions. First, there is the alleged endogeneity of credit as against the exogeneity of commodity and fiat money; it is suggested that this argument represents a failure to think about endogeneity/exogeneity in terms of the appropriate decision variables of the actors in different sorts of monetary regime. In the case of fiat money, especially, this points to the need to expand the model space to consider 'non-economic' variables, and maybe to privilege historical understanding over formal modelling altogether.

A somewhat similar conclusion emerges from consideration of the second question: the functioning of the banking system in the standard mark-up model of credit-money endogeneity. It is argued that this is a naive model of a complex, regulated oligopoly, particularly when considering the interactions between commercial financial institutions and policy-makers. Thirdly, the dependence on social convention of the classes of asset regarded as money is examined. The asset composition of money is usually regarded as an empirical matter; here it is argued that this view is symptomatic of the inability of neo-classical economics to think about social relationships other than in terms of atomistic commodities. Winnett follows Keynes in focusing on the primacy of the abstract unit-of-account aspect of money, particularly as sustained by conventions surrounding the money wage rate, which confer a strategic role on the money rate of interest. This approach goes well beyond simply treating the rate of interest as a parameter, as in the standard endogeneity arguments.

In conclusion, the case is made for the fruitfulness of the analogy between money and language, as social institutions having dimensions of both conventional structure and evolutionary process.

Malcolm Sawyer's central purpose, in Chapter 5, is to consider the contributions of the four major originators of post-Keynesian pricing theories, roughly half a century after their publications. The authors discussed are Means, Kalecki, Hall and Hitch, and Sweezy. They are to some degree considered in chronological order, but also by the extent of their departure from orthodoxy.

Sawyer shows that each of these authors made quite distinct contributions, which should not be pushed together. Also, orthodox economists tended to place a price rigidity interpretation on their work, which interacted with a similar interpretation of the work of Keynes. Yet, with the possible exception of Means, their work (as that of Keynes) does not support a price-rigidity interpretation.

The contribution of Means is seen to be threefold: first, the distinction between market-dominated and administration-dominated prices; second, the removal of the auctioneer in administration-dominated pricing; and third, the relative stability of prices in the face of demand variations.

Kalecki retained the pursuit of profits and a loose form of profit maximisation as the objective of firms, though the working assumption of constant administration-dominated costs was reinforced by difficulties of exact calculation by firms. He introduced the distinction between cost-determined and demand-determined prices, which Sawyer argues is superior to the flex-price/fix-price dichotomy with which it has been confused. The key contribution of Kalecki is seen here as the idea that the real product wage is set in the product market rather than the labour market.

Sweezy developed the perceived ('imagined') demand curve. There are indications that his theory was based on interviews with business people. Whilst Sweezy clearly sought to provide an explanation for price stickiness, this was an explanation based on the decisions made by firms and not imposed upon them. Further, he clearly indicated that firms will seek to supply the demand forthcoming at the price which they set.

Hall and Hitch cast doubt on the general applicability of the conventional analysis of price and output pricing in terms of marginal cost and marginal revenue. They raised questions of what is meant by marginal revenue and marginal cost (for example, over what time span?), and the nature of demand curve (actual or perceived). Prices were seen as set by the application of a rule of thumb, labelled 'full-cost' pricing. Price–cost margins are then seen as relatively stable, but not prices (unless costs are also stable).

Sawyer concludes with the observation that any price inflexibility which may be involved in these theories (with the possible exception of Means) derives from endogenous stability rather than imposed rigidity.

The significance of endogenous stability is quite different from that of imposed rigidity.

Chapter 6 is also concerned with pricing policy. Jerzy Osiatyński traces the development of the relation between price and the degree of monopoly in Kalecki's theory. Kalecki's macroeconomic theory was designed to explain economic growth and specifically the business cycle, which Kalecki saw as an intrinsic feature of a mature capitalist economy. Formally it is independent of his microeconomics: Kalecki's theory of price and the distribution of national income between wages and profits, since total output does not depend on prices and distribution, nor do prices and distribution depend on aggregate output. But the key determinants of aggregate output and growth lie in the expenditure decisions of capitalist firms, and Kalecki is unique in providing a microeconomic theory which he sought to refine and make consistent with his macroeconomics.

In this chapter, four successive models of prices and distribution are presented. In all of them a key assumption is that firms operate at less than full capacity. But in the earliest models (1929–38), there is a rising marginal cost curve, prices are determined by competition, and the relative share of wages in national income is fixed. This was the basis on which Kalecki criticised the pre-Keynesian policy of promoting a general reduction in wages in order to increase employment. Subsequently (1938–9) Kalecki modified this model to introduce the notions of imperfect competition that he came across in his research in Poland and in Cambridge. He then proposed that marginal costs are approximately constant up to the point where output reaches full capacity utilisation, and he assumed that firms seek to maximise profits.

But in this second model, Lerner's degree of monopoly, which Kalecki adopted, turns out to be merely the inverse of the price elasticity of demand, and there are problems in aggregating this for the economy as a whole. Kalecki therefore proposed a third model in 1939 and 1940. This time he had oligopolistic firms setting prices according to those of their competitors, while still seeking to maximise profits. Here again Kalecki found that it was not possible to avoid ambiguity about the role of the price elasticity of demand and arbitrariness in defining industrial boundaries. Kalecki quickly abandoned this approach, and from 1943 he held to a microeconomics in which he distinguished between services and manufacturing, whose prices are fixed by firms in those sectors, and the primary industries in which prices are demand-determined, while uncertainty causes firms to avoid adherence to any particular form of profit maximisation.

This theory still leaves certain gaps and apparent inconsistencies. The new notion of degree of monopoly has been held by some to be somewhat vague, stretching to include the political power of capitalists, and there are aggregation problems with it. But it remains in general a sound foundation for a critical alternative to contemporary pre-Keynesian economics.

Amitava Dutt, in Chapter 7, 'Rentiers in Post-Keynesian Models', examines the role of the rentier class, defined as the class which obtains its income from interest, in the economy using post-Keynesian models of accumulation and distribution. The models considered belong to the post-Keynesian tradition in the sense that they emphasise the importance of class distinctions, effective demand, uncertainty, and the endogeneity of credit money at an interest rate determined exogenously by power relations between different groups.

The models consider a closed economy producing one commodity with labour, capital and a fixed-coefficients technology. Workers earn only wage income and are in unlimited supply, rentiers earn interest from bank deposits, and capitalists earn the surplus income. Wage earners do not save, while rentiers and capitalists save fixed proportions of their income. Banks borrow from rentiers and lend to firms; the central bank stands ready as a lender of last resort. Firms produce at full capacity if there is sufficient demand, or produce according to demand at a price given in the short run. They make investment plans based on the rate of profit, the real rate of interest and the rate of capacity utilisation. Over time the money wage responds positively to the gap between the real wage and the wage firms wish to pay if there is excess capacity, or according to the excess demand gap if there is full capacity. In the short run the wage, price, capital stock and rentier wealth are fixed, while in the long run they change, implying changes in the real wage and the rentier share in capital.

Two models are analysed in turn: one with excess capacity and the other with full capacity utilisation. In the model with excess capacity in the short run output adjusts to clear the goods market. In the long run, with the desired real wage of workers responding to labour-market pressures, the market is stable if the saving rate of capitalists is higher than that of rentiers; but if the rentiers have a higher saving rate, the economy will be balanced on a knife-edge: either the rentier share in capital will eventually diminish and the rate of capital accumulation and the wage share in income will increase, or the rentier class will dominate, with adverse consequences for accumulation and distribution. In the model with full capacity utilisation with desired accumulation greater than saving, actual accumulation will be savings-determined. In the long run the stability of the model depends on the speed at which the real wage adjusts to the propensities of capitalists and the rentiers; if the rentiers have a higher propensity to save, greater wage flexibility is stabilising, whereas the opposite is true when capitalists have a higher saving propensity. The implications of changes in the interest rate are also examined.

Richard Damania and Douglas Mair turn their attention to the incidence of taxation in Chapter 8. Their specific problem is to model the effects of substituting a poll tax for a property tax. In neo-classical economics, tax incidence is concerned with the effects of a fiscal change on the distribution of private real incomes viewed from either the 'sources of income' side or the 'uses of income' side, whereas post-Keynesian theory argues that the macroeconomic effects of broad-based taxes cannot be ignored. The theory of income distribution underpinning neo-classical tax incidence theory is marginal productivity theory, and are generally developed on the assumptions of full employment and fully competitive product and factor markets. The post-Keynesian model presented in this chapter can accommodate conditions of less than full employment and can operate under oligopoly.

The neo-classical theory of the incidence of the property tax is examined and is demonstrated to be suffering from a number of theoretical shortcomings which render it suspect as a theoretical basis from which to establish the burden of either a property tax or a poll tax. The neo-classical 'traditional' and 'new' views of property tax incidence are compared and a number of limitations are identified.

An alternative post-Keynesian theory of tax incidence, based on a 1937 paper of Kalecki as expanded and developed by Asimakopulos and Burbidge, is presented. This short-period model examines the macroeconomic effects of substitutions between a profits tax, a consumption tax, a tax on wage income and a tax on rentier income and is here extended to include a property tax and a poll tax. Two variants of the model are presented, identifying effects on prices, consumption, savings and the level of employment under competitive conditions and under oligopoly. The model predicts that the short-period effects of substituting a poll tax for a property tax under oligopolistic conditions will be to reduce profits, workers' consumption and the level of output or employment but to increase rentiers' consumption.

In Chapter 9, Paul Auerbach looks at the market mechanism. He argues that the 'market' and the 'plan' are traditionally offered up in the literature as alternative and opposing methods of economic governance. According to one tradition stretching from Engels to John Kenneth Galbraith, the use of the market mechanism in the twentieth century has been giving way to the predominance of those 'islands of planning' to be found within the giant firms of capitalism. Planning, according to this school, involves a series of technical and administrative mechanisms which have a logic of their own and substitute for market co-ordination.

An alternative, free-market approach has, curiously enough, a great deal in common with the planning school. For free-market advocates such as Ronald Coase, the firm (an administrative entity) only exists when the costs of using the market are too high. Implicitly, in this approach 'markets' are always in existence in a ubiquitous manner to serve as alternatives to administrative co-ordination (planning).

In truth, however, the separation made between the market and the plan is a false one. In the modern world there is little indication that modern economies are being progressively dominated by ever more planned, vertically integrated enterprises. The development of planning and ever more sophisticated forms of managerial co-ordination continue to be complemented by the growth and enrichment of markets in goods and services.

The planning approach fails to note that rational planning under capitalism has never been a purely technical problem of co-ordination, but has taken place in the context of competitive pressures and a consideration of the market alternatives available to the firm. On the other hand, the free-market approach fails to see the crucial role of planning and administrative co-ordination in the creation and expansion of markets.

Improvements in planning techniques, therefore, may result in the appearance not only of larger, more sophisticated administrative entities (vertically integrated firms), but in an enhancement of the role of markets as well, as the actions of individual firms enrich individual markets and create new ones. The emergence of the multinational corporation after the Second World War is often seen as a victory for 'internalisation' – a vertically integrated mode of behaviour dominating the use of market relationships. In fact, this flood of multinational activity was complemented by an equal expansion in international trade; present-day multinationals can make greater use of the market – can perform using less vertically integrated structures – precisely because the activities of *other* firms and multinationals have created markets for the services they wish to use.

The traditional dichotomy between planning and the market is, therefore, part of a more complex relationship. The simultaneous growth in the modern world of both richer markets and more sophisticated planning must be seen in the context of the fact that these alternative modes of governance are not merely rivals, but are complementary in their development.

In Chapter 10, Peter Reynolds explores some issues associated with the international co-ordination of macroeconomic policies in a world economy consisting of an industrialised core and a periphery producing primary products. Price changes in the industrial sector are largely cost-determined while primary-sector prices respond more directly to changes in demand.

Expansion and recession in the industrial (core) countries affect the prices of commodities produced in the periphery, and periphery incomes. These effects feed back on the industrial countries in a potentially destabilising way, which policy co-ordination between the industrial countries makes worse. The argument also takes account of the effects of changes in interest rates on the ability of less developed countries to maintain debt repayments.

The relationship between the rates of expansion of industrial production in individual countries and the rate of growth of world industrial production as a whole is examined by considering the effects of changes in the degree of international macroeconomic synchronisation on the cyclical pattern of world industrial production and hence on the behaviour of commodity prices. It follows that inflationary pressures will be at their greatest when domestic expansion is accompanied by the expansion of world industrial production as a whole. Conversely, if lower economic activity or restrictive monetary policies in the developed countries have indirect effects on their industrial output *via* the income of primary producers, then synchronised recession along with high interest rates in the developed countries could have a self-reinforcing impact far more damaging on output in both world sectors than many economists would believe. The greater the degree of synchronisation, the greater will be the recessionary impact. Comparing the period 1960–71 with the period 1972–88, it is apparent that the later period, which experienced much more volatile behaviour in commodity prices, was also characterised by an increase in the extent to which the major industrial countries experienced synchronisation in their business cycles.

Some very tentative policy conclusions include support for schemes directed at commodity price stabilisation, along with recognition that one route towards greater stability may be to reduce the extent to which macroeconomic policies are synchronised internationally. Secondly, the return to a regime of fixed exchange rates is supported, but paying due consideration to the arguments advanced, by both Keynes in the

1940s and Kaldor more recently, for the establishment of an adequately funded agency responsible for the stability of commodity prices.

We could not finish this introduction without expressing our thanks to the members of the Study Group, whose enthusiastic support has been invaluable, and to the authors in this volume, for their chapters and also for refereeing each other's work. Finally, but not least, we are extremely grateful to Edward Elgar and his colleagues for their support and encouragement, not only in the production of this book but more generally in our efforts to promote post-Keynesian ideas.

1. Human Logic in Keynes's Thought: Escape from the Cartesian Vice

Bill Gerrard

I INTRODUCTION

In recent years there has been a resurgence of interest in the life and work of John Maynard Keynes. One important aspect of this resurgence is the emergence of a new wave of Keynesian fundamentalism associated with Carabelli (1988), Fitzgibbons (1988) and O'Donnell (1989) amongst others. The 'old' Keynesian fundamentalism of Robinson (1964) and Shackle (1967) viewed Keynes's revolutionary break from orthodox economics as being rooted in his treatment of uncertainty and expectations. These earlier writers saw Chapter 12 of the *General Theory* on the nature of long-term expectations as containing 'Keynes's ultimate meaning' (Shackle, Ch. 11). This interpretation of Keynes has much in the way of supporting textual evidence. In particular Keynes chose to highlight expectations and uncertainty in his *QJE* 1937 summary of the *General Theory*, accusing orthodox theory of being 'one of those pretty polite techniques which tries to deal with the present by abstracting from the fact that we know very little about the future' (*JMK* XIV: 115). The point of departure for the 'new' Keynesian fundamentalism is the attempt to show that the origins of the revolutionary aspects of Keynes's economics can be traced back to his early philosophical writings.

The new Keynesian fundamentalism is making an important contribution to the understanding of Keynes's thought by shedding light on aspects which have been much neglected in the past. However, many economists, even among those of a post-Keynesian persuasion, who are most likely to be sympathetic, are left cold by this new fundamentalism, which they consider to be of purely academic interest with no practical relevance. There is some justification in their concerns. The problem with much of the new fundamentalism is that it has become infected by the excessive scholasticism of the early Keynes. There is a need to view Keynes's early philosophical thought with the same attitude as Keynes himself came to adopt in his later writings. Keynes retained the essential elements of his early philosophical beliefs throughout his life, but he came to see their limitations. In particular Keynes's later perspective was laden with experiences; he became more practically-minded, seeing his early beliefs as too rationalistic. The new Keynesian fundamentalism will only make a significant contribution to the understanding of human behaviour if it approaches Keynes's early beliefs in the spirit of the later Keynes. This is the approach of the present chapter, which deals with some of the meta-theoretical themes in Keynes's thought. The aim is a practical one. It is argued that these themes are suggestive of an attitude of mind and methods of enquiry appropriate to those actively seeking an alternative to mainstream economics.

The structure of the chapter is as follows. Section II outlines the rationalist mode of thought and its limitations with particular reference to the Cambridge revolt against formalism of which Keynes was part. Section III considers Keynes's own revolt against formalism as recorded in his essay 'My Early Beliefs'. Sections IV–VI deal with specific aspects of Keynes's move beyond formalistic analyses. Particular emphasis is put on the vagueness of knowledge (Section IV), the limitations of the mathematical method (Section V), and Ramsey's distinction between formal logic and human logic (Section VI). Section VII provides some conclusions, arguing for the need to adopt a particular 'Keynesian' attitude of mind.

II THE REVOLT AGAINST FORMALISM

Keynes's revolt against formalism can be viewed as an escape from the grip of what could be termed the Cartesian Vice. By the Cartesian Vice is meant an approach to knowledge that is purely rational and contemplative in nature. Descartes formulated the rationalist approach in reaction to the scepticism induced by the deceptions of appearances. The earth appeared to be flat and motionless but science had shown that reality is otherwise. For Descartes it was rational thought, not sense-data, that provided the infallible foundations for certain knowledge. Rational thought could furnish propositions which are beyond doubt, 'I think, therefore I am' being the prime example. From such infallible foundations, implications are derived by logical deduction, in particular the mathematical method. The rationalist mode of thought goes hand-in-hand with the adoption of a reductionist approach in which observed phenomena are explained in terms of a set of first principles. The emphasis is necessarily on that which is amenable to precise definition and quantification. Furthermore, an atomistic ontology is the natural presupposition of this rationalist approach. Atomism implies that complex wholes can be reduced to the sum of their parts, a necessary prerequisite for the reductionist approach.

The Cartesian Vice of stressing the rationality of the world led to what Keynes called 'extravagant scholasticism'. One expression of this in academic circles is the emphasis on theory rather than empirical evidence. This is reflected in the adoption of an aprioristic methodology in which basic axioms are taken to be undeniable truths, beyond empirical criticism. Empirical testing is not seen as determining the validity of theories, only their applicability in particular circumstances. It is a methodology to which most economists remain firmly wedded. More generally the Cartesian Vice is reflected in the separation of theory and practice. The Cartesian concern lies with understanding the order of things rather than with the ability to control and change things. The Cartesian philosopher adopts a medieval, pre-scientific attitude, seeking to understand the world, not change it. The effects of the Cartesian Vice were summed up well by Sartre when he said in another context: 'The separation of theory and practice resulted in transforming the latter into an empiricism without principles; the former into a pure, fixed knowledge' (1968: 22).

The revolt against the formalism of the Cartesian mode of thought was characteristic of many of the intellectual developments associated with Cambridge in the first half of the twentieth century. Formalism had reached its peak at the beginning of the century with the publication of Russell's *The Principles of Mathematics*, and, with Whitehead, *Principia Mathematica*, Moore's *Principia Ethica* and Wittgenstein's *Tractatus Logico-Philosophicus*. These volumes represented attempts within their respective disciplines to provide precise and clearly formulated foundations from which conclusions are rigorously derived by logical analysis. They aimed to rid their respective disciplines of those controversies generated by what they considered to be the two obstacles to intellectual progress – vague definitions and non-logical arguments.

The Cambridge revolt against formalism can be seen clearly in the writings of Ramsey and the later writings of Whitehead in their criticisms of excessive scholasticism (Winslow 1986, 1989). Whitehead, for example, criticised conventional philosophy for its attachment to what he called the Dogmatic Fallacy, the belief that philosophical hypotheses are clear, obvious and irreformable when in fact all familar ideas are infected with an incurable vagueness. Likewise Ramsey argued that: 'The chief danger to our philosophy, apart from laziness and woolliness, is scholasticism, the essence of which is treating what is vague as if it were precise and trying to fit it into an exact logical category' (quoted in *JMK* X: 343).

The later Wittgenstein also underwent a change in his attitudes to formalism. In his early work Wittgenstein recognised the existence of vagueness but his reaction was to seek to limit philosophical discourse to that which is amenable to precise and rigorous analysis, all else being considered as beyond the scope of that whereof the philosopher may speak. The later Wittgenstein sought to transcend the limitations of his earlier formalistic correspondence theory of language. *Philosophical Investigations* develops the notion of language-games in which meaning is seen as part and parcel of life and hence cannot be treated as a subject capable of precise formulation and analysis in any complete sense. This approach to the question of meaning was in part anticipated by Ramsey in his statement that 'meaning is mainly potential', that definitions do not 'explain what we have hitherto meant by our propositions but rather . . . they show how we intend to use them in future' (quoted in *JMK* X: 341). Ramsey himself had to overcome his own attachment to scholasticism:

> I used to worry myself about the nature of philosophy through excessive scholasticism. I could not see how we could understand a word and not be able to recognise whether a proposed definition of it was or was not correct. I did not realise the vagueness of the whole idea of understanding . . . (*Ibid.*)

This is not to say that these writers denied any validity to formalistic techniques. It was the religion of formalism that they came to deny: the belief in the attainability of certain, complete and precise knowledge. They retained the methods of formal analysis but always in full awareness of the inherent limitations of these methods due to the vagueness of knowledge. As Ramsey said, to reject scholasticism is not to embrace 'laziness and woolliness'. Formal analysis has an important role to play in the acquisition of human understanding, but one which is limited in crucial ways.

III KEYNES'S EARLY BELIEFS

Keynes's own revolt against formalism is charted in his essay 'My Early Beliefs' (*JMK* X: Ch. 39) written for the Bloomsbury Memoir Club in September 1938. In this essay Keynes re-examined his own beliefs and those of his closest friends when they were undergraduates at Cambridge. Keynes described those early beliefs as a 'religion' dealing with 'one's attitude to oneself and the ultimate' (p. 436). This religion was derived from Moore's *Principia Ethica*, which was published in 1903 at the end of Keynes's first year at Cambridge and came to have a dominant influence on his early beliefs. Keynes described the religion derived from Moore as follows:

> Nothing mattered except states of mind, our own and other people's of course, but chiefly our own. These states of mind were not associated with action or achievement or with consequences. They consisted in timeless, passionate states of contemplation and communion, largely unattached to 'before' and 'after'. Their value depended, in accordance with the principle of organic unity, on the state of affairs as a whole which could not be usefully analysed into parts . . . The appropriate subjects of passionate contemplation and communion were a beloved person, beauty and truth, and one's prime objects in life were love, the creation and enjoyment of aesthetic experience and the pursuit of knowledge. Of these love came a long way first. (*JMK* X: 436–7.)

Thus even in his early beliefs Keynes recognised limitations to the reductionist methodology. States of mind were not considered as atomistic in nature and hence could not be usefully broken down into their constituent parts for the purposes of analysis. Rather states of mind adhered to the 'principle of organic unity'.

Keynes described these early beliefs as a religion. But that was not how he saw them at the time:

> I have called this faith a religion, and some sort of relation of neo-platonism it surely was. But we should have been very angry at the time with such a suggestion. We regarded all this as entirely rational and scientific in character. Like any other branch of science, it was nothing more than the application of logic and rational analysis to the material presented as sense-data. Our apprehension of good was exactly the same as our apprehension of green, and we purported to handle it with the same logical and analytical technique which was appropriate to the latter. Indeed we combined a dogmatic treatment as to the nature of experience with a method of handling it which was extravagantly scholastic. Russell's *Principles of Mathematics* came out in the same year as *Principia Ethica*; and the former, in spirit, furnished a method for handling the material provided by the latter. (*Ibid.*: 438–9.)

In retrospect Keynes saw his early beliefs as formalistic, derived exclusively by 'the application of logic and rational analysis'. He came to see these early beliefs as 'dogmatic' and 'extravagantly scholastic'. By 'extravagantly scholastic' Keynes meant the attempt to make precise those notions which are inherently vague:

> It was all under the influence of Moore's method, according to which you could hope to make essentially vague notions clear by using precise language about them and asking exact questions. It was a method of discovery by the instrument of impeccable grammar and an unambiguous dictionary. 'What exactly do you mean?' was the phrase most frequently on our lips. If it appeared under cross-examination that you did not mean exactly anything, you lay under a strong suspicion of meaning nothing whatever . . . So we spent our time trying to discover precisely what questions we were asking, confident in the faith that, if only we could ask precise questions, everyone would know the answer. (*Ibid.*: 440.)

The later Keynes did not repudiate his early beliefs and remained wedded to this 'religion' throughout his life. Rather he came to see the limitations of his early beliefs:

> I see no reason to shift from the fundamental intuitions of *Principia Ethica*; though they are much too few and too narrow to fit actual experience which provides a richer and more various content. (*Ibid.*: 444.)

While remaining committed to his 'religion', the later Keynes recognised the need to take a more general and less exact view of the process of life, treating experience as a series of actions through time:

> It seems to me looking back, that this religion of ours was a very good one to grow up under. It remains nearer the truth than any other that I know, with less irrelevant extraneous matter and nothing to be ashamed of; though it is a comfort today to be able to discard with a good conscience the calculus and the mensuration and the duty to know exactly what one means and feels. It was a purer, sweeter air by far than Freud cum Marx. It is still my religion under the surface. I read again last week Moore's famous chapter on 'The Ideal'. It is remarkable how wholly oblivious he managed to be of the qualities of the life of action and also of the pattern of life as a whole. He was existing in a timeless ecstasy. (*Ibid.*: 442–3.)

Keynes also recognised that his early beliefs embodied too narrow a view of human nature, a view which he came to describe as 'this thin rationalism skipping on the crust of the lava, ignoring both the reality and the value of the vulgar passions' (p. 450). He came to see human nature as an amalgam of both the rational and the irrational. His early beliefs had recognised only the former:

> this pseudo-rational view of human nature led to a thinness, a superficiality, not only of judgment, but also of feeling. It seems to me that Moore's chapter on 'The Ideal' left out altogether some whole categories of valuable emotion. The attribution of rationality to human nature, instead of enriching it, now seems to me to have impoverished it. It ignored certain powerful and valuable springs of feeling. Some of the spontaneous, irrational outbursts of

> human nature can have a sort of value from which our schematism was cut off. (*Ibid*.: 448–9.)

In 'My Early Beliefs' the later Keynes characterises his early beliefs as 'extravagantly scholastic', while at the same time incorporating those beliefs into a more general account of human nature capable of providing better guidance for action. It is a record of a process of transcendence which Keynes repeated in several other areas of his intellectual thought.

IV THE VAGUENESS OF KNOWLEDGE

The revolt against formalism is the rejection of the belief in the attainability of certain, complete and precise knowledge. Instead knowledge is seen as having an inescapable vagueness. This vagueness has to be accepted and embraced. Formalism offers only an illusory and misplaced concreteness. Wildon Carr summed the sentiment up well when he remarked that 'it is better to be vaguely right than precisely wrong' (quoted in Rothschild 1947: 320). It is echoed by Keynes in the *General Theory* in his notes on mercantilism, when he refers to:

> the brave army of heretics . . . who, following their intuitions, have preferred to see the truth obscurely and imperfectly rather than to maintain error, reached indeed with clearness and consistency and by easy logic but on hypotheses inappropriate to the facts. (*GT*: 371.)

Keynes recognised at least three aspects to the vagueness of human knowledge. First, knowledge is always provisional in the face of an unknowable future. This is the problem of uncertainty enshrined in Hume's famous statement of the problem of induction. Keynes recognised that many of our current decisions depend on judgements about the future. These judgements can never be justified objectively on purely logical grounds. They are always rooted in our subjectively-determined beliefs and fluctuating degrees of confidence. Secondly, knowledge is incomplete because of 'the complexities and interdependencies of the real world' (*GT*: 298). Even if the world is atomistic, so that the reductionist project is legitimate, the multitude of causal factors involved will always render our explanations incomplete. Thirdly, knowledge cannot be formulated fully if phenomena are not atomistic in nature but rather are organic. Organic unities can only be grasped intuitively and as wholes. An organic unity can be analysed only in terms of fragments of form. By its very nature, an organic unity defies complete reduction to its constituent parts. An organic whole is always more than the sum of its parts. The first two aspects of the vagueness of knowledge correspond to what Loasby (1976) has termed respectively the problem of ignorance and the problem of complexity. The organicist aspect to the vagueness of knowledge bears some relation to Polanyi's notion of a tacit dimension to knowledge: 'we always know more than we can tell'. Organic unities may be known intuitively but cannot be told in any complete sense. The usual emphasis in Keynesian writings has been on the problem of uncertainty but all three aspects of the inherent vagueness of human knowledge were recognised by Keynes. For Keynes human knowledge is always fallible, characterised by uncertainty and incompleteness, both in form and in content.

V BEYOND CARTESIANISM

The Cartesian Vice arises out of an unacceptably narrow conception of the world. Rationalism fails to take account of the human condition, of the thickness of experience, of the need to act, of the vagueness of knowledge. An alternative dictum to that of Descartes is 'I live, therefore I am'. Life consists of thought and action. We seek not only to understand the world but also to change it. Knowledge is vague; our understanding is always fallible, made up of uncertain truths held on a provisional basis. But the vagueness of knowledge does not mean that knowledge is not possible. The rejection of rationalism does not imply scepticism. Knowledge is uncertain but it is still justified belief. Knowledge is grounded in experience, justified on both cognitive and practical grounds. Knowledge is cognitively justified if it is consistent with both our theoretical systems and the available empirical evidence. Cognitively justified beliefs are seen as providing an understanding of the perceived patterns of order in the world. Such knowledge must be realistic in the sense of 'fitting the facts', recognising of course that facts are not objective but are always the product of human perception. Knowledge is practically justified if it provides guidance for actions which achieve designated goals. This is the instrumental or technological aspect of knowledge. This account of human knowledge transcends the limitations of not only Cartesian rationalism but also empiricism and pragmatism. Each of these philosophical accounts of knowledge has highlighted one aspect to the exclusion of all others. This more general account of human knowledge could be described as reconstructed pragmatism in the sense that a belief is justified if 'it works' both cognitively and practically.

The development of Keynes's thought is an exemplar of the process of transcending the limitations of the Cartesian Vice. 'My Early Beliefs' records how the later Keynes came to see his early philosophy as too Cartesian in its concern with rationality and precision and in its failure to take account of action and consequences as well as other aspects of human experience. This process of transcendence is clearly evident in the transition of Keynes's thought from the *Treatise on Probability* to the *General Theory*. The *Treatise* sought to go beyond the limits of formal logic by extending its application to the realm of uncertain knowledge (probability). The *Treatise* also represented a move beyond the traditional preoccupation with numerical probabilities. By highlighting the importance of non-numerical probabilities, Keynes showed that probability has both quantitative and qualitative aspects. The *General Theory*, in turn, transcended the *Treatise* by moving from the abstract logical analysis of probability to an experience-laden account of human behaviour under uncertainty.

Keynes's attitude to the mathematical method also exemplifies his transcendence of Cartesianism:

> The object of our analysis is, not to provide a machine, or method of blind manipulation, which will furnish an infallible answer, but to provide ourselves with an organised and orderly method of thinking out particular problems; and, after we have reached a provisional conclusion by isolating the complicating factors one by one, we then have to go back on ourselves and allow, as well as we can, for the probable interactions of the factors among themselves. This is the nature of economic thinking. Any other way of applying our formal principles of thought (without which, however, we shall be lost in the wood) will lead us into error. It is a great fault of symbolic pseudo mathematical methods of formalising a system of economic analysis . . . that they expressly assume strict independence between the factors involved and lose all their cogency and authority if this hypothesis is disallowed; whereas, in ordinary discourse, where we are not blindly manipulating but know all the time what we are doing and what the words mean, we can keep 'at the back of our heads' the necessary reserves and qualifications and the adjustments which we shall have to make later on, in a way in which we cannot keep complicated partial differentials 'at the back' of several pages of algebra which assume that they all vanish. Too large a proportion of recent 'mathematical' economics are mere concoctions, as imprecise as the initial assumptions they rest on, which allow the author to lose sight of the complexities and interdependencies of the real world in a maze of pretentious and unhelpful symbols. (*GT*: 297–8.)

Again what is important to note is that Keynes does not deny all validity to the mathematical method. Indeed Keynes made limited use of the mathematical method throughout his work in economics, the derivation of the fundamental equations of the *Treatise on Money* being the most noteworthy example. What Keynes sought to do was to prevent the blind usage of mathematics. He saw mathematics as a particularly powerful tool for deriving implications from a set of precisely formulated premises. But the mathematical method cannot determine the validity of the premises themselves. The danger is that precision becomes so attractive that the tail comes to wag the dog with premises being selected on the basis of their amenability to mathematical manipulation rather than their empirical relevance. Also, as Keynes pointed out, the precision of the mathematical method may make it unsuitable for dealing with 'the complexities and interdependencies of the real world' so characteristic of economic phenomena and which render economic knowledge vague and provisional.

In highlighting the limitations of the mathematical method Keynes followed Marshall, who also possessed great abilities in its application and indeed taught mathematics at St John's College before he took up economics. Marshall was greatly attracted by the benefits of mathematics being applied to economics:

> a training in mathematics is helpful by giving command over a marvellously terse and exact language for expressing clearly some general relations and some short processes of economic reasoning; which can indeed be expressed in ordinary language, but not with equal sharpness of outline. (Marshall 1920: 781.)

But Marshall came more and more to appreciate the limitations of applying the mathematical method to economics. He stressed the need to translate mathematical analyses into English and to assess their empirical relevance, as he made clear in a letter to Bowley in 1906:

> I had a growing feeling in the later years of my work that a good mathematical theorem dealing with economic hypotheses was very unlikely to be good economics, and I went more and more on the rules – (1) Use mathematics as a shorthand language, rather than as an engine of inquiry; (2) Keep these till you have done; (3) Translate into English; (4) Then illustrate by examples that are important in real life; (5) Burn the Mathematics; (6) If you can't succeed in (4), burn (3). This last I did often. (Quoted in Kaldor 1985: 58–9.)

As Loasby (1989: 68–70) has pointed out, Marshall's recognition of the tension between the benefits and dangers of formal analysis is clearly seen in the assessment of his own static equilibrium demand-and-supply theory:

> The theory of stable equilibrium of normal demand and supply helps indeed

> to give definiteness to our ideas; and in its elementary stages it does not diverge from the actual facts of life, so far as to prevent its giving a fairly trustworthy picture of the chief methods of action of the strongest and most persistent group of economic forces. But when pushed to its more remote and intricate logical consequences, it slips away from the conditions of real life . . . The Statical theory of equilibrium is only an introduction to economic studies; and it is barely even an introduction to the study of the progress and development of industries which show a tendency to increasing return. Its limitations are so constantly overlooked, especially by those who approach it from an abstract point of view, that there is a danger in throwing it into definite form at all. But, with this caution, the risk may be taken . . . (Marshall 1920: 461.)

The point is not to deny all validity to formalist methods. Rather it is the need to appreciate their limitations arising out of the inescapable vagueness of human knowledge about economic processes which are uncertain, complex and organic in nature.

Keynes always stressed the need to combine abilities in logical analysis with the art of selecting the appropriate assumptions. In stark contrast to the currently dominant methodology in mainstream economics, he argued for the importance of realistic assumptions. Most economists profess an attachment to Friedmanite instrumentalism, a methodology by which models are judged with regard to the goodness of their predictions, not the realism of their assumptions. The denial of any need to test your assumptions sits well with the adoption of the Cartesian perspective, which treats the foundations of a model as true *a priori*. Keynes's methodology is more akin to that of the behavioural approach in economics associated primarily with the work of Herbert Simon (1976). Simon argues that there is a need to replace the traditional highly restrictive assumption of optimising agents with the more general assumption that agents are satisficers, seeking a 'good' solution rather than the 'best' one. As Simon puts it, there is need to replace the assumption of substantive rationality with that of procedural rationality. If such an approach to the study of human behaviour is adopted, it follows that model-builders must be concerned with the decision rules which agents employ to resolve complex choice situations. The most useful models will be those which make realistic assumptions about the decision rules actually used. The choice of assumptions must, therefore, be based on experience, not theoretical expediency.

Overall, Keynes, both in his thought and in his life in general, is the outstanding repudiation of Cartesianism in economics. He combined the intellectual concern for theory and empirical realism with the practical concern for policy formulation. Keynes was no Cartesian philosopher. He sought to understand the world in order to change it.

His theory is not a 'pure, fixed knowledge' but rather it is vague and provisional; his practice is not 'empiricism without principles' but rather combines theory with a pragmatic awareness of the limitations imposed by the uncertainties, complexities and organic nature of the real world.

VI FORMAL LOGIC VERSUS HUMAN LOGIC

The distinction between formal logic and human logic is due to Ramsey. It is discussed by Keynes in his 1931 review of Ramsey's *The Foundations of Mathematics*. Formal logic is a 'logic of consistency' concerned with the rules of consistent thought. Human logic, on the other hand, is a 'logic of truth' concerned with the study of 'useful mental habits'. Formal logic has a highly limited scope of application, a scope which Keynes had extended to deal with non-conclusive argument in his *Treatise on Probability* by developing a (formally) logical theory of probability. Human logic is a more general field of study concerned not with the problem of valid (i.e. internally consistent) arguments but with the problem of realistic (i.e. externally consistent) arguments. Useful mental habits are adopted for reasons which need to be studied and subjected to critical evaluation. These reasons are more than just a concern for logical consistency. Thus human logic extends beyond the limits of formal logic but it is not merely 'descriptive psychology'; there is a normative aspect to human logic. Ramsey argued that useful mental habits, such as induction, are justified on pragmatic grounds. Keynes appears to have interpreted Ramsey as adopting a practically-based pragmatism. Keynes deemed this type of pragmatism an insufficient account of the justification of induction and other useful mental habits. This criticism of Ramsey seems to imply that Keynes believed that there is also a cognitive and realistic justification for useful mental habits, a view which has been described above as one of reconstructed pragmatism. Keynes, however, may not have been entirely fair in his interpretation of Ramsey on this point. Ramsey defined pragmatism in the following way: 'The essence of pragmatism I take to be this, that the meaning of a sentence is to be defined by reference to the actions to which asserting it would lead, or, more vaguely still, by its possible causes and effects' (quoted in *JMK* X: 338). The concern for 'effects' suggests a practical pragmatism but the reference to 'causes' may be interpreted as a concern for cognitive justifications.

Ramsey developed the distinction between formal and human logic as a critique of Keynes's (formally) logical theory of probability. Keynes accepted Ramsey's argument that, whereas the study of the relations between degrees of belief is a matter of formal logic (do degrees of belief form an internally consistent system?), the study of the basis of particular degrees of belief belongs to the realm of human logic. Indeed Keynes went as far as to say that 'Ramsey may have been pointing the way to the next field of study when formal logic has been put in good order and its highly limited scope properly defined' (*JMK* X: 339). From this standpoint the *General Theory* can be seen as an exercise in human, not formal, logic. Likewise the notion of language-games, so central to the philosophy of the later Wittgenstein, can be seen as an exemplar of human logic in contrast to the formal logic of Wittgenstein's earlier correspondence theory of language. Human logic represents the rejection of the Cartesian Vice and the acceptance that knowledge is experience-laden (and, of course, experience is knowledge-laden). As such, human logic is a concept worthy of further refinement within Keynesian circles and beyond.

The distinction between formal and human logic is useful in casting light on the debates about the nature of science. The problem of induction, as Ramsey pointed out, is a problem only from the perspective of formal logic. One cannot justify the inference of the general from the specific on purely logical grounds. But this does not invalidate induction as a useful mental habit. To accept that induction does not yield infallible knowledge does not mean that it cannot provide any reliable knowledge. To argue this is to embrace scepticism, the inverse of rationalism and, as such, a symptom of the Cartesian Vice. Past experience provides a vital guide for future action. We adopt the principle of continuity in the absence of any reason to do otherwise. The need to act necessitates the need to make judgements on the basis of available evidence, irrespective of the lack of any formally logical justification for so doing.

Likewise Popper's methodology of falsificationism can also be better understood through the use of the distinction between formal and human logic. Falsificationism is only a solution to the problem of induction from the perspective of formal logic. As a practical method it is in the same sort of predicament as the inductive method of verificationism. Given the conglomerate nature of theories, an observed falsification is always a falsification of a particular conjunction of target and auxiliary hypotheses, the problem known as the Duhem–Quine thesis. The interpretation of the results of empirical testing always involves a conventional decision to treat some part of the existing body of knowledge as beyond doubt for current practical purposes. This is a useful mental habit, the justification of which lies in the realm of human, not formal, logic.

There is no purely formal logic of science. The study of science lies, in part, in the field of human logic. Science involves the continuous search for a provisionally acceptable consistency between theoretical systems and available empirical evidence, a process which is always historically contingent and subject to social, political, economic and institutional influences. Science is a fallible, human enterprise and always involves much more than the blind application of some formal set of rules designated to be the Scientific Method. It follows, therefore, that, although formal methodological rules have some role to play, such rules are not, and never can be, the sole arbiter of scientific disputes. To claim otherwise is to reduce science to a 'thin rationalism' which leaves out of account the very richness and creativity that is so characteristic of actual scientific practice.

VII SOME CONCLUDING THOUGHTS

The themes developed above are suggestive of a particular attitude of mind and methods of analysis appropriate to those who seek to move beyond the confines of mainstream patterns of thought. First, there is a need for intellectual humility and acceptance of the inevitable fallibility of human knowledge. There is no Archimedean point with which to lift our knowledge into the rarefied sphere of objective truth. As Newton once remarked, all we can ever hope to find is a few pebbles on the shore. Secondly, there is a need for open-mindness and the repudiation of TINA (There Is No Alternative). We must always carry with us a critical awareness of the limitations of our theories, or, at the very least, be open to the possibility of the existence of such limitations. The dogmatic adherence to a set of supposedly undeniable truths closes the mind and creates bounded vision. Thirdly, there must be tolerance of differences. The aim should not be to deny any validity whatsoever to alternative perspectives but, rather, to explore the limitations of each, seeking, where possible, to generate a synthesis which overcomes these limitations. The tolerance of pluralism offers a more general presupposition than reductionism. To use a distinction suggested by Dow (1985), there is a need to replace the Cartesian/Euclidean mode of thought with the Babylonian mode of thought.

With regard to specific methods of analysis two points have emerged in the above discussion. First, the limitations of formalist techniques such as the mathematical method must be recognised. Secondly, models should be developed with regard to their empirical realism and practical significance. Knowledge should be justified on cognitive and practical grounds – the doctrine of reconstructed pragmatism. These are the attitudes of mind and methods of analysis that seem to emerge out of Keynes. They also underlie the notion of what I have called elsewhere a post-classical synthesis (Gerrard 1989).

Two quotations sum up this 'Keynesian' attitude. The first is by Dickinson on the type of attitude associated with Cambridge, quoted approvingly by Keynes in his essay on Ramsey:

> It is a type unwordly without being saintly, unambitious without being inactive, warmhearted without being sentimental. Through good report and ill such men work on, following the light of truth as they see it; able to be sceptical without being paralysed; content to know what is knowable and to reserve judgment on what is not. The world could never be driven by such men, for the springs of action lie deep in ignorance and madness. But it is they who are the beacon in the tempest . . . (Quoted in *JMK* X: 340.)

The second quotation is by Russell, quoted in part by Dow (1985):

> Science tells us what we can know, but what we can know is little, and if we forget how much we cannot know we become insensitive to many things of great importance. Theology, on the other hand, induces a dogmatic belief that we have knowledge where in fact we have ignorance and by doing so generates a kind of impertinent insolence towards the universe. Uncertainty, in the presence of vivid hopes and fears, is painful, but must be endured if we wish to live without the support of comforting fairy tales. It is not good either to forget the questions that philosophy asks, or to persuade ourselves that we have found indubitable answers to them. To teach how to live without certainty, and yet without being paralysed by hesitation, is perhaps the chief thing that philosophy, in our age, can still do for those who study it. (Russell 1946: 14.)

These two quotations capture the central Keynesian themes of this chapter: the vagueness of knowledge, the repudiation of the Cartesian Vice, the appreciation of the thickness of human experience in an uncertain world, and, above all, that the denial of rationalism and the belief in certainty need not result in extreme scepticism and the paralysis of action. Keynesians, in the spirit of Keynes, should always seek to combine the recognition of human fallibility with an optimism that we can always try to do better, in both theory and practice.

REFERENCES

Carabelli, A., 1988, *On Keynes's Method*, Macmillan, London/St Martin's Press, New York.

Dow, S.C., 1985, *Macroeconomic Thought: A Methodological Approach*, Basil Blackwell, Oxford.
Fitzgibbons, A.J., 1988, *Keynes's Vision: A New Political Economy*, Oxford University Press, Oxford.
Gerrard, B., 1989, *Theory of the Capitalist Economy: Towards a Post-Classical Synthesis*, Basil Blackwell, Oxford.
Kaldor, N., 1985, *Economics Without Equilibrium*, University College Cardiff Press, Cardiff.
Keynes, J.M., 1973–89, *The Collected Writings of John Maynard Keynes*, 30 vols, ed. D.E. Moggridge, Macmillan, London/St Martin's Press, New York. (*JMK* in text.)
Vol. VII: *The General Theory of Employment, Interest and Money*, 1936. (*GT* in text.)
Vol. X: *Essays in Biography*.
Vol. XIV: *The General Theory and After: Part II, Defence and Development*.
Loasby, B.J., 1976, *Choice, Complexity and Ignorance*, Cambridge University Press, Cambridge.
Loasby, B.J., 1989, *The Mind and Method of the Economist*, Edward Elgar, Aldershot.
Marshall, A., 1920, *Principles of Economics*, 8th edn, Macmillan, London/ Porcupine Press, Philadelphia.
O'Donnell, R.M., 1989, *Keynes: Philosophy, Economics and Politics: The Philosophical Foundations of Keynes's Thought and their Influence on his Economics and Politics*, Macmillan, London.
Ramsey, F.P., 1931, *The Foundations of Mathematics*, Routledge & Kegan Paul, London.
Robinson, J., 1964, *Economic Philosophy*, Penguin, Harmondsworth.
Rothschild, K.W., 1947, 'Price Theory and Oligopoly', *Economic Journal*, 57, 299–320.
Russell, B., 1946, *A History of Western Philosophy*, Allen & Unwin, London.
Sartre, J.P., 1968, *Search for a Method*, Random House, New York.
Shackle, G.L.S., 1967, *The Years of High Theory*, Cambridge University Press, Cambridge.
Simon, H.A., 1976, 'From Substantive to Procedural Rationality', in S.J. Latsis, ed., *Method and Appraisal in Economics*, Cambridge University Press, Cambridge.
Winslow, E.G., 1986, ' "Human Logic" and Keynes's Economics', *Eastern Economic Journal*, 12, 413–30.
Winslow, E.G., 1989, 'Organic Interdependence, Uncertainty and Economic Analysis', *Economic Journal*, 99, 1173–82.

2. From Keynes's Vision to Keynesian Economics

Athol Fitzgibbons

I INTRODUCTION

Anyone who studies Keynes's *General Theory* in the original soon finds that his followers 'improved' his theory with what they thought was greater rigour. However the seeming logic of a systematiser often overlooks the scope of the original idea, and the Keynesians have typically painted on a more narrow canvas than did Keynes. For example Keynesianism is not part of a system of political economy, despite its political implications. By comparison even Keynes's technical economic theory makes better sense within a wider context.

Before he became an economist Keynes was a philosopher, whose *Treatise on Probability* launched the modern philosophy of the subject. The young Keynes delivered papers on moral theory, he wrote essays on politics, and he was the author of a scholarly and innovative essay on the political philosophy of Edmund Burke. Keynes's writings on these subjects were not published, evidently because they were thought to be irrelevant to his economics. But recently economists have understood that Keynes's economics of uncertainty draws on his philosophy of probability, which reflects in turn the more general outlook I have called Keynes's vision. By cross-referencing Keynes's economics with his philosophic and political ideas, we can revise Keynes's intellectual pedigree and consider what implications there are for Keynesian economics.

II THE PROBLEMS OF KEYNESIANISM

Keynes criticised British economic policy in the 1920s because the attempt to preserve the price of sterling in terms of gold had caused excessively high rates of interest and unemployment. The *General Theory*, which was written during the Great Depression, gave theoretical reasons for the policies he had previously recommended. It argued that unemployment was inevitable in a laissez-faire economy because uncertainty would sabotage the tendency to a full employment equilibrium. Keynes was often tentative about what was the best cure for unemployment, but he recommended low interest rates and, in the immediate circumstances of post-war Britain, a defined programme of deficit spending.

In the decades following the publication of the *General Theory* Keynesian ideas spread and were applied to the problems of the post-war world. The techniques of the Keynesian synthesis, which combines the neo-classical method with Keynes's, were used to 'fine tune' the major economies of the West. But, although unemployment and inflation were distinctly lower during the Keynesian period than they are now, Keynesian policies have met widespread opposition.

One reason is the difficulty of expressing Keynes's system in formal theoretical terms. The attempts to formulate a mechanistic Keynesian system have, often despite the interpreters' intentions, taken Keynesianism further away from Keynes and back towards classical economics. As a result the *General Theory* is now widely believed to be only a special instance of the classical general case, in which wage and price rigidities forestall progress to a classical equilibrium.

Apart from the theoretical difficulties there has been political hostility because Keynesian policies have been used all over the world to promote the growth of big government, and are associated with high taxes and the welfare state. Despite references to 'Keynes-neutrality', Keynesian policies were used to promote centralist goals, the reaction against which has given a strong impetus to rationalist economics.

Keynes's reputation as a socialist seemed further confirmed by Joan Robinson's doctrine, which combined Keynes with Sraffa and Kalecki. She succeeded in showing that the neo-Keynesians, or the 'bastard Keynesians' as she called them, had misrepresented Keynes in a way which put a gloss on laissez-faire. The conventional picture had omitted Keynes's scepticism towards laissez-faire and his differences from neo-classical method, including his emphasis on uncertainty and economic change. She concluded that Keynes had irrationally baulked at the socialistic conclusions which the *General Theory* obviously implied: ' "The Social Philosophy towards which the General Theory might lead" is markedly less radical than the argument of the book has led the reader to expect' (Robinson 1962: 82).

When the political mood in the West subsequently swung against economic intervention there was a corresponding swing in sentiment against Keynes. Yet the monetarist claims that the macroeconomy can be understood in equilibrium terms are hard to reconcile with the world's continuing experience of booms and recessions, and changing fortunes in the markets for equities and foreign exchange. It has often been remarked that the raw facts of the world seem more consistent with John Maynard Keynes's theories, despite the theoretical and political shortcomings of the Keynesian system.

The exegesis of Keynes's works indicates that many of these alleged shortcomings, both theoretical and applied, arose out of developments which were added on after Keynes. The major theoretical objection, that Keynesianism is only a special case of classical economics, wrongly identified Keynes's theories with the mechanistic IS–LM model. IS–LM is a neo-classical system to the extent that it omits uncertainty, speculation, and other features which reflect Keynes's philosophy of judgement and change, to which classical economics does not subscribe.

As for the political objections to Keynes, though it is true that he was not committed to laissez-faire, his politics might nevertheless appeal to the modern pragmatic sentiment. Keynes was the author of a new system of political economy which justified practical action in terms of an extended process of reason. Keynes's new doctrine did have some similarities to socialism, and in particular he accepted (though he learnt this from the ultra-conservative Edmund Burke) that there were no limits in principle to the power of the state beyond what some high ideals of justice might provide. He was also a Utopian who conceived of a future when the economic problem would be solved, and he was, within limits, an egalitarian who proposed a modest British welfare system.

But despite these correspondences the doctrine of pragmatism to which Keynes subscribed was much older than socialism, and had different aims and assumptions. In particular Keynes opposed economic centralism, he stressed individualism, and concluded that his Utopia would be best advanced by laissez-faire. Allan Meltzer is right to argue (Meltzer 1989) that the post-war policy of macroeconomic fine tuning was not conceived by Keynes.

After the Second World War Keynesian policies successfully maintained full employment without excessive inflation. Nevertheless they imposed costs and the pendulum has swung to a more laissez-faire orientation. The danger is that Keynes's original doctrine, which followed from philosophic insights of a very general nature, could be lost in the process. His social and economic ideals are a matter of substantial intellectual interest. But Keynes's attempts to draw out the significance of economic uncertainty, including his refutation of Say's Law and his system of pragmatism on policy issues, can be ignored by macroeconomists only at great peril, because they are the only systematic account of the effects of economic change.

III THE IDEALS AND GENERAL CHARACTER OF KEYNES'S SYSTEM

It is a matter of significance therefore that Keynes cannot be claimed by any school of Keynesians, if only because his method of economic analysis was central and unique. Keynes's philosophy was not formulated along the lines of natural science, but in terms of an old duality, of practical wisdom based on ideals, versus the transience of the world:

> The old world which took its rise at the dawn of civilisation is at last passing away. . . . Our [absolute] goods will remain as they must always remain, but our duties will change. . . . While the Good is changeless and apart, the ought shifts and fades and grows new shapes and forms. (*Modern Civilisation*, quoted in Fitzgibbons 1988: 68.)

Keynes once described himself as being 'on the extreme left of celestial space'; he meant that traditional philosophy, which was celestial space, had been misused to promote conservatism, the sanctity of property, and other 'outworks' of civilisation which had become outmoded. When he was a young man (he later recanted his own irreverence, but it is indicative of his thought) Keynes attacked the Christian church, on the grounds that it was a conventional religion; and he likewise opposed traditional sexual rules and the laws of inheritance, on the grounds that they were remnants of the feudal system.

Nevertheless the young Keynes did not find his essential truths in Marx and Freud, whom he was grateful to have escaped, but in Plato and the 'religion' of G.E. Moore. Keynes rejected materialism in general, which is why he rejected both socialism and laissez-faire: 'State Socialism . . . is in some respects a clearer, in some respects a more muddled, version of just the same philosophy as underlies nineteenth-century individualism' (*JMK* IX: 290). He conceived that, if the lofty ideals of traditional philosophy could be more purely expressed, they would provide an idealistic justification for economic growth; and his idealism also led him to believe that it was possible to strike a technical balance between liberal and egalitarian goals.

In short there was a carefully thought out philosophic system beneath the economic theory iceberg. Keynes's intellectual interests focused on the age of reason somewhat more than two hundred years ago, when the modern world-view was formed. Keynes's ambivalence to the Age of Reason is expressed most notably in his essay on Edmund Burke, but also in his references to socialism and laissez-faire. Keynes rejected the reductionism and mechanical outlook of that age and described its new ideals of liberty and equality as conditional rather than absolute Goods.

Keynes repeatedly said that the significance of economic growth was that it opened new possibilities for individualism and moral development: 'If there is no moral objective in economic progress, then it follows that we must not sacrifice, even for a day, moral to material advantage' (*JMK* IX: 268). For the first time since the neolithic revolution in prehistorical times there was sustained economic growth. Capital formation was proceeding on a scale a hundredfold greater than anything previously known, and in some foreseeable future, perhaps 50 or 100 years ahead if population growth and war could be avoided, Keynes anticipated that the economic problem would be solved. This did not mean that there would be unlimited commodities, but he anticipated that there would be a material surplus sufficient for the pursuit of aims that had always been higher than the economic, and which had been beyond the range of the general population because of economic need.

The moral error which economic need imposed was, in Bloomsbury terms, 'purposiveness', or 'doing good', instead of 'being good'. Keynes understood purposiveness as a calculating, goal-oriented egoism, which he identified with the utilitarian ethic. When the economic problem had been solved it would be widely recognised that this pseudo-rational egoism was no longer required. The eventual resolution of the economic problem would permit most people to live by the values which previously only an aristocratic minority could afford. The pursuit of virtue and the Good in all its forms would be recognised as the only motives that reasonable people could adopt:

> For purposiveness means that we are more concerned with the remote future results of our actions than with their own quality or their immediate effects on our own environment. . . . [When the economic problem is solved] I see us free to return to some of the most sure and certain principles of religion and traditional virtue. (*JMK* IX: 329–30.)

There was a tension between these Utopian objectives and the economic constraints, because, whatever was right in the absolute moral sense, the requirements of economic growth were avarice and usury and the love of money; 'Fair is foul and foul is fair,' said Keynes, echoing the witches in *Macbeth*, 'for foul is useful and fair is not' (*JMK* IX: 331).

Laissez-faire was not an Ideal, but on technical grounds it seemed to be the most effective way to reach one.

However the purposive mentality which economic growth required was inappropriate to politics, because the practice of justice was essential to public life. Keynes learnt, again from Edmund Burke, that the violation of an absolute standard of justice had material consequences. Mechanistic minds would fail to anticipate the complexity of political events and overlook the undercurrents which injustice would set in train:

> In only one way can we influence those hidden currents [of political fate] – by setting in motion those forces of instruction and imagination which change the climate of opinion. The assertion of truth, the unveiling of illusion, the dissipation of hate . . . must be the means. (*JMK* II: 188.)

Keynes wanted to combine liberty with idealism and practical wisdom with economic growth. Rational intuition was to be expressed in politics while instrumental minds created the economic conditions required for the future.

IV BACKGROUND TO THE ECONOMICS OF UNCERTAINTY

It should not be surprising therefore that the theme of Keynes's first great book, the *Treatise on Probability*, was the *logical theory of probability*, which simply amounted to an argument that the intuition could be aided by reason. He might equally have called his the theory of rational expectations; but Keynes did not restrict himself, as economic rationalists do, to quantifiable situations. Even when a situation was quantitatively unknown, he argued, it was possible to make a defensible judgement of what was *probably* true.

The logical theory of probability had a very wide range. It applied to practical life, to the law, to the entrepreneur, to creative science, and wherever a mixture of art and reason was required. The scientist, Keynes said, drew on the same abilities as the artist, except that scientists took longer to mix the paints.

Rational intuition meant Keynes could reject two extreme positions, utter nihilism and complete quantification, which are both represented in economics today. The first extreme was the more profound and the second the more common, which is also the situation today. First, Keynes rejected the notion that a probability judgement is never based on sufficient assumptions to reach a logical conclusion. According to this nihilist philosophy, a probability judgement is either an emotional response, or else it is based blindly on a convention. Keynes knew this position as David Hume's philosophy of probability. It is a paradox that economists attribute it to Keynes himself – but he rejected it because nihilism was based on a false theory of causation and was unworkable in life.

Keynes admitted that to the extent that there is uncertainty it is impossible to guarantee that a particular course of action will lead to the best result. Nevertheless the nihilists had failed to understand that the process of arriving at the best course of action could proceed in a logical and systematic manner. Keynes quoted Herodotus with approval:

> There is nothing more profitable for a man than to take good council with himself; for even if the event turns out contrary to one's hope, still one's decision was right, even though fortune has made it of no effect: whereas if a man acts contrary to good council, even though by luck he gets what he had no right to expect, his decision was not any the less foolish. (*JMK* VIII: 339–40.)

Roy Weatherford's survey of the philosophy of probability expresses Keynes's point more exactly: 'Clearly Keynes is using the word "rational" to mean something much more like "in accordance with the Laws of Thought" than like "leading to success in practice" ' (Weatherford 1982: 122).

After rejecting nihilism Keynes refuted those statisticians who (anticipating the new classical economists) claimed that all probability judgements can be given a quantitative value. Keynes showed that the axiomatic basis of probability was inadequate for the conclusions which the statisticians reached; the principle of non-sufficient reason, which could be assumed in structured games of chance, did not extend to the real world. Keynes then gave examples of unquantifiable probabilities. What, for example, is the quantifiable probability that a scientific statement, such as the theory of evolution, is correct? How can we quantify the prospect that a particular ship, which has disappeared off the coast of Africa, will be found?

Yet in many such cases where quantification had no meaning a reasonable judgement could still be offered. It was reasonable to subscribe to the theory of evolution, even if it was not meaningful to calculate that the odds were ten to one it was true. Because the statisticians had not recognised that practical life drew on a wider notion of rationality, they had to define uncertainty away.

In the *General Theory*, Chapter 12, Keynes established the context of uncertainty by arguing that a profit-maximising entrepreneur often did not have sufficient objective information to calculate his best course. In 'former times' such uncertainty was not important, because an entrepreneur thought of investment 'as a way of life'. By comparison modern business, which was dominated by large institutional investors, salaried managers and speculators, had lost its animal spirits or entrepreneurial rationale.

The wider concept of rationality in the *Treatise on Probability* is implicit in Keynes's references to 'animal spirits', but the *General Theory* extended the notion. The *Treatise* had analysed the requirements for logical probability judgements and refuted false theories of probability. The *General Theory* considered a case in which the requirements for a logical approach to probability were too stringent, because of uncertainty, and false approaches were adopted *en masse*. The stock exchange speculators had not developed a logical way of dealing with uncertain knowledge. They tried to be rational economic men and to rely on quantitative calculations of the future, but ultimately they depended on 'false rationalisations' which were unwarranted by the real state of knowledge.

Typically investors estimated future profits by assuming that the parameters of the present would more or less continue into the future. When their expectations were disappointed investment could become highly volatile. Here was the root cause of the instability of laissez-faire:

> [Action] based on so flimsy a foundation . . . is liable to sudden and violent changes. . . . New fears and hopes will, without warning, take charge of human conduct. The forces of disillusion may suddenly impose a new conventional basis of valuation. . . . At all times the vague panic fears and equally vague and unreasoned hopes are not really lulled, and lie but a little way below the surface. (*JMK* XIV: 115.)

Since investment was highly volatile, swings in expectations could destabilise the whole economy through the investment multiplier. The purposive psychology of rational economic man promoted economic growth within a stable context, but Keynes's philosophy challenged the context which rational economic man assumed.

V A PHILOSOPHY OF PRACTICAL ACTION

Keynes's method amounted to a rejection of excessive abstraction. He regarded the economy as uncertain because, like the practical world in general, its atomic details were complex and interactive beyond the possibility of full comprehension. Classical economics had abstracted from the mind-boggling buzz of the real world to formulate a manageable theory. Keynes's response was that the classics had gone too far; their theoretical simplification crucially assumed that they could reduce the economic system to simple categories, whereas in fact their simplification altered the nature of the theory.

He conceded that it was valid to abstract from complexity for practical purposes if nothing depended on the principle involved. However it was illegitimate of classical economics to conclude that the economy really was an abstract system, and he stressed that the validity of his own theory did not depend on abstraction *per se*:

> These partly insoluble difficulties of quantitative description do not arise in our causal analysis, which is *strictly logical* in itself and is subject, in practice, not to insoluble difficulties, but only to the actual imperfections of our knowledge. (*JMK* XXIX: 73.)

Because there were only analogies between theoretical categories and the facts, economics could not be more than a lean theory hung on a few central ideas. The role of theory was to provide a framework for the intuition, which was the only way to account for the changing details of practical life:

> Hence the extreme complexity of the actual course of events. Nevertheless . . . if we examine any actual problem along the lines of the above schematism, we shall find it more manageable; and our practical intuition (which can take account of a more detailed complex of facts than can be treated on general principles) will be offered a less intractable material on which to work. (*GT*: 249.)

The *General Theory* introduced real-world complexity through the spectrum of rates of interest. There was not one abstract rate of interest, but many rates of return on many different assets. Abstract classical method had represented the interest rate as the reward for savings, but there were only returns on particular assets, rather than a rate of interest on savings as such. The rate on money was a particularly critical rate of return, because the liquidity premium put a floor under the whole spectrum of interest rates.

Keynes placed the most volatile element, money, at the very centre of the economy. Given expectations, the money market set 'the' rate of interest; and given expectations again, the rate of interest set the level of investment.

VI CONCLUSIONS

Keynes was one of the rare few who have enlarged the central scheme of economic reasoning. He applied his insight to the terrible economic problems of his time and made important contributions to the toolbox of economic theory. However the very general nature of Keynes's philosophy makes it a source of inspiration rather than a theory in itself; and the differences between Keynes and the Keynesians, which are theoretical, methodological and political, suggest that a definitive version of Keynesian economics is unlikely to emerge.

But the absence of a universal Keynesian theory is a sign that it is still a living doctrine. Adam Smith's dream of a universal system of economics and jurisprudence, which would supposedly parallel Newtonian physics, was only an epistemological excess from the Age of Reason. There can be no general theory of economics, because no formula can anticipate the problems of the future.

REFERENCES

Fitzgibbons, A.J., 1988, *Keynes's Vision: A New Political Economy*, Oxford University Press, Oxford.

Keynes, J.M., 1973–89, *The Collected Writings of John Maynard Keynes*, 30 vols, ed. D.E. Moggridge, Macmillan, London/St Martin's Press, New York. Citations in the text are indicated by *JMK* and a volume number, with the exception of the *General Theory of Employment, Interest and Money*, vol. VII, which is indicated by *GT*.

Keynes, J.M., 'Modern Civilisation' and 'Egoism', in the unpublished writings of J.M. Keynes. The Provost and Scholars of King's College Cambridge, in the King's College Library.

Meltzer, A., 1989, *Keynes's Monetary Theory*, Cambridge University Press, Cambridge.

Robinson, J., 1962, *Economic Philosophy*, Penguin, Harmondsworth.

Weatherford, R., 1982, *Philosophical Foundations of Probability Theory*, Routledge & Kegan Paul, London.

3. On Keynes's Ethics

Suzanne W. Helburn*

I INTRODUCTION

This chapter addresses an important aspect of Keynes's early philosophical work – his ethics – and in particular the influence of G.E. Moore. In Robert Skidelsky's biography and other recent books, Keynes's early work in philosophy has come under increasing scrutiny (Skidelsky 1983, Lawson and Pesaran 1985, Fitzgibbons 1988, Carabelli 1988, O'Donnell 1989). Attention has centred mainly on Keynes's method and attempts to relate his *Treatise on Probability* to his economics. However, Skidelsky, Fitzgibbons and O'Donnell have all discussed Keynes's ethics, recognising it as central to his methodology and politics.

Ethical considerations are important on two levels in Keynes's economics. First, his views on ethics underlie his political philosophy and therefore his attitude about public (professional) duty, so that they affect his approach to the acquisition of economic knowledge and to economic policy formation. Second, his view of actual commonsense morality and the ethical behaviour of economic agents affects his theory of economic performance.[1]

This chapter is concerned only with the first level. Understanding ethical presuppositions of Keynes's work is important because he considered economics a moral science involving the exercise of practical wisdom about economic and political issues. Keynes's methodological stance, recently an important area of investigation for economists, is necessarily based on his ethics, on the rational basis for moral judgement. Thus ethics is more fundamental than method, because it incorporates the methodological considerations.

I argue below that Keynes should not be considered a utilitarian or an act-consequentialist, because as a young man he rejected utilitarianism in favour of an ethics of virtue. This is a position articulated recently by Athol Fitzgibbons (1988). This chapter provides evidence from Keynes's 'Juvenilia' of his move away from G.E. Moore, who had an early influence on Keynes's ethics, and it helps resolve some apparently contradictory aspects of Keynes's ethics. In particular, I address three interrelated questions which have been raised in recent conflicting interpretations of Keynes's ethics. To what extent, and in what form, is egoism present in Keynes's ethics? Did Keynes resolve the apparent discordant demands of his private life and public life? How adequate is it to categorise him as a utilitarian, or, in O'Donnell's words, as an 'act-consequentialist'? These questions can also be discussed in terms of the relative influence on Keynes's moral philosophy of the nineteenth-century Cambridge utilitarians – Henry Sidgwick and G.E. Moore – versus the ancient Greek philosophers – Plato and Aristotle. This chapter seeks to show that the subtlety of Keynes's thinking about ethics argues against classifying him as a disciple of Moore, or, indeed, as an adherent of any particular historical system of morality.

My argument emphasises the importance of Greek philosophy and plays down utilitarianism and act-consequentialism in Keynes's ethics. It also raises the possibility that Keynes's views have particular significance for current debates in moral philosophy. Alasdair MacIntyre has written with great cogency about the failure of modern systems of morality to provide a rational basis for ethical life, advocating a return to the tradition of the virtues as a way to sustain moral life in contemporary society (MacIntyre 1981). Bernard Williams has criticised the pseudo-rationality of contemporary theories of morality and has advocated a return, in modified form, to the ancient Greek approach to ethics which emphasised character development and human well-being (Williams 1985). Because a similar argument is made about Keynes below, Williams's defence of ancient Greek moral philosophy, and his scepticism about the possibility of constructing rational systems of morality, will be outlined to help frame Keynes's position.

II HISTORICAL BACKGROUND

Undoubtedly, Keynes's ethical deliberations are an outgrowth of the nineteenth-century Cambridge philosophical debates, which were dominated by two issues. The first related to disagreements among intuitionists and utilitarians over the nature and source of ethical knowledge. Is moral obligation based on certain duties or expectations about behaviour, or on the ends achieved, the welfare produced? And is intuition based on a moral sense the source of knowledge, or can such knowledge be derived from rational scientific procedures? Intuitionists accepted deontological first principles (which relate to rules of good behaviour and of one's duty) based on intuition as the source of this knowledge. Utilitarians (and egoists) accepted welfarism – achieving what is best through evaluating consequences.[2]

The second issue involved the relation between morality and egoism.[3] Intuitionists, often justifying or building on religious faith, rejected egoism outright or incorporated it in their theology. Utilitarians tended to assume a harmony of interests between the agent' welfare and that of society. Bentham accepted psychological egoism as an empirical fact, but argued that actions most conducive to the general welfare also tend to promote the greatest happiness of the agent (Sidgwick 1960: 244). When they do not, the simple expediency of sanctions will induce the appropriate behaviour. Mill recognised that, although the general happiness is a good to the aggregate of all persons, there has to be some motivation, in the form of sanctions, to induce individuals to act for the good of the whole. These sanctions he thought derived from fellow-feeling and a recognition by individuals that they are part of the whole (*ibid.*: 245–50).[4]

In *The Methods of Ethics*, Henry Sidgwick believed he resolved the debate between intuitionists and utilitarians in favour of the latter. Dissatisfied with the sloppy thinking of intuitionists, he sought a rational basis for ethics and a method for testing or systematising commonsense morality. Schneewind argues that Sidgwick's major objective was to test the claim that only utilitarianism can provide a rational method for determining moral obligation (Schneewind 1977: 8). Sidgwick accepted the intuitionist position that first principles in ethics must rest on some fundamental moral intuition. However, he showed that 'intuitionism, rigorously pressed, yields utilitarianism' and that only the basic principle of utilitarianism is self-evidently certain (*ibid.*: 329). Schneewind claims that Sidgwick created the prototype of modern ethical theory in adopting scientific standards for theorising.

Although Sidgwick resolved the debate between intuitionism and utilitarianism to his satisfaction, he made more apparent the conflict between egoism and utilitarianism. He identified what he called a 'dualism of the practical reason in ethics based on the fact that it is just as rational to pursue one's own good as to pursue universal good' (Sidgwick 1960: 300). Not only does reason require individuals to be both prudent and utilitarian, Sidgwick also claimed that empirical evidence (commonsense morality) indicates that morality is both egoistic and utilitarian. This conclusion creates a profound problem for ethics. By demonstrating that there is no rational way to choose between one's own good and universal good, Sidgwick's conclusions called into question the existence of a moral order.

In *Principia Ethica* Moore also wrestled with the conflict between intuitionism and utilitarianism, and between egoism and morality. Moore separated the ethics of ends, that is, consideration of what things ought to exist for their own sakes, from the ethics of action, that is, consideration of the actions which people ought to perform to increase goodness. He rejected hedonism and any other definition of goodness, arguing that questions about intrinsic value are determined by intuition. He concluded that the most valuable things 'are certain states of consciousness, which may be roughly described as the pleasures of human intercourse and the enjoyment of beautiful objects' (Moore 1959: 188). Moore also claimed that the greatest goods are complex organic unities, states of affairs which include not only states of mind of one or more persons, but knowledge, emotions and objects of contemplation such as works of art.

Moore adopted the utilitarian criterion that actions should aim at achieving the best state of affairs for the universe. However, he rejected intuition as a source of knowledge about correct action, arguing that what one ought to do depends on actual consequences, predictions of which must be based on evidence of probable results. He argued, however, that, because of the complexity of the greatest goods and the inadequacy of our knowledge of the distant future, there is rarely a rational basis for choosing between alternative actions. Therefore, he advocated, on utilitarian grounds, following a few conventional rules of conduct which have generally proved useful in producing better total results than other alternatives, and he recommended egoism as a doctrine of means: individuals should pursue their own good, while nevertheless obeying conventional moral rules.

III DISAGREEMENTS IN INTERPRETING KEYNES'S ETHICS

Principia Ethica was published in the spring of 1903, during Keynes's first year at Cambridge. The book immediately became the centre of discussion among the Apostles, a select, secret discussion society of which both Moore and Keynes were members. The Apostles were profoundly affected by Moore's book; however, if Moore's philosophy formed, exclusively, the basis of Keynes's ethics, Keynes scholars must explain the apparent contradiction between that philosophy which emphasises pursuit of personal life and his active public life.

Robert Skidelsky interprets Keynes as very much in the tradition of Moorean ideal utilitarianism (Skidelsky 1983, 1987). He argues that

Keynes never resolved the weaknesses in Moore's ethics – how to reconcile one's duty to society with the basically apolitical ideal of pursuing truth, beauty and love in one's personal life. Skidelsky argues that throughout his life Keynes struggled to find a balance between these two sets of moral claims; thus he detects a strong strain of egoism. Keynes had to make a separate case for the pursuit of economics and politics, and Skidelsky considers Edmund Burke the inspiration for his political utilitarianism.

While recognising Moore's influence on Keynes's values, Athol Fitzgibbons emphasises Keynes's idealism and identifies Burke and Plato as Keynes's 'intellectual paragons' (Fitzgibbons 1988: 195). He claims that Keynes attempted to apply to the modern world the pre-modern idealist tradition in political philosophy, the central tenet of which is that the state should be ruled by reason and true ideals. This tradition is embodied in Edmund Burke's political theory. Keynes, according to Fitzgibbons, bridged the theoretical gap in Moore's ethics identified by Skidelsky by reintroducing intuition as a source of objective knowledge about means. Fitzgibbons asserts that, by arguing in the *Treatise on Probability* that probabilities are *knowable* by intuition but are not necessarily *quantifiable*, Keynes refutes Moore's grounds for distinguishing between the proper knowledge base for value judgements and judgements about conduct. In so doing Keynes destroys the validity of utilitarianism based on scientific, quantifiable working out of the effects of alternative actions, because he shows that judgements about conduct normally cannot be determined by a consequential calculus (*ibid.*: 41). Like ancient Greek idealist philosophy, Keynes's ethics and political theory are based on motives and 'experience' rather than outcomes or consequences.

R.M. O'Donnell argues that Keynes remained essentially a Moorean throughout his life, but he rejects Skidelsky's argument about the split in Keynes's loyalties between public and private life (O'Donnell 1989: 117). He claims that Keynes's corrections of *Principia Ethica*, by developing a sounder philosophic justification of act-consequentialism, provided an adequate foundation for Keynes's ethics and political theory.[5] O'Donnell classifies the philosophy of practical reason developed by Keynes in *Treatise on Probability* as a probabilistic form of act-consequentialism, based on Moore's ideal utilitarian values rather than on the hedonist values of classical utilitarianism. O'Donnell notes, however, that Keynes never opposed rule making as such; rather his purpose 'was the restoration of individual judgement as the arbiter in *all* cases, and not merely, as with Moore, in some cases' (*ibid.*: 119).

IV WILLIAMS'S CRITIQUE OF MODERN SYSTEMS OF MORALITY

Sidgwick's work illustrates the important influence of scientific method and values on ethical theory in late nineteenth-century Cambridge. The utilitarian system of morality was consciously developed to conform to the standards of rationality used in science. As noted above, Bernard Williams has recently criticised modern systems of morality such as utilitarianism (Williams 1985). He prefers the ancient Greek approach to ethics, which permits a wider range of ethical considerations and is grounded in a concern to live a rational, satisfactory human life. In this view, what is ethically desirable must be the agent's dispositions or character traits. Because Aristotle recognised humans as part of a social whole, well-being included the exercise of practical reason and moral wisdom in civic life. Since the agent's dispositions are the ultimate supports of ethical values, this view focuses on the virtues which must be developed to promote well-being, and no clear distinction is made between moral excellence and other forms of human achievement.

Williams contrasts this broad view of ethics with the narrower, modern reductionist 'systems of morality' based on social expectations and designed to establish a rational basis for moral obligation. They are reductionist because the demands of logic require the reduction of all ethical considerations to one principle to permit comparison of alternative actions. This conception of rationality cannot take into account multiple ethical considerations. Williams notes, however, that there are several incommensurable kinds of considerations included in conceptions of the ethical: considerations of duty, of what is best, of ethical characteristics of actions, and of virtue. Morality systems, 'rationalistic' conceptions of rationality, give the false impression that every decision can be based on grounds that can be incontrovertibly justified.

Although modern moral philosophers consider Aristotle's ethics to be egoistic, Williams argues that this assessment springs from the moralistic view that motivation, to be ethical, must be based on a sense of obligation. In contrast, Aristotle (and Plato) had an inside account of ethics in which what is ethical is so much part of the self in the good person that ethical considerations take precedence over other wants. Hence, goodness comes naturally.

Williams's criticism of modern ethical systems parallels Keynes's objection to economists' slavish emulation of the methodology of the physical sciences. Anna Carabelli has argued that Keynes's reliance on practical reason for his own economics has much in common with older forms of rational discourse grounded in Aristotelian practical logic

(Carabelli 1988). The following analysis of Keynes's 'Juvenilia' shows that he was critical of a similar tendency in ethical theorising, and shows that Keynes gravitated to an ethics which emphasises individual character development. The papers examined were written between 1904 and about 1909. They include his Apostles essays, notes on *Principia Ethica*, which he titled 'Miscellanea Ethica' and which he developed into the long essay called 'A Theory of Beauty', a short critique of Moore written in April 1906, and his long essay on 'The Political Principles of Edmund Burke'.

V THE DEVELOPMENT OF KEYNES'S VIEWS OF WHAT OUGHT TO EXIST

The following summary shows a consistent development of Keynes's views on what ends one is obligated to pursue, starting with Moore's position and ending up arguing in favour of character traits rather than specific states of mind such as contemplation of beauty or enjoyment of friendship. It also shows Keynes's struggle to incorporate egoism into an ethical viewpoint, but to avoid a strictly egoist position.

Although Moore accepted the utilitarian obligation to promote the maximum good for the universe, he argues in *Principia Ethica* that it is next to impossible to know how to do so because the greatest goods are complex organic unities which we cannot completely comprehend, and because we cannot predict the full long-run consequences of our actions. Commenting in 'Miscellanea Ethica' that Moore had reduced us to moral impotence, Keynes set about re-establishing our moral powers in a series of arguments which legitimise egoism by moving towards an ethics of virtue.

A first step was to eliminate organic unities. In an early essay, 'Beauty', dated 20 April 1904, Keynes questions Moore's discussion of beauty. He criticises Moore's tendency to treat beauty as attaching to everything 'of which the admiring contemplation is good', to consider beauty a quality of the object, and to assume that beauty has intrinsic value, even when there is no one to appreciate it. In 'Miscellanea Ethica' and 'A Theory of Beauty', written between August and October 1905, Keynes distinguishes between objects of contemplation and the mental state such objects inspire. He calls the object which inspires good feeling 'fit' and the feeling itself 'good'.

Keynes argues that we ought to create both fit objects and good states of mind. However, separating goodness from fitness permits Keynes to demonstrate that goodness is additive; hence increases in the goodness of individuals also increase goodness in the universe. Keynes argues that goodness refers only to mental states of conscious beings. Since the universe is not a conscious being capable of mental states, the ethical unit must be the individual. This move effectively reinstates egoism as an end. It also permits the argument that people, acting to improve themselves, also increase the total good in the universe. Keynes recognises, however, that fitness is still subject to the principle of organic unity.[6]

Keynes uses the concept of fitness to discuss which human characteristics should exist and incorporates into what ought to exist a broader, more complex set of mental traits. Fitness, he points out, is a characteristic of a state of mind when it is an object of contemplation. Thus states of mind can be both fit and good. In the discussion that ensues, Keynes stresses the importance in ethical deliberations of moral excellence, or dispositions to act. He emphasises that states of mind are not necessarily 'fit in proportion as they are good'; there is no *a priori* reason to suppose that fitness, 'moral beauty', must be proportionate to 'moral excellence', the ability to experience appropriate good feelings. He argues that the beauty of the mind is different from 'solid moral worth', and agrees with Plato that 'the peculiar beauty of the opening mind of youth is . . . a most fit object of affection'. He speculates that as men grow older their minds develop more intrinsic value, that, possibly, the mental qualities of youth which are considered beautiful are mere surface qualities which 'do not depend upon a subtle and penetrating knowledge of character'. On the other hand, he suggests that the increased strength of the adult mind might make it a more fit as well as a more excellent object of our love, so that the most excellent mind is also the most beautiful. Keynes comes back to this topic in another Apostles paper, 'Posterior Analytics', where he again defends the good (analytic, self-conscious, reflective) mind which is 'appreciative of details . . ., the valuation and knowledge of motives, the understanding of evil as well as of good, and a certain curiosity'. He remarks that we would 'scarcely change without it'.

In his essay, 'Egoism', written in February 1906, Keynes meets head-on Moore's utilitarian premise of the invariable connection between universal good and ought. He argues that Moore assumes what he should prove. When goodness refers to states of consciousness rather than to pleasure, Keynes asks why a person must give up his own goodness for the general good; he points out that Moore does *not* assert that 'personal goodness *consists* in the advancement of universal goodness'. And he comments that before the Christian era all 'thoughtful and reflecting persons' were egoists, because it never occurred to them that a person could ever have any goal except his own well-being. Keynes suggests that possibly Moore confuses 'rational motive as a ground of action and psychological motive as an efficient cause of action. We may be strong enough to sacrifice our own pleasure, but never strong enough deliberately to sacrifice our own goodness. We ought, but we can't.'

In a short note to himself written in April 1906, Keynes argues that Moore bases his refutation of the egoist on the assumption that 'ought' means 'this will produce in the long run the greatest amount of *good* on the whole'. Keynes says that Moore treats his basic assumption as analytic (necessarily true by definition), when it is in fact synthetic (a judgement about the world which can only be probable). He considers this to be cheating since it is very difficult to prove or persuade that this is a universal *a priori* synthetic judgement (necessarily true *and* about the world). Keynes argues, however, that some synthetic judgement must be at the basis of ethics and his problem with Moore comes when he, Keynes, treats the above judgement as synthetic. He says, 'I think I know now . . . what states of mind are good in themselves, but I still waver as to what ought to exist. And my attempt to identify the two has constantly led to difficulties.' He points out that in the history of philosophy there have been several qualities of value which have competed for the criterion of that which ought to exist for its own sake. Keynes concludes that Moore, by assuming that his judgement is analytic, is able to conclude that other philosophers have committed the 'naturalistic fallacy' of treating goodness as a natural property. This is an important criticism and one which might have influenced Moore to give up the notion that 'ought' means 'productive of the greatest good'.[7]

Two other Apostles essays seem to be intended to question Moore's emphasis on states of mind and his relative disregard of pleasure. In 'Prince Henry or Prince Rupert?', dated 28 November 1908, Keynes stages a Socratic dialogue to dramatise an argument, made earlier in 'Miscellanea Ethica' and 'A Theory of Beauty', that goodness is not purely a mental phenomenon. Prince Rupert convinces Prince Henry that strong emotions move our bodies, and that such sensations are a criterion for the genuineness of a state of mind, commenting that, in fact, most bad taste is the result of judgements formed in the absence of feeling! In a sardonic Apostles essay titled 'Paradise', Keynes notes that Moore hardly considered pleasure good at all, but that he recognised the value of punishment and argued that the pain of punishment, which in itself is a negative, could actually bring about an improvement in the state of affairs. Keynes seems to be pointing to an inconsistency in Moore's position on pleasure and pain which enabled him to play down pleasure and psychological motivation. He says, 'George Moore may be right that pain is bad and pleasure is not good.' But if this were so, why is punishment effective?

Keynes may have stated his fully developed position about what has ethical value and ought to be created in an undated, untitled paper, which he reread on 22 January 1921. Here he argues that dispositions of character are desirable for their own sake. Keynes uses 'good' to refer to states of consciousness in isolation, 'desirable' to refer to other things of value, and 'the good' (which is correlative to 'ought') to include both the good and the desirable. He calls things which are desirable 'states of affairs', because they are organic unities, and claims that they have ethical value which does not depend solely on the states of mind within them. Attributes which belong to states of affairs are beauty, harmony, justice, tragedy, virtue, consistency, truth and their opposites. For instance, only persons can be virtuous, not because of single states of consciousness, but rather as an attribute of their conduct as a whole. Unjust states of affairs exist in complex conditions where unjust men are powerful. Keynes argues that we need some knowledge to make ethical judgements; because we do not have a very clear conception of the states of mind of others, our judgements usually refer to the whole state of affairs. He thinks that our feelings relate to these organic unities rather than to states of mind. Furthermore, he warns that disregarding external relations and restricting judgements of intrinsic value to states of mind drives us, 'more than we actually are, to egotism'.

In summary, the foregoing discussion indicates a consistent development over three or four years of Keynes's position about what ends we are obligated to pursue. Starting from Moore's ideal utilitarian position that the greatest goods are certain states of consciousness related to appreciation of beauty and the pleasure of friendship, Keynes moves to a fuller description of character traits and states of affairs which are just, harmonious and so on. He also defends egoism, but clearly, from the last essay quoted, he wants to avoid a purely egoist point of view. Keynes's ethics seems to have metamorphosed from ideal utilitarianism to an ethics of virtue, in which one's obligation is to develop ethical dispositions, and in which ends and means are not so clearly distinguished as they are in utilitarian morality.

VI CIVIC DUTY

Keynes developed his attitudes about public life by the time he left Eton.[8] His most extensive writing on political theory during this period was his long essay on Edmund Burke's political philosophy. Keynes discusses and approves of Burke's modified political utilitarianism, insofar as he maintains that the only legitimate goal of political activity is the happiness of the people. Keynes also shares Burke's disdain for politics based on abstract principles which ignore actual circumstances. He emphasises, however, that Burke's own political views were principled, and that Burke could not be considered, ethically, a utilitarian because he believed in fixed standards of right and wrong.

Burke's political philosophy constitutes an ethical theory of the state in which political authority is vested in a principled elite, and in which democratic institutions serve solely to check abuse of power. I have argued elsewhere that Keynes adopted the logic, but not the content, of Burke's political philosophy (Helburn 1991). Virtuous men are crucial to Burke's and Keynes's political elitism, and, interestingly, in the 1904 essay Keynes quotes an 'admirable passage' of Burke's describing the 'whole duty of man' which emphasises the traits of the good member of the polis and seems to parallel Keynes's emphasis on the virtues:

> we are born only to be men. We shall do enough if we form ourselves to be good ones. It is therefore our business carefully to cultivate in our minds, to rear to the most perfect vigour and maturity, every sort of generous and honest feeling, that belongs in our nature, to bring dispositions that are lovely in private life into the service and conduct of the commonwealth; so to be patriots as not to forget we are gentlemen. To cultivate friendships, and to incur enmities. To have both strong, both selected: in the one to be placable, in the other immovable. To model our principles to our duties and our situation. To be fully persuaded that all virtue which is impracticable is spurious; which leads us to act with effect and energy, rather than to loiter out our days without blame and without use. (Keynes 1904b: 9–10.)

Few of the Apostles papers focus on civic duty.[9] However, 'Modern Civilisation', written on 28 October 1905, is an important early statement indicating Keynes's commitment to public duty.[10] In this essay Keynes criticises the conservative basis of Burke's politics, especially the view that duties are unchanging. He contends that economic progress is likely to transform what had seemed most fundamental to morality in the past. Although ultimate goods, 'founded on the nature of things and of goodness', are eternal, Keynes argues that duty, what we ought to do, is a matter of circumstance. He recognises that not all actions should be decided individually, because duty is guided by rules (based on past experience) which have such general validity that they ought to be accepted. But he argues that 'there is coming a revolution in duty', because rapid economic development is increasing the scale of the social organism and converting the whole world into one unit. Just as changes in the scale in production require different technology, so, in social life, changes in scale require new methods. 'Duty', Keynes says, 'is our method in social life', and with fundamental social change, duties must change. He concludes that 'Plato will remain the prophet of those who live apart from the machine. But in the Kingdom of moralities and duties the Galilaean will himself be conquered . . . by the irresistible trend of human affairs and the need for an adequate and relevant morality.' It is important to note that in this essay Keynes rejects Burke's claim of the universality of duty and the contemporary system of morality. However, he recognises that duty must be based on rules and he does *not* defend act-consequentialism.

VII KEYNES AND CONSEQUENTIALISM

Keynes questions Moore's practical ethics of conduct as early as 1904, in 'Ethics in Relation to Conduct', where he first raises his objection to Moore's conclusion that there is little rational ground for choosing between alternative actions to increase universal good. Moore acknowledges that one often can rank actions in terms of their immediate consequences; however, he argues that one cannot know the long-run effects. In contrast Keynes argues that if, with given knowledge of the situation, one alternative is likely to provide more benefit in the short run, and if nothing is known about long-run effects, it is rational to choose the alternative providing the most short-run benefit.

In Chapter 26 of the *Treatise on Probability* Keynes refines this analysis. Superficially, this appears to clear the way for consequentialist thinking. However, most of the chapter is in fact a critique of consequentialism conceived of as a comparison of quantitative estimates of expected values. Keynes demonstrates that estimates of mathematical expectations are based on intuition. Moreover, these estimates must be revised to allow for the weight of the argument and for moral risk, both of which also have an intuitive component.

Assuming that greater goodness of a part makes greater goodness in the whole more probable (an assumption Keynes considers problematic), he argues that a fundamental problem exists in the use of mathematical expectation (*JMK* VIII: 312). He questions whether quantities of goodness are subject to laws of mathematics. Indeed, even degrees of probability are often not subject to the laws of mathematics. And even if it is possible to sum mathematical expectations, Keynes argues that comparison of such results might not give the most rational judgement. Taking expectations alone disregards the weight of the argument – the amount of evidence available to support the expectation. The element of risk is also disregarded. For instance, the undesirability of an action might increase more than proportionately to its uncertainty: 'We may doubt whether the moral value of speculative and cautious action respectively can be weighted against one another in a simple arithmetical way' (*ibid.*: 314).

Keynes argues that one must be able to 'make direct quantitative judgments of probability and goodness jointly. . . . If therefore, the question of right action is under all circumstance a determinate problem, it must be in virtue of an intuitive judgment directed at the situation as a whole' (*ibid.*: 312). He points out that the difficulty in taking weight and risk into account derives from 'the lack of any principle for the calculation of the degree of their influence' (*ibid.*: 315). He concludes:

> The judgment of goodness and the judgment of probability both involve somewhere an element of direct apprehension, and both are quantitative. We have raised a doubt as to whether the magnitude of 'oughtness' of an action can be in all cases directly determined by simply multiplying together the magnitudes obtained in the direct judgments. . . . The hope, which sustained many investigators in the course of the nineteenth century, of gradually bringing the moral sciences under the sway of mathematical reasoning, steadily recedes. (*Ibid.*: 316.)

As noted above, O'Donnell considers Keynes an act-consequentialist, claiming that Keynes corrected the procedure for determining probable consequences (O'Donnell 1989: 107). This is true; however, Keynes held that the procedure depends on intuition at each crucial point, and mere technical, that is, mathematical, comparison of alternatives is usually not justified. The quality of judgement depends on the quality of intuition. Broadening the definition of act-consequentialism to include Keynes's method makes it almost meaningless. Even the procedures for comparing consequences described in Chapter 26 of the *Treatise on Probability* are only possible when alternative outcomes can be reduced to one standard of value. Furthermore, it can be argued that, for Keynes, rational (and moral) action involves a continuous process of trying to achieve the best result under continually shifting circumstances. In particular, mathematical problem solving has limited usefulness when knowledge of what is possible changes with the circumstances and 'the best' is a moving target.

Getting the best solution with limited foresight requires both intellectual powers, flexibility and the will to see a project through to the most successful conclusion possible. Thus, categorising Keynes as an act-consequentialist detracts from this central feature of his ethics, in which it is motives rather than outcomes, experience and good judgement rather than mechanistic problem-solving – the qualities of the decision-maker – which are important.

VIII 'MY EARLY BELIEFS' AND KEYNES AS AN IMMORALIST

In 'My Early Beliefs' Keynes restates views developed earlier in the 'Juvenilia', indicating considerable continuity in the development of his ethics. In this essay Keynes distances himself from many of his youthful excesses, although he refuses to recant on the basic intuitions of his early beliefs. Nevertheless, the good-humoured but sometimes mocking tone only takes the sting out of what amounts to profound self-criticism.

In the 'Juvenilia' Keynes had moved away from Moore's narrow emphasis on isolated states of consciousness and argued that desirable character traits ought to exist for their own sake. In 'Prince Henry or Prince Rupert?' he also emphasised the importance of emotions. In 'Egoism' he had apparently rejected the universalist obligation to maximise the good in the universe if it required sacrificing one's own good. In 'Modern Civilisation' he defends public duty, but, calling duty our method in social life, he emphasised that it changes according to circumstance. All of these views reappear in 'My Early Beliefs'.

Keynes summarises the Apostles' 'religion', 'one's attitude towards oneself and the ultimate' and their 'morals', 'one's attitude towards the outside world and the intermediate', and sums up Moore's influence with the remark, 'We accepted Moore's religion, so to speak, and discarded his morals' (*JMK* X: 436). The religion, according to Keynes, involved timeless passionate states of contemplation and communion, largely unattached to 'before' and 'after', and endless discussions, which they considered 'entirely rational and scientific', ordering states of consciousness according to their relative value (*ibid.*: 438–9). Keynes says he continues to accept the fundamental intuition of *Principia Ethica*; however, in retrospect he considers them 'too few and too narrow':

> Indeed it is only states of mind that matter, provided we agree to take account of the pattern of life through time and give up regarding it as a series of independent, instantaneous flashes, but the ways in which states of mind can be valuable, and the objects of them, are more various, and also much richer, than we allowed for. (*Ibid.*: 449–50.)

Three moral principles were discarded: Moore's utilitarian criterion which obligated a person to act to produce the 'most probable maximum eventual good', the Benthamite calculus and the duty to obey general moral rules. Because the Apostles denied any obligation to obey moral maxims, Keynes says they were, 'in the strict sense of the term, immoralists' (*ibid.*: 445–6).

Keynes does not repudiate the early rejection of the utilitarian criterion. Nor does he disavow his rejection of Benthamite calculus, which he says is 'based on an over-valuation of the economic criterion'. Indeed he claims it had destroyed 'the quality of the popular ideal'. Keynes is objecting to the effect on people's values (character?) of over-valuing economic goals. He does not object to pursuit of pleasure *per se*, but to the value system encouraged by Benthamism, which emphasises economic reward, encourages forward-looking, goal-oriented 'purposiveness', and thereby inhibits people from living in the present and enjoying the truly human pleasures such as friendship and the contemplation of beauty.

He considers his early disregard for traditional rules of conduct a mistake, admitting that the group's faith in individual judgement was based on the false assumption that human nature is reasonable.

> We were not aware that civilisation was a thin and precarious crust erected by the personality and the will of a very few, and only maintained by rules and conventions skilfully put across and guilefully preserved. We had no respect for traditional wisdom or the restraints of custom. . . . It did not occur to us to respect the extraordinary accomplishment of our predecessors in the ordering of life . . . or the elaborate framework which they had devised to protect that order. (*Ibid.*: 447–8.)

That faith in rationality, he remarks, led to a 'superficiality, not only of performance, but of feeling' (*ibid.*: 448) which left out 'powerful and valuable springs of feeling' as well as many fit objects of contemplation 'related to the order and pattern of life among communities'.

> I can see us as water-spiders, gracefully skimming, as light and reasonable as air, the surface of the stream without any contact at all with the eddies and currents underneath . . . this thin rationalism skipping on the crust of the lava, ignoring both the reality and the value of the vulgar passions, joined to libertinism and comprehensive irreverence, too clever by half . . . a regular skin poison. (*Ibid.*: 450.)

This is a Burkean evaluation amounting almost to a recantation, and the stress on emotions is interesting in the light of his criticisms in the Apostles papers of the inadequate attention given to feeling.

These statements, however, need to be interpreted in the light of his admission earlier in the essay, 'I remain, and always will remain, an immoralist' (*ibid.*: 447). The argument in this chapter suggests that we avoid interpreting this statement in a moralistic sense. It is more accurate to consider Keynes's ethics closer to an ethics of virtue which focuses on dispositions of character rather than social expectations. This ethics emphasises that individuals make a difference in social life, and that their effectiveness is based on inner dispositions which involve a mixture of intellectual and moral excellence – wisdom, spirit or courage, and control – over more immediate human appetites. It is in this sense that Keynes calls himself an 'immoralist', in the 'strict' sense of the word. His actions, and sense of duty, are governed by inner dispositions rather than by external moral expectations.

Keynes confesses that, while the complete repudiation of customary morals and traditions might have been wrong, he cannot change (because his character is already formed). The persisting need to think for himself stems from his individualism, and he admits as much, remarking that 'we carried this individualism of our individuals too far' (*ibid.*, 448). However much he might recant on human reasonableness, he never gives up his fundamental faith in individuals, at least certain individuals. His faith in individual will, creativity and character is unabated even though he becomes more aware of human fallibility.

That Keynes valued personal dispositions of character is evident in his biographies and obituaries for friends. Keynes speaks of 'a rare quality of excellence' in A.F.R. Wollaston, Chancellor of the University:

> some quality of his actions in themselves as distinct from their causes or consequences. . . . This aptitude for beauty in action could not, of course, have found its full expression if it had not been combined with many other qualities. Perhaps the most necessary was concentration on the surrounding circumstances rather than on himself. (*Ibid.*: 347–8.)

And he says about William Herrick Macauley that he was

> a man of remarkable character and powers, of a nearly infallible judgment both of intellect and of right feeling on all matters falling within the strict range of his attention, never untrue in the least degree to his own standards, and dealing with all according to his own honour and dignity. . . . Chiefly, perhaps, we shall remember him as a man whom many of the principles of behaviour and feeling, which we most admire, ruled spontaneously, without there being required any choice or decision in the matter. (*Ibid.*: 351, 356.)

Perhaps the most significant comment is Keynes's explanation of Alfred

Marshall's long delay in publishing the *Principles*. Here Keynes clearly states why trying too hard to 'do good' is actually self-defeating.

> Marshall was too anxious to do good. He had an inclination to undervalue those intellectual parts of the subject which were not *directly* connected with human well being or the condition of the working classes or the like, although *indirectly* they might be of the utmost importance, and to feel that when he was pursuing them he was not occupying himself with the *Highest*. (*Ibid*.: 200.)

IX CONCLUSIONS

Keynes converted Moore's ideal utilitarianism to a rational ethics of virtue which emphasised well-being, that is, how one should live one's whole life. If Carabelli is right about the Aristotelian influence on his method of analysis, Keynes may have been similarly influenced by Aristotle's ethics. This is, nevertheless, consistent with political utilitarianism, because it incorporates both private and civic moral responsibility, as well as prudence, as defined by Burke. It means that Keynes resolved Moore's (and Sidgwick's) inability to choose rationally between doing good and being good. It also explains Keynes's defence of egoism. It provides a firmer psychological basis for action than does utilitarianism. Utilitarianism is a very demanding morality, requiring people to act for the good of the whole at all times. However, it provides no reason to expect people to be so altruistic, which accounts for the moralising which Keynes and his friends probably found so trying. Finally, this interpretation explains Keynes's own claim that, 'in the strict sense of the term' he was an immoralist. He rejected a 'system' of morality but *not* a moral life.

Keynes also rejected the Benthamite tradition, which defines goodness and evil strictly in terms of pleasure and pain, emphasising economic values and the hedonic calculus. Not only did Keynes consider the procedure often impossible or inappropriate, he also held that using it as a guide to action encourages 'purposiveness' and over-emphasises materialist values, negatively affecting character by inhibiting the formation of more human values and, therefore, more productive and satisfying lives.

Keynes rejected consequentialism as usually defined and practised – basing judgements of probability on a summing-up of mathematical expectations. True, he was always concerned about consequences, but he warned about the use of pseudo-rational methods, that is, the inappropriate use of mathematical calculation. Rather, he counted on intuition and moral courage, and a broad spectrum of methods, including critical reflection and discussion. Thus I disagree with O'Donnell's description of the philosophy of practical reason developed by Keynes in *Treatise on Probability* as a form of act-consequentialism. However, O'Donnell is quite right in arguing that Keynes's purpose was 'the restoration of individual judgement as the arbiter in *all* cases, and not merely . . . in some' (O'Donnell 1989: 119). Even as a young man, and particularly as he grew older, Keynes did accept moral rules and maxims, and not always merely as useful means. The final pages of 'My Early Beliefs' indicate what he might have learned from Burke about the value of conservancy and an ordered society.

The view of Keynes's ethics presented here provides a deeper understanding of his politics and his goals for economics. The *General Theory* is a repudiation of the economic theory which Keynes says furnished a scientific justification for *laissez-faire* for the nineteenth-century Utilitarians (*JMK* IX: 277–8). Keynes recognised the need for an interventionist liberal politics which promotes both the happiness of the people and also, to the extent possible, their well-being. His was an elitist politics, and he might be described as he characterised Burke: 'Politically he may, without serious inaccuracy, be described as a utilitarian; for, with the exception of occasional lapse, he sets before himself the happiness of the community as the sole and ultimate end of government' (Keynes: 1904b). The principle of expediency which he followed was similar to Burke's: policies should be designed by the elites to fit the circumstances and the temper of the times. Such practice enables the elites to manage progress so as to make it consistent with *their* values.

In the 1930s Keynes described his own politics as on the extreme left of celestial space, presumably to indicate his visionary hopes for a post-capitalist world and his desire to encourage changes consonant with this vision. His elitism and limited tolerance of democratic practice and working-class politics give his politics a decidedly conservative edge. Nevertheless his conscious integration of ethical considerations, political philosophy and social sciences into practical reason created a powerful rational basis for twentieth-century interventionist liberalism.

NOTES

* I wish to acknowledge the help of Judith Allan, who made the Keynes manuscripts available to me at the Marshall Library in Cambridge, and the help of Dr Michael Halls with the papers in the Modern Archives at King's College Library. Permission to quote from the unpublished manuscripts in the J.M. Keynes papers in King's

College Library was kindly granted by King's College, Cambridge University. In addition I have benefited greatly from discussions about this paper with Athol Fitzgibbons, Anna Carabelli, Gary Stahl, James Smith and Bruce Watson.

1. Marshall, as is well known, also recognised the effect of ethical behaviour on the performance of the economy. He recognised that economic and social progress in capitalist society depended on the concurrent development of high moral character, 'economic chivalry', among the capitalist class, and even among the working classes. In his evolutionary theories of social development, his optimism was based on the assumption that economic and moral progress represented an interactive, self-reinforcing process (Marshall 1920: Ch. XIII).
2. Utilitarians seek to maximise the good in the universe; egoists, who, in a sense, reject the ethical point of view, seek what is best for their own individual welfare.
3. By egoism I mean the position that each person should pursue his or her own best interests. This is a teleological viewpoint in that it assumes persons are goal-oriented to pursue their own welfare. It is also consequentialist in that it assumes that persons should act according to a consideration of all the consequences of their action.
4. Interestingly, advocates of *laissez-faire* politics (and some neo-classical economists) inverted this reasoning to argue that pursuit of self-interest in fact yields the greatest good for the greatest number. This latter view ignores the fact that some persons have to be concerned about the good of the social whole, and early utilitarians did recognise this by assuming altruism among moral agents.
5. Act-consequentialism seems to mean that the moral agent should make judgements based on the consequences of each act. It would seem that this is another term for act-utilitarianism, the position that one is obligated to take that action which yields the greatest good for the universe. It is not clear to me why O'Donnell chooses this term rather than act-utilitarian to describe Keynes, unless he means to indicate Keynes also used consequentialist reasoning to determine actions which would promote his greatest personal good.
6. In 'Miscellanea Ethica' Keynes notes that the quality of fitness is observable, perfectly objective and admits of degrees. Therefore it can be assessed, whereas the goodness of states of mind cannot be assessed by others. Keynes argues that 'the fitness of an object is in precise proportion to the goodness of the best feeling it can inspire'. There are, for instance, unfit objects for which the appropriate feeling is bad. It would seem that in making judgements of value, Keynes thought that ranking the fitness of objects of contemplation becomes a proxy for ranking the corresponding goodness of states of mind, so that it is possible to overcome the problem of objective ranking of states of mind.
7. Moore rejected this notion in his 'A Reply to My Critics' (Schilpp, 1942). See Williams 1985: 206 n. 12.
8. See the quote from a speech Keynes made on liberalism during his last year at Eton in Skidelsky 1985: 102.
9. There are some exceptions. In his essay on 'Toleration', written in 1904, he discusses whether or not the principle of toleration, as a public policy, should be universally accepted. In 'Have we a Panacea?' he defends liberal politics based on rational, step-by-step problem-solving, but worries about competing against political movements which sway the public with panaceas.
10. The essay is undated, but O'Donnell dates it 28 October 1905.

REFERENCES

Bateman, B., 1988, 'G.E. Moore and J.M. Keynes: A Missing Chapter in the History of the Expected Utility Model', *American Economic Review*, vol. 78, 5.

Carabelli, A., 1988, *On Keynes's Method*, Macmillan, London/St Martin's Press, New York.

Fitzgibbons, A.J., 1988, *Keynes's Vision: A New Political Economy*, Oxford University Press, Oxford.

Helburn, S.H., 1991, 'Keynes and Burke', in B. Bateman and J. Davis, eds, *Keynes and Philosophy*, Edward Elgar, London.

Keynes, J.M., 1904–10, Juvenilia manuscripts housed in the Modern Archives at King's College Library, Cambridge:
1904a 'Beauty'.
1904b 'The Political Principles of Edmund Burke'.
1904c 'Ethics in Relation to Conduct'.
1904 'Toleration'.
1905 'Miscellanea Ethica'
1905 'A Theory of Beauty'.
1905 'Modern Civilisation'.
1906 'Egoism'.
1906 Untitled paper on Moore's meta-ethics.
1908 'Prince Henry or Prince Rupert?'
n.d. 'Paradise'.
n.d. 'Posterior Analytics'.
1910 No title, on desirable states of affairs.

Keynes, J.M., 1973–89, in D.E. Moggridge, ed., *The Collected Writings of John Maynard Keynes*, 30 vols, Macmillan, London/St Martin's Press, New York. (*JMK* in text.)
Vol. VIII: *A Treatise on Probability*, 1921.
Vol. IX: *Essays in Persuasion*, 1931.
Vol. X: *Essays in Biography*, 1933
Vol. VII: *The General Theory of Employment, Interest and Money*, 1936. (*GT* in text.)

Lawson, T. and H. Pesaran, eds, 1985, *Keynes' Economics: Methodological Issues*, Croom Helm, London & Sydney.

MacIntyre, A., 1981, *After Virtue*, 2nd edn, University of Notre Dame Press, Notre Dame, Indiana.

Marshall, A., 1920, *Principles of Economics*, 8th edn, Macmillan, London/Porcupine Press, Philadelphia.

Moore, G.E., 1942, 'A Reply to my Critics', in P.A. Schilpp, ed., *The Philosophy of G.E. Moore*, Open Court Publishing Co., La Salle.

Moore, G.E., 1903, *Principia Ethica* (1959 edition), Cambridge University Press, Cambridge.

O'Donnell, R.M., 1989, *Keynes: Philosophy, Economics and Politics: The Philosophical Foundations of Keynes's Thought and their Influence on his Economics and Politics*, Macmillan, London.

Schneewind, J.B., 1977, *Sidgwick's Ethics and Victorian Moral Philosophy*, Clarendon Press, Oxford.

Sidgwick, H., 1884, *The Methods of Ethics*, Macmillan, London.

Sidgwick, H., 1960, *Outline of the History of Ethics*, 6th edn, enlarged, Beacon Press, Boston, Mass.

Skidelsky, R., 1983, *John Maynard Keynes, Volume I: Hopes Betrayed, 1883–1920*, Macmillan, London.

Skidelsky, R., 1987, 'Keynes' Political Legacy', in A. Kilmanock, ed., *The Radical Challenge*, Deutsch Publications, London.

Williams, B., 1985, *Ethics and the Limits of Philosophy*, Harvard University Press, Cambridge, Mass.

4. Some Semantics of Endogeneity

Adrian Winnett*

I INTRODUCTION: THE LIMITATIONS OF THE SPECIAL CASE

Many post-Keynesians now work with the assumption that the money supply is endogenous. Quite varying interpretations are put on this assumption; the purpose of this chapter is to question some, at least, of these interpretations. This questioning will serve as a peg on which to hang some wider reflections on the procedures of post-Keynesian economics. In particular, I want to develop the argument that some versions of the endogeneity assumption draw post-Keynesians into diversionary disputes with their neo-classical colleagues and inhibit the development of their own distinctive approach. By this I mean that the phrasing of the assumption is such that they are already operating within the confines of a basically neo-classical model, arguing about the shape or independence of the money supply function (Davidson 1990). They are then trapped, an opportune word, within the confines of a special case. The obvious, not unrelated, parallel is with the narrowing of debate associated with the re-interpretation of liquidity preference as a theory of the demand for money. The task then, as Keynes well understood, is to revise our conceptual categories so that the special case and the general case change places.

II MONETARY THEORY AND VALUE THEORY

The central role accorded to the assumption of endogeneity by post-Keynesians represents the convergence of two main, related lines of argument. Firstly, there is the question of the most adequate way to develop a critique of the quantity-theoretic foundations of monetarism, as both theory and policy. Secondly, there is the question of the relationship between interest rates and prices in non-neo-classical as compared with neo-classical models. I refer to these as the monetary-theoretic and value-theoretic questions, respectively.

On the first question, endogeneity in the sense of the monetary authorities' inability to control the money supply – or, at least, to control it at any acceptable cost[1] – is clearly sufficient to rule out monetarism as a policy (Kaldor 1982). But this argument is often transposed into an analytical context, where it is supposed to discredit much more general neo-classical arguments, such as those of dichotomisation of monetary and real sectors, and monetary neutrality. In short, having failed to establish a convincing divide between quantity-theoretic and Keynesian arguments on the demand for money side, it is as though an easier route appears to be open on the supply of money side. Serious discussion of endogeneity tends to drop from sight at this point, and it appears simply to be a justificatory assumption for parametric money interest rates – an alternative to a liquidity trap in the money demand function. Reflection on the prolonged debates around the latter issue should readily convince us that there is, in fact, no easy route from an assumption about the shape of one function to general statements about the adequacy of general neo-classical monetary models. Post-Keynesians would, of course, reply that they do not accept many of the other assumptions of such models; the point, though, is that in posing the problem in terms of demand and supply functions for money, they have already made very large concessions to the neo-classical point of view, and they have denied themselves many possibilities for showing how their assumptions might form a coherent alternative.

This leads into the second, value-theoretic issue. The centrepiece of the neo-classical model is its theory of relative price determination; ultimately, it is this model which underpins the most general neo-classical propositions about the role of money in the economy. The most direct challenge to this central model comes from those theories which emphasise the dependence of relative prices on some distributional parameter, where the parameter is not itself determined within the pricing model. The best articulated of these models are the neo-Ricardian ones, though more partial models of mark-up pricing share many of the same features (Moore 1989). Indeed, the attempt to introduce monetary features into the former must lead to some convergence between them. This is because the neo-Ricardian models are specified in process space, whereas the mark-up models are specified in agent space, and, at some point, monetary factors such as asset and liability positions have, presumably, to be specified in relation to the latter.[2] Whether and how this bridge-building should take place must be a major agenda item for all those interested in developing an alternative to neo-classicism. At present I am interested in a more limited issue: the way in which the money interest rate is to be integrated into neo-Ricardian models. Following Sraffa's (1960: 33) by now notorious suggestion, the interest rate can be treated as a parameter determining the rate of profit.

The most straightforward account along these lines is provided by Pivetti (1990). He makes clear that the money wage rate has also to be taken as exogenous, and the interest rate is then set to determine the rate of profit and therefore the purchasing power of the wage in terms of commodities. In effect, the monetary authorities, in setting the interest rate, represent some sort of collective consciousness of the capitalist class in the determination of income distribution.[3] Generously interpreted, this seems a satisfactory response to a standard objection against accounts of this sort, which is that the income distribution appears to be sorted out on financial markets and not on the shop floor, the ostensible site of distributional struggles. Not so satisfactory, perhaps, is the implication that in an inflationary environment, the monetary authorities have to set a real rate of interest; this is not so easy to justify in terms of the standard endogeneity arguments to which Pivetti appeals in parametrising the interest rate, and, more generally, it suggests that the value-theoretic question has not been thoroughly re-assessed to allow for monetary influences.

Indeed, there are major issues to do with exactly how the interest rate enters such models. Pivetti simply assumes that the profit rate is marked up over the interest rate to reflect the risks and costs of employing productive as against financial capital; this argument is also familiar from mark-up models of industrial pricing. A somewhat more sophisticated account is provided by Franke (1988), who distinguishes between owned capital and borrowed capital, so that prices reflect a rate of profit which is a weighted average of the profit rate on owned capital and the interest rate; these last two rates determine the ratio between owned and borrowed capital. For any wage rate, there will then be a (possibly complex) relationship between the profit rate on owned capital and the interest rate. So the interest rate cannot simply be set to close the model since there are two degrees of freedom. One of these could be eliminated by assuming balanced growth and invoking a 'Cambridge' saving function to link growth and profits. Another sort of complication is that discussed by Panico (1988), who assumes that financial capital is provided by a specialised sector which earns the going profit rate by marking up lending rates over borrowing rates.

These exercises really illustrate two points. First, the relationship between the profit rate and the interest rate is likely to be of some complexity in multi-sector production models, even if these introduce monetary factors in a fairly naive way. Assuming parametric interest rates is not such a transparently obvious closure of the model as it may first appear. Second, perhaps closure is a misguided quest anyway, both in principle and particularly if it has to be bought at the expense of modelling procedures which deploy assumptions that appear to lead far from what seems appropriate to understanding monetary economies. The way in which money is represented seems to be driven very much by the perceived requirements of the model.

Whether the issue is looked at from the monetary-theoretic or the value-theoretic side, the *analytical* work is being done by the parametrisation of the money interest rate.[4] But however persuasive the usual endogeneity arguments are from a policy point of view, they simply cannot carry the analytical demands that are being made on them. (Exactly why we might wish to continue to use them as policy arguments is a point to which I return.) This will be clear if the monetary- and value-theoretic arguments are thought of in terms of Wicksell's pure credit money economy – the prototype 'horizontalist' model, in Basil Moore's phrase. In Wicksell's model (1936) the money rate is fixed independently of the natural rate, at least in the short run. This generates price level dynamics within a completely neo-classical world; nothing has happened to disturb the workings of the real economy. The process is the same as would take place with a steadily growing, exogenous money stock. This is, of course, due to the assumption of a natural rate.

If we now turn to models which explicitly abandon the capital-theoretic assumptions behind the natural rate, there is no convincing explanation of how monetary factors are at work in the model in ways which could justify the weight placed on the money rate as a 'closure' of the model. In short, we need to think in terms of models – perhaps too restrictive a phrase – within which monetary factors are pervasive. Simply thinking in terms of the shape of the money supply function is an inadequate way of discriminating monetary from 'real' economies. I now wish to reflect a little more fully on why this is so. I consider three issues: the alleged exogeneity of commodity and fiat money as against credit money; the way in which the functioning of the banking sector is conceptualised in models of endogeneity; and the social conventions surrounding the definition of monetary assets. These will each provide pointers as to how we might proceed.

III COMMODITY AND FIAT MONEY

The distinction between endogeneity and exogeneity is to do with the causal structure of models. This in itself should give post-Keynesians pause for thought as to the usefulness of such a distinction (Dow 1988). But for the moment I will continue to think in these terms. This means that great care is needed in specifying the model space. The endogeneity or exogeneity of credit money is described in interest rate–money stock space because these are the decision variables of the relevant institutions. In the same way we could define decision variables and therefore model spaces for commodity money and, more problematically, for fiat money. There is no reason why a definition of endogeneity that is appropriate to credit money should tell us anything at all about the endogeneity of other types of money. But there is a persistent tendency to think in terms of commodity and fiat money as somehow created outside the system and of credit money as created within it. This tells us more about the adequacy of our ways of attempting to deal with monetary systems than about endogeneity and exogeneity.

Consider commodity money; presumably commodity money (gold) must be produced and/or have significant non-money uses. Either way its price must be determined as part of the pricing process of all commodities. If gold is produced, the money price level in equilibrium must be consistent with the money wage rate being the marginal product of labour in the gold industry. The argument for exogeneity in these cases is that the stock cannot alter by a significant amount in a finite time, other than by unforeseen discoveries. The former is justified by an assumption of sharply rising marginal costs on existing resources. But if the price level is to change by a finite amount in a finite time this implies that marginal costs will alter significantly as production flows adjust to cover changed levels of depreciation of the stock and/or non-money uses which are not unit price-elastic. And discoveries, of course, amount to a shift in the marginal cost function. More fundamentally, it is plausible to think of the discovery process as responsive to economic variables, as is now standard in economic modelling of natural resources. This view seems historically reasonable. So even as between stationary states, and *a fortiori* growing steady states, there is no necessity to think of the money price level as determined by an exogenous stock of commodity money.

In the same way that discussions of credit-money endogeneity are appropriately phrased in terms of the decision variables of the credit industry, so should discussions of commodity-money endogeneity be phrased in terms of the decision variables of commodity-money producers (and non-money-use consumers). Indeed classical monetary theory was often strongly horizontalist – in the relevant model space – in assuming a constant marginal cost of gold production! Glasner (1985, 1989) has recently argued that the core classical monetary theory was *not* the quantity theory, but a theory of commodity money, extended, through some sort of real bills doctrine, to include competitively issued paper money.[5] The quantity theory was a special theory applicable to inconvertible paper money, not an attempt to show that paper could or should behave like gold.

How the special case of inconvertible paper money – fiat money – became paradigmatic for monetary theory is an interesting question. I suppose the answer is that it is the easiest type of money to regard as an exogenous variable in the conduct of neutrality exercises and the like. It seems to fit in naturally with the way in which economic decisions are conceptualised in the neo-classical world and with the desire to abstract supposedly fundamental explanatory forces – preferences and technology – from explicit institutional reference. To accept this sort of model as a starting-point is therefore to impose serious distortions on any ensuing discussion. Instead, it is better to look at the origins of debates surrounding inconvertible paper and especially at their context of wartime inflation and post-war dislocation in early nineteenth-century Britain. Here there is no lack of institutional reference: money was perceived as a creature of the state, manipulated for political ends. This is, of course, generally true, but the nature of the manipulation is peculiarly obvious and direct in the case of inconvertible paper, which is associated historically with periods of crisis in the financing of the state. This suggests that far from being the 'purest' form of money, fiat money is the most highly politicised, and the most unlikely to be understood in isolation from the way politico-economic institutions operate, often in somewhat extreme conditions, where the state has either acquired exceptional control over civil society or is close to disintegration.

Thus, if we wish to think in terms of the endogeneity or exogeneity of fiat money, we will certainly have to extend the boundaries of the model to include some aspects of the political economy of the state. Such discussions as there are by economists tend to collapse the issue into one of the costs and benefits of inflation, though some of these treatments begin to raise wider questions (Gordon 1975); of more interest are the detailed accounts offered by historians, for instance of policy-making after the Napoleonic Wars (Hilton 1977). Yet the salience of these discussions for the understanding of the historical evolution of monetary processes has not been properly appreciated. All too often fiat money is represented as a sort of evolutionary stage between commodity and credit money.

IV CREDIT MONEY AND THE BANKING INDUSTRY

I turn now to credit-money regimes. These are the focus of attention for those who believe that endogeneity of the money supply is, or should be, a crucial point of differentiation between post-Keynesians and more conventional monetary economists (see, especially, Moore 1988 for an exhaustive discussion and numerous references). Moore takes particular exception to the 'verticalist' model of a high-powered monetary base, controlled by the monetary authorities, supporting the money supply through a credit-creation multiplier dependent on fixed reserve ratios and other assumed constants. This may be thought of rather mechanically or, more plausibly, as the response of a reserve-constrained monopolistic industry, though the latter is liable to behave in ways inconsistent with the strict verticalist model.

In the verticalist model the banking sector is said to be a quantity setter and a price taker. Against this it is argued that the banking sector is, in fact, a price setter and a quantity taker. Both of these seem pretty appalling models of a complex, regulated oligopoly. The horizontalist argument is that the banking sector's creation of assets necessarily creates monetary liabilities, and that assets are created on demand. Commercial banks set an interest rate and at this rate their operating procedure is to meet their customers' demands for loans. Likewise, the central bank sets an interest rate at which it passively meets demands for reserves. (Liability management complicates the picture, since banks are clearly not passive quantity takers in the relevant markets. The argument seems to be that banks satisfy their residual demand for funds in these markets, but at rates ultimately dependent on the actions of the central bank.)

There are clearly numerous detailed problems with this story (some of which are to do with the way in which liability management is handled), including the apparent lack of constraint on central bank interest-rate strategies other than those flowing from the reactions of other central banks. But I will mention two general issues.

First, in financial markets, credit rationing is clearly observed to take place. This suggests that banks are *both* price setters *and* quantity setters; it is misleading to believe that they have to be one or the other. The usual explanation for credit rationing is that if interest rates were set to satisfy all demands for loans it would increase the probability of default, in the absence of very good information about all borrowers (Stiglitz 1987). This is perfectly consistent with under-utilised lines of credit or with banks seeking out borrowers, and seems to me quite reasonable as a post-Keynesian argument! More generally banks' lending and borrowing strategies may evolve in quite fundamentally new directions as the financial system develops, invalidating any general account of the way in which they set interest rates and meet loan demands (Chick 1986; again, liability management is a relevant issue: Goodhart 1989). Therefore this first issue disputes the usefulness of thinking in terms of outcomes as having to lie on price–quantity schedules, and of taking announced or understood operating procedures as adequate interpretations of those outcomes.

The second issue, to which I now turn, is again to do with institutional strategies in an industry like banking. Here I wish to focus more on relations between the central bank and the commercial banks, though analogous points might arise in terms of relations among commercial banks and of their relations with other parts of the financial system, and some of the foregoing issues of credit rationing and borrowing–lending strategy might similarly characterise central bank activities.

There has been periodic argument as to whether the alleged endogeneity of the monetary base is a result of specific central bank operating procedures or of more general rules of the game, such as lender of last resort facilities. What I wish to suggest is that the appropriate way to approach this question is to think of the central bank and the commercial banks as players in a politico-economic game. There are some very good accounts of particular episodes, notably Moran's analysis (1984) of Competition and Credit Control and the secondary banking crisis. This shows how the rules of the game were negotiated and renegotiated in British banking in the 1970s. There are a number of more formal models of 'policy credibility' (Blackburn and Christensen 1989) which suggest insights into these processes of institutional change. For example, in repeated games in which players' motivations are uncertain, it is easy to establish patterns of collusion followed by defection, with the timing of defections partly dependent on the time horizon of the players. Again, there is a well-known conflict between the desire of a principal to secure an agent's compliance, requiring discretionary action, and the inconsistencies that this can generate over time, requiring rules (O'Flaherty 1990).

I am not sure that these more formal models tell us any more than does careful historical description and analysis. But the point is the one made earlier in relation to fiat money: that it is essential to expand the boundaries of the model beyond what is conventionally regarded as economic. Indeed, this may well imply the abandonment of anything like model-building in the usual sense. Within a given institutional set-up, it can then make sense to ask whether certain strategies are feasible or whether they will lead to institutional breakdown, and how this might be resolved. Wojnilower's 'credit crunches' and Minsky's 'financial fragility' are attempts to capture some of the financial limits to institutional stability in the United States, but with perhaps insufficient attention to the role of the political system in the financial process (Wojnilower 1980, Minsky 1982). Only within this politico-economic context is it possible to ask if money supply control is a feasible institutional strategy, and to conclude that *sometimes* it may not be. But sometimes it may be, and we should not rush to general conclusions from particular historical circumstances.

These arguments are necessarily at a far more specific institutional level than is captured by general statements about the nature of credit money. What is quite clear is that defining endogeneity in terms of the elasticities of money supply functions in interest rate–money stock space is adequate neither to the general phenomenon of credit money as a pervasive feature of transactions in some economies nor to the historical specificities of banking sector responses to monetary policy. Rather it develops a mode of thinking about these issues which is irredeemably shaped by objections to a particular model of the money supply process, and in so doing tacitly accepts the same modelling conventions. By way of contrast, some interpretations of credit money endogeneity sensibly take it in a very diffuse way that more or less identifies as endogenous any process by which money balances are brought into existence as a result of successfully implemented expenditure decisions (Wray 1990). This is quite consistent with a wide range of possible responses by the financial sector to the financing of expenditure plans and therefore of relationships between stocks of financial instruments and interest rates. This might be called a neo-Schumpeterian view, in its focusing on the creation and destruction of credit-money balances as expenditures are consummated, but freed from Schumpeter's identification of this process with transitory bursts of innovatory investment around a stationary-state benchmark (Schumpeter 1934, Schefold 1986).

V MONEY AND SOCIAL CONVENTION

I have so far tried to show that there is not a single way of defining endogeneity and exogeneity by which we can place commodity money and fiat money on one side of the line and credit money on the other; I have also suggested that the notion of endogeneity as a characteristic of money supply functions is a very misleading way of approaching the issues even – maybe especially – within a credit-money regime. I now want to turn to the last of the three issues I mentioned: the dependence on social convention of the class of financial instruments regarded as money. In a sense, this is the deepest sort of endogeneity, but it is conventionally regarded as a somewhat trivial issue, resolvable empirically. On the contrary, I believe this attitude is symptomatic of a failure properly to consider the nature of money as a social institution. A proper consideration can do no better than to begin with the view with which Keynes opens his *Treatise on Money*:

> Money-of-Account, namely that in which Debts and Prices and General Purchasing Power are *expressed*, is the Primary Concept of the Theory of Money. . . . Money itself, namely that by delivery of which debt-contracts and price-contracts are *discharged*, and in the shape of which a store of General Purchasing Power is *held*, derives its character from its relationship to the Money-of-Account, since the debts and prices must first have been expressed in terms of the latter. . . . Perhaps we may elucidate the distinction between *money* and *money-of-account* by saying that the money-of-account is the *description* or *title* and the money is the *thing* which answers to the description. Now if the same thing always answered to the same description, the distinction would have no practical interest. But if the thing can change, whilst the description remains the same, then the distinction can be highly significant. (*JMK* V: 3–4.)

Keynes is here talking about the continuity of the money 'thing' over time. Starting from a similar distinction, Sayers argues that there is also a necessary imprecision in the way in which the money 'thing' is defined at any time:

> Money is the standard by which we measure the exchange values of things and in which debts are denominated. This is the abstract sense in which we use the term. . . . When we say that our economic system has acquired its present shape on the basis of a general assumption that the value of money is reasonably stable, it is of this abstract sense that we are thinking. Yet when we say that in order to achieve this stability in the value of money, we must control the supply of money, we have switched away from the abstract sense of money to its other, concrete sense. . . . We have switched from an unambiguous abstraction to a class of marketable objects whose boundary has neither sharpness nor certainty nor permanence. (Sayers 1960: 710–11.)

The standard approach is almost directly opposed to this. Very little attention is paid to money in the 'abstract sense' of a measure of price and standard of indebtedness. Instead, 'moneyness' is thought of as a collection of tangible characteristics, which various financial instruments may offer in different degrees. Financial innovation is thought of in terms of introducing instruments offering new permutations of characteristics. We can choose where to draw the line around the stock of monetary instruments according to the extent to which those instruments offer 'monetary' characteristics. This is regarded primarily as an empirical issue, once we have settled on the appropriate characteristics.

Behind this approach is the inability of neo-classical economics to think of social phenomena other than in terms of atomistically definable commodities and their associated markets. There are monetary phenomena, so these must be explicable in terms of monetary commodities. I need hardly add that accepting this framework, by arguing about the shape of money demand or supply functions, for example, is to be already on a slippery slope. There appears to be a sort of commonsense licence for this, since there are, indeed, plenty of financial instruments, some of them called money. But 'moneyness' is, of course, far more than this; in part, it is a complicated and fundamental social convention, which cannot be understood simply by thinking up a theoretical commodity for which there appears to be a rough empirical correlate. What might be called the Keynes–Sayers argument is that the convention is primarily founded on the aspect of 'moneyness' embodied in the abstract unit of account. Social processes lead to the evolution of various financial instruments which reflect this convention, by enabling purchasing power, in terms of the unit of account, to be transferred from place to place and from date to date with varying degrees of success.

VI INTEREST RATES AND MONEY WAGES

I now wish to develop an important argument from Keynes's *General Theory* (1936) which attempts to show that, in a capitalist economy, there is a special relationship between the particular way in which the abstract monetary convention operates and the returns to financial instruments.

To prepare the way for this, I briefly take up a point which I made at the beginning of the chapter. There I cautioned against the idea that simply fixing the money interest rate made much difference to the basic workings of the standard, conventional model. Provided the money price level is free to adjust, pegging the money interest rate is really neither here nor there. And this is true for unorthodox models also, such as the neo-Ricardian model. To make a difference, in the sense that 'real' variables depend essentially on monetary variables, we have to fix *two* nominal variables. All this is very obvious and elementary. So post-Keynesians tend to work both with an exogenously determined money interest rate and with an exogenously determined money wage rate (for example, Rogers 1989). The former, as we know, is justified by an appeal to extreme money supply endogeneity. The latter is usually – and often rather casually – related to some more specific wage contract version of the Keynes–Sayers type of argument on the primacy of the monetary standard of value. The important points from the present point of view are: first, that the rationalisations of interest rate exogeneity and money wage rate exogeneity are essentially independent of each other; and second, that the way in which the latter is rationalised ultimately depends on arguments which take a different, and perhaps more plausible, view of the appropriate model to adopt in seeking to understand the workings of a monetary economy. If we could develop an argument that showed some close connection between the behaviour of the money wage and of the interest rate, this would indeed show that money was 'essential'. In effect, there would be a nexus of monetary relationships from which the workings of the economy could not be abstracted.

It was exactly this type of argument which Keynes attempted to outline in Chapter 17 of the *General Theory*. I do not wish to suggest that Keynes had the last word on the subject, rather that Chapter 17 shows one possible way to proceed. It is particularly germane to the present chapter, since the horizontalist argument is often presented as an acceptable alternative to the supposed difficulties of liquidity preference explanations of inflexibilities in interest rates, and Chapter 17 is the ultimate generalisation of liquidity preference.[6] In this chapter, Keynes, following Sraffa (1932), developed a tortuous analysis, using own interest rates, of 'the essential properties of interest and money'. The gist of the argument is straightforward enough (see, for example, Kregel 1980 for a very clear account). Each asset, broadly defined, has an own rate that is the sum of its net user yield, carrying cost and liquidity premium. As stocks of assets increase, own rates decline as yields decline and carrying costs increase.[7] Since in equilibrium stocks are adjusted so that all the own rates must be equal, the asset with the most slowly declining own rate will 'rule the roost' – all the other own rates will eventually have to conform with this asset's own rate. Keynes identified the asset as money, which has a substantial liquidity premium and negligible carrying costs.

This analysis does not directly explain why the own rate on money is reluctant to decline; here Keynes identified peculiar characteristics of money, including low elasticities of production and substitution against changes in its labour price. The first of these has been dismissed by those who believe the money supply to be endogenous. This is a misunderstanding. Keynes is asserting that, except for genuine commodity money, money is not a produced commodity in any ordinary sense: incentives to alter the stock do not depend on the relation between its price and the money wage rate. Though Keynes's 'essential properties' are phrased in terms of the characteristics of a commodity, they really point to the underlying futility of thinking of money in this way. As Kregel puts it:

> the conditions necessary for the existence of a monetary economy take precedence over the physical properties of the durable that plays the role of money in such an economy. The essential properties are less important as a classificatory aid in identifying what serves as money than as a definition of the conditions required of a monetary production economy . . . (Kregel 1980: 45.)

So although Keynes's story reads like a classical account of convergence to a stationary state, it is perhaps better thought of as an attempt to describe structure as the end result of process. I will shortly suggest that it might be preferable to keep structure and process analytically distinct, at least to begin with.

How then are these essential properties related to money in the abstract sense as a unit of account? Keynes argued that the high liquidity premium on money enhances the expectation that wage rates will be relatively sticky in terms of money, and this expectation reinforces the liquidity premium. As Lerner explained in one of the earliest and best discussions of Chapter 17:

> This is the essential lesson of the chapter. The usefulness of money depends intimately on a certain degree of stability in its purchasing power. This stability encourages the making of contracts and the development of other institutions that help to establish a rigidity of the general price level. The rigidity in turn gives further stability to the purchasing power of money so that its position in the economy reinforces itself in the mould of custom. (Lerner 1952: 192.)

Thus the significance of the money rate of interest and the stickiness of the money wage rate are closely related, defining the structure of the monetary economy. As Townshend (1937) pointed out, this type of perspective has truly radical implications: the theory of value has become a monetary theory, and the continuing stability of the price system is ultimately a matter of the maintenance of certain social conventions.[8]

Notice that we are now in a capitalist world, defined by the prevalence of the wage relationship. Other sorts of conventions would have to be present to sustain other sorts of monetary regimes. We have seen, for example, that Keynes's essential properties of money do not apply, strictly, to genuine commodity money, and presumably other conventions would then be necessary to sustain the abstract function of money as a unit of account. Of course it may be that a universal unit-of-account function is not very significant in some commodity-money systems, in which money is *simply* a medium of exchange, in the sense of a component in a sophisticated system of barter, or in which it circulates only in restricted and partitioned spheres of exchange. One of the advantages of the Keynes–Townshend story is that it suggests how we might characterise a distinctively capitalist monetary economy by linking together types of pricing conventions and types of monetary regime. Some of the very general accounts of the nature of money tend to neglect the distinctiveness of various types of monetary economy. There may be other ways of doing this: for example, what I earlier called the neo-Schumpeterian view focuses on the nature of the credit-generating process as the differentiating feature of capitalist money. This relies on a view of capitalism as a dynamic process of exploitation of investment opportunities – a view which is perhaps complementary to the rather dismal Chapter 17 story. But 'moneyness' is a multi-faceted social phenomenon, and there should be room for many such perspectives – as well as Keynes and Schumpeter, Marx and Simmel beckon.

VII CONCLUSION: MONEY AS LANGUAGE

I hope that the title of this chapter may evoke that of a famous paper, which first appeared in 1957, by the economic anthropologist, Karl Polanyi: 'The Semantics of Money Uses'. Polanyi pointed out that in non-capitalist societies money was an imperfectly unified system, and that what we now analytically distinguish as the functions of money were, in fact, carried out in socially separated ways. This was the framework for numerous insights, some of which I find helpful, some not. One passing remark which I do find helpful is that we can think of modern money as like a language.[9] This has now become almost a commonplace, but it still provides a useful way of organising some thoughts on the issues raised in this chapter.

Polanyi used the analogy with language to draw attention to the unified structure of capitalist monetary systems. To me, the analogy with language suggests, rather, the usefulness of adopting multiple perspectives in discussing a social institution as complex as money. As with many social institutions, of which language is the paradigm case, it may be useful to think of money as having both structure and process.[10] The structure is a set of relatively persistent conventions and understandings. Within the structure, the elements are impermanent events with a capacity for evolution. Money in the abstract sense functions through sets of social conventions and understandings that sustain continuing economic activity; money in the concrete sense consists of the transitory and evolving collections of financial instruments created and transferred in the course of that activity. The former is a structure, and the latter, a process; and, as has been suggested in this chapter, both have types of analysis appropriate to them. It may be that there are integrative modes of explanation which can be developed from this distinction, but they would certainly look very different from reductive representations of money in terms of the shapes of supply and demand functions.

NOTES

* I wish to thank Philip Arestis, Vicky Chick, Sheila Dow and Tom Rymes for helpful comments.

1. I do not take seriously the point of view that *any* cost is acceptable to control inflation.
2. Tom Rymes has drawn my attention to the difficulty of specifying the real output and associated price of the banking sector in a multi-sector model, and the difficulties that this entails for mark-up pricing.
3. Dutt (this volume) assumes that the level of the interest rate represents the power of the rentier class.
4. I talk simply of *the* interest rate. Kalecki (for example, 1965) has an interesting derivation of the long rate from the short rate, designed to show the relative stability of the former against cyclical fluctuations in the latter. This is, no doubt, relevant to some of the issues discussed later, but is not pursued further.
5. Glasner's work is part of an extensive reappraisal of the theory and history of 'free banking'. Though post-Keynesians would, rightly, question the premises of this reappraisal, there is no doubt that it has yielded many insights of relevance to the present chapter – some of which I hope to pursue elsewhere.
6. An issue I have not discussed is the consistency, at some level of explanation, of liquidity preference and money supply endogeneity (Dow and Dow 1989, Wray 1990).
7. I ignore some serious capital-theoretic issues, which merit extended consideration.
8. If Sraffa's suggestion about the money rate of interest was to be taken *really* seriously, this would be quite consistent as a description of Sraffian prices, in contrast with the rather deterministic standard picture of them as somehow rooted in the physical necessities of production.
9. Carabelli (1988: 167–72), who also emphasises the significance of the unit of account

aspect of money in Keynes's work, argues for a parallel with Wittgenstein's philosophy of language.

10. Again, drawing on the linguistic analogy, it may be useful also to distinguish structure and *agency*; this may offer a way of handling another problem bedevilling post-Keynesianism, that of uncertainty. Such distinctions are central to Tony Lawson's recent work.

REFERENCES

Blackburn, K. and M. Christensen, 1989, 'Monetary Policy and Policy Credibility: Theories and Evidence', *Journal of Economic Literature*, 27, 1–45.

Carabelli, A., 1988, *On Keynes's Method*, Macmillan, London/St Martin's Press, New York.

Chick, V., 1986, 'The Evolution of the Banking System and the Theory of Saving, Investment and Interest', *Economies et Sociétés* (Cahiers de l'ISMEA, Série Monnaie et Production), 3, 111–26.

Davidson, P., 1990, 'Endogenous Money, the Production Process and Inflation Analysis', in L. Davidson, ed., *Money and Employment*, Macmillan, London.

Dow, S.C., 1988, 'Money Supply Endogeneity', *Economie Appliquée*, 41, 19–39.

Dow, A.C. and S.C. Dow, 1989, 'Endogenous Money Creation and Idle Balances', in J. Pheby, ed., *New Directions in Post-Keynesian Economics*, Edward Elgar, Aldershot.

Franke, R., 1988, 'Integrating the Financing of Production and a Rate of Interest into Production Price Models', *Cambridge Journal of Economics*, 12, 257–71.

Glasner, D., 1985, 'A Reinterpretation of Classical Monetary Theory', *Southern Economic Journal*, 52, 46–67.

Glasner, D., 1989, 'On Some Classical Monetary Controversies', *History of Political Economy*, 21, 201–29.

Goodhart, C.A.E., 1989, 'Has Moore become too Horizontal?', *Journal of Post Keynesian Economics*, 12, 29–34.

Gordon, R.G., 1975, 'The Demand for and the Supply of Inflation', *Journal of Law and Economics*, 18, 807–36.

Hilton, B., 1977, *Corn, Cash, Commerce*, Oxford University Press, Oxford.

Kaldor, N., 1982, *The Scourge of Monetarism*, Oxford University Press, Oxford.

Kalecki, M., 1965, *Theory of Economic Dynamics*, revised edn, Allen & Unwin, London.

Keynes, J.M., 1930, *A Treatise on Money*, Macmillan, London. (*JMK* V in text.)

Keynes, J.M., 1936, *The General Theory of Employment, Interest and Money*, Macmillan, London.

Kregel, J.A., 1980, 'Markets and Institutions as Features of a Capitalistic Production System', *Journal of Post Keynesian Economics*, 3, 32–47.

Lerner, A.P., 1952, 'The Essential Properties of Interest and Money', *Quarterly Journal of Economics*, 66, 172–93.

Minsky, H.P., 1982, *Inflation, Recession and Economic Policy*, Wheatsheaf, Brighton.
Moore, B.J., 1988, *Horizontalists and Verticalists: The Macroeconomics of Credit Money*, Cambridge University Press, Cambridge.
Moore, B.J., 1989, 'The Effects of Monetary Policy on Income Distribution', in J.A. Kregel and P. Davidson, eds, *Macroeconomic Policies and Problems of Income Distribution*, Edward Elgar, Aldershot.
Moran, M., 1984, *The Politics of Banking*, Macmillan, London.
O'Flaherty, B., 1990, 'The Care and Handling of Monetary Authorities', *Economics and Politics*, 2, 25–44.
Panico, C., 1988, *Interest and Profit in the Theories of Value and Distribution*, Macmillan, London/St Martin's Press, New York.
Pivetti, M., 1990, 'On the Monetary Explanation of Distribution', in K. Bharawadwaj and B. Schefold, eds, *Essays on Piero Sraffa*, Unwin Hyman, London.
Polanyi, K., 1968, 'The Semantics of Money Uses', in G. Dalton, ed., *Primitive, Archaic and Modern Economies*, Doubleday, New York.
Rogers, C., 1989, *Money, Interest and Capital*, Cambridge University Press, Cambridge.
Sayers, R.S., 1960, 'Monetary Thought and Monetary Policy in England', *Economic Journal*, 70, 710–24.
Schefold, B., 1986, 'Schumpeter as a Walrasian Austrian and Keynes as a Classical Marshallian', in H.-J. Wagener and J.W. Drukker, eds, *The Economic Laws of Motion of Modern Society*, Cambridge University Press, Cambridge.
Schumpeter, J., 1934, *The Theory of Economic Development*, 1961 reprint, Oxford University Press, New York.
Sraffa, P., 1932, 'Dr. Hayek on Money and Capital', *Economic Journal*, 42, 42–53.
Sraffa, P., 1960, *Production of Commodities by Means of Commodities*, Cambridge University Press, Cambridge.
Stiglitz, J.E., 1987, 'The Causes and Consequences of the Dependence of Quality on Price', *Journal of Economic Literature*, 25, 1–48.
Townshend, H., 1937, 'Liquidity-Premium and the Theory of Value', *Economic Journal*, 47, 157–69.
Wicksell, K., 1936, *Interest and Prices*, 1965 reprint, Kelly, New York.
Wojnilower, A.M., 1980, 'The Central Role of Credit Crunches in Recent Financial History', *Brookings Papers on Economic Activity*, 2, 277–326.
Wray, L.R., 1990, *Money and Credit in Capitalist Economies*, Edward Elgar, Aldershot.

5. On the Origins of Post-Keynesian Pricing Theory and Macroeconomics

Malcolm C. Sawyer*

I INTRODUCTION

The second half of the 1930s saw the publication of a series of seminal contributions on pricing, many of which can now be seen to have provided the foundations for post-Keynesian pricing theories. Many of these contributions have entered the mainstream of microeconomics in the sense that they are often taught, even though they do not fit in easily with neo-classical economics. Whilst the mark-up pricing elements of these approaches play some role in macroeconomics, it is generally a rather marginal and misunderstood one (as argued below). The major purpose of this paper is to review these contributions and to indicate the important differences between them, as well as the significant similarities.

The contributions discussed here were initially published within three years of the publication of the *General Theory*. Keynesian economics has often been associated with price rigidity and the view that malfunctioning of the economy arises from such rigidity. It is clear that Keynes did not appeal to either (product) price rigidity or imperfect competition in order to explain unemployment (for further discussion see Sawyer 1992b). Chapter 21 of *General Theory* indicated considerable price flexibility, with prices changing with (1) costs, generally to maintain the relationship between prices and wages for a given level of demand (that is, a constant real wage) or (2) with changes in demand, for a given schedule of costs. Keynes treated the nominal wage as the *numeraire*, which has often been confused with an assumption of rigidity of money wage (and which is in effect just the opposite in that this allows the money wage to take any value). However, it soon became accepted that '[a]t the core of the Keynesian polemics of the past ten years and more is the relationship between price flexibility and full employment'. Further, '[t]here always exists a sufficiently low price level such that, if expected to continue indefinitely, it will generate full employment' (all in italics in original) and 'in a static world with a constant stock of money, price flexibility assures full employment' (Patinkin 1951).

The approaches to pricing considered here interact with such a view, as they appeared to provide explanations for price rigidity so that a Keynesian economics could proceed on the assumption of price rigidity, irrespective of Keynes's own assumptions. The interaction was reinforced by the publication of the works considered here about the same time as the *General Theory*. It is argued here that at most these contributions only involve price rigidity with respect to changes in demand conditions and that any such rigidity results from the decisions of the producers; it is not imposed by some external agency. In the neoclassical approach, price changes arise only in response to excess demand, and a denial of the impact of demand on price appears superficially to exclude the possibility of price adjustments. It will become evident below that much confusion arises from introducing arguments from one framework (such as price constancy with respect to demand from imperfect competition) into another (for example, price rigidity imposed on atomistic competition). It is argued that any constancy of price has quite different origins and different consequences in the context of price-setting firms than the imposition of price rigidity has in the atomistic competitive context.

The four contributions from the 1930s discussed here are Means (1933, 1935, 1936), Kalecki (1938, 1943), Hall and Hitch (1939) and Sweezy (1939). The common features of these contributions include a focus on the setting of prices in an environment which does not involve atomistic competition and (in varying degrees) some attention to imperfect information. This chapter has four main sections. Section II provides a consideration of the nature of the contributions of the abovementioned authors.[1] Section III discusses the relationship between approaches to pricing and macroeconomic analysis. Section IV considers some of the differences between the four approaches, with an emphasis on the objectives of firms and their time-horizons for decision-making purposes. Section V reflects on the nature of prices as encapsulated in these approaches with contrasts drawn with the Walrasian general equilibrium view of prices.

II APPROACHES TO PRICING

A Means

We begin with the contribution of Means, which for our purposes contains three important ideas.[2] The first could be summarised as the consequences of the absence of a Walrasian auctioneer, whose role is the continual adjustment of price to reach equilibrium between demand and supply. This was not a contrast between a mythical auctioneer and the real world but rather between markets where prices are settled by haggling between buyers and sellers and those where prices are set by the seller. 'Means considered erroneous the assumptions that prices are always determined by the interaction of buyers and sellers and that they change in a highly flexible manner' (Samuels and Medema 1989: 170). In some situations, of which the oriental bazaar is an example, price is set in the process of trade by haggling. In these cases, '[p]rice does not *precede* a trade, but is determined *in* trade and therefore flexibility of price can be assumed to exist' (Means 1933: 131) as a result of the haggling which leads to a sale. In contrast, 'prices are fixed by administrative action for periods of time' (*ibid*.: 135) prior to trade, and the price set would not usually lead to an equilibrium between supply and demand. These administered prices would be seen as a characteristic of most markets in an industrialised economy.

The second (and related) feature was the contrast drawn between 'market-dominated price' (prices made by interaction of a large number of buyers and sellers *and* administered prices in which one or more market-priced raw material constitutes a substantial part of the product's costs) and 'administration-dominated price' (all other prices). The 'market-dominated' prices would be expected to change more frequently than the 'administration-dominated' ones, and this was the original basis for Means's classification of industries in terms of one of the types of price regimes (for example, Means 1936).

This leads into the third feature, namely that 'market-dominated' prices were more responsive to demand than 'administration-dominated' ones, so that the former rose (relative to the latter) during the upswing of the business cycles and fell during the downswing. (This idea was later to form the starting-point of Eichner's approach, as indicated in Eichner 1973: 1187.)

> [T]he administered price thesis specifically held that in business recessions administered prices showed a tendency not to fall as much as market prices while the recession fall in demand worked itself out primarily through a fall in sales, production, and employment. Similarly, since administered prices tended not to fall as much in a recession, they tended not to rise as much in recovery while rising demand worked itself out primarily in a rising volume of sales, production, and employment. (Means 1972: 292–3.)

Thus Means linked changes in price with changes in output, and the implication would appear to be that variations of output will be much greater when administered prices apply than otherwise for a particular variation in demand. This implication arises, though, only from consideration of price and output decisions, which in turn have implications for the level of aggregate demand. There may be many other differences between sectors, notably over investment behaviour. It would appear that variations in output and employment over the business cycle would be more severe under a regime of administered prices than under market-dominated prices, but this says nothing about the average level of output and employment. Thus, as with a number of recent approaches (for example, Okun 1981), that of Means would appear to leave the average level of economic activity unexplained.

Means (1936: 34) argued that 'an administered price and a monopoly price are quite different aspects of price'. Administered prices were seen as both inevitable and impeding the functioning of the economy.

> [I]nflexible, administered prices have acted as an impediment to that automatic readjustment which is supposed to occur through price changes and which is supposed to keep an economy in approximate balance with full use of our economic resources. (*Ibid.*: 33.)

However, inflexible prices were inherent in modern technology so that questions of whether administered prices were right or wrong were irrelevant. Further, '[a]ccording to the rules of the laissez faire game, they [administered prices] could not be expected to come down [in a depression]. I am only saying that inflexible administered prices are incompatible with automatic economic adjustment' (*ibid.*: 35).

Means does not provide any clear account as to why inflexible prices would have these undesirable effects, though it can be inferred that inflexibility would clearly create problems in an atomistic competitive economy. In a number of respects, Means comes closest of the authors considered in this chapter to the later caricature of Keynes's economics as Walrasian general equilibrium with rigid prices.

B Kalecki

Kalecki's approach to pricing went through a number of versions, which have been fully discussed in Kriesler (1987). Our remarks here relate particularly to the earlier versions, though most would apply more generally. Kalecki retained the pursuit of profits and a loose form of profit maximisation as firms' objective, though the working assumption of constant average direct costs was reinforced by difficulties of exact calculation by firms (Kalecki 1940). Kalecki's approach can be summarised as follows: prices are set as a mark-up over average direct costs (which include the costs of materials and manual labour) where the size of the mark-up depends on the 'degree of monopoly'. As first approximations, both the mark-up and average direct costs are taken as constant with respect to output, but that is not an integral part of the theory. However, those approximations do have the effect of providing a sharp distinction between micro- and macro-effects. The share of profits in national income becomes a microeconomic effect, derived as a summation over the pricing decisions of firms, whilst the volume of profits is a macroeconomic effect, determined by the aggregate level of expenditure but which cannot be determined by any appropriate summation over firms.

Of the four approaches considered here, Kalecki's approach could be considered the closest to a neo-classical approach. It retains profit maximisation (though subject to certain caveats) and has a strong affinity with the view that industrial structure (varying from monopoly through to perfect competition) has an impact on profitability, which many view as the basis of the neo-classical approach to industrial economics. Further, Kalecki was more concerned with the factors external to the firm determining price in relation to average direct costs. He was little concerned (at least in his writings) with the process by which prices were decided upon.

Kalecki (1943) introduced the distinction between cost-determined and demand-determined prices. Some (notably Robinson 1977) have seen this as paralleling the flex-price/fix-price distinction made by Hicks, Okun and others. But there are some important differences between the two dichotomies, notably that Kalecki indicates that cost-determined prices, while unresponsive to demand changes, do respond to cost changes, whilst the forces which might move fix-prices are left unspecified. There is some parallel between this dichotomy and that of Means indicated above, with both indicating that the way prices are set and behave varies across different sectors of the economy.

It is argued here that Kalecki's main contribution in respect of price is the idea that the setting of product prices has implications for the distribution of income and the level of real wages. This could be seen from Kalecki (1938) where price determination was directly linked with the distribution of income between wages and profits.

In his review of the *General Theory* Kalecki highlighted Keynes's use of the wage unit as the *numeraire* and the demonstration that 'a movement of wages induces a proportional movement of prices. . . . If the fall in nominal wages due to unemployment leads to an equi-proportional fall in prices, there is no tendency to absorb unemployment' (Kalecki, as translated in Targetti and Kinda-Hass 1982). Further, there is the independence of production and employment from movements in nominal wages. The idea that price movements offset any nominal wage movements, which can be described as real wages being determined in the product market, has become a major feature of the post-Keynesian approach. But it is not generally realised that such a view is a feature of (virtually) all theories of imperfect competition where the price set depends on money wages (and other costs) and the level of demand (see Sawyer 1992c).

C Sweezy

Sweezy (1939) is best known for the kinked demand curve as an explanation of price inflexibility (which also appears in Hall and Hitch 1939, discussed below). The appearance of this article illustrates the perception in the 1930s of rigidity of price and the search for an explanation.

> [T]he theory was advanced that there exists a kink in the demand curve for the product of an oligopolist and that this kink goes far to explain price rigidities in oligopolistic industries. [Further,] the theory is an ingenious rationalisation of the price rigidities that were reported in many statistical studies of prices during the thirties, and no doubt this explains its popularity. (Stigler 1947: 410.)

Sweezy's approach was intended to be a generalisation of the way business people behaved. It retained the assumption of profit maximisation with the focus on the equality between marginal cost and marginal revenue, though there was an emphasis on 'a systematic inquiry into the nature of imagined demand curve' (Sweezy 1939: 404). The kink in the imagined demand curve (which would now be more usually called the perceived demand curve) arose, of course, from the perception by the firm that a price rise would not be followed by rivals whereas a price reduction would be followed. The resulting gap in the marginal revenue curve (at the prevailing level of output) generates a degree of price inflexibility in the face of both demand and cost changes. As Sweezy noted, 'any disturbance which affects only the position of the marginal cost curve may leave short-run equilibrium of price and output entirely unaffected' (*ibid.*: 406).

A change in demand feeds through into mainly quantity changes rather than price changes. 'It seems clear that any such shift [in the perceived demand curve] will first make itself felt in a change in the quantity sold at the current price' (*ibid.*: 407). But there are also changes in perceptions associated with shifts in demand – when demand rises, the gap between the two marginal revenue curves is diminished as the upward elasticity is lower and the downward elasticity is higher than before. Conversely, when demand declines, the gap opens up. The argument is then that price tends to be relatively rigid for low levels of demand but can rise for high levels of demand. Sweezy suggested that his analysis could be developed to throw light on the issue of rigid prices.

Sweezy's approach has been criticised for only analysing movements in price relative to an initial situation. This criticism arises from a neoclassical perspective where the relevance of history is denied and where equilibrium is unaffected by the disequilibrium path. In contrast, Sweezy stressed that imagined demand curves 'can only be thought of with reference to a given starting point' (*ibid.*: 409), so that the history of prices in an industry is relevant for the current level. There can be a large number of price–output combinations which, if reached, would constitute equilibrium in that there are no endogenous forces making for a change. The influence of the previous history of an industry on the prices set in that industry is a common theme in the contributions being discussed here.

Some elements of kinked demand–type arguments have surfaced in recent years (for example, Hahn 1978) to seek to explain price stickiness. The conjectures which firms hold are then such as to make them reluctant to change price. However, Hahn's models relate to situations of atomistic competition in which firms encounter quantity constraints, with the essential feature that the conjectures held by the firms mean that it is perceived not to be worthwhile to vary price. This is rather different from the position of Sweezy that firms are prepared to meet the demand which arises at the price which they set.

D Hall and Hitch

In a number of respects, the paper of Hall and Hitch (1939) represented a more radical approach than the others considered in this chapter, with a departure from profit maximisation as the objective of a firm. In particular, it cast 'doubt on the general applicability of the conventional analysis of price and output policy in terms of marginal cost and marginal revenue, and [suggested] a mode of entrepreneurial behaviour which current economic doctrine tends to ignore' (Hall and Hitch 1939: 12), whereas both Kalecki and Sweezy retained profit maximisation as a working assumption. In their paper, Hall and Hitch questioned the meaning of marginal revenue and marginal cost (for example, to what time span do they relate?) and the nature of demand curve (actual, perceived). However, one of the reasons they give for firms following the full-cost approach to pricing is a kinked demand curve argument, parallel to that of Sweezy, which clearly makes use of the marginal revenue and cost concepts.

They argued that the majority of firms do not aim for the maximisation of profits through the equalisation of marginal revenue and marginal cost. Instead, in the determination of prices, firms 'try to apply a rule of thumb which we shall call "full cost", and . . . maximum profits, if they result at all from the application of this rule, do so as an accidental (or possibly evolutionary) by-product' (*ibid.*: 19).

Much of the attention of Hall and Hitch was on the procedure for setting price. They provided a generalisation for the setting of the full-cost price: 'prime (or direct) cost per unit is taken as the base, a percentage addition is made to cover overheads . . . and a further conventional addition . . . is made for profit' (*ibid.*: 19). However, they thought that it was impossible to deduce the full-cost price from 'the technical conditions of production and the supply prices of the factors' (*ibid.*: 19–20). Thus, while it is possible to portray price as a mark-up over average costs, it is not possible to formulate the precise factors which determine the extent of the mark-up. There is a degree of stability in pricing policies of firms, though '[p]rices in an industry become "unstable" as soon as any of the competitors form an idea of a profitable price which is markedly different from the existing prices' (*ibid.*: 28).

Hall and Hitch argued that a full understanding of prices at any particular time can only be reached by allowance for the history of the industry concerned. They conclude that prices have a tendency to be stable and 'will be changed if there is a significant change in wage or raw material costs, but not in response to moderate or temporary shifts in demand' (*ibid.*: 33).

Although it is not stated explicitly, it would appear that firms are viewed as generally satisfying the demand which is forthcoming at the full-cost price. In periods of high demand, it is acknowledged that price may be moved up when firms find it difficult to satisfy demand.

III PRICING AND MACROECONOMICS

The four approaches briefly surveyed above share a number of features. The first is that they all refer to situations of imperfect competition in the general sense that some of the key attributes of perfect competition are absent. The situation of imperfect competition may involve fewness of numbers and/or product differentiation. The crucial point, which is explored below, is that any conclusion (especially on any notion of inflexibility of prices) cannot be readily translated over into atomistic competition.

The second common feature is that the Walrasian auctioneer is absent: rather prices are set by producers in pursuit of their own objectives and changed when the producers think fit. Those who set the price do so in their own interests; similarly if prices do not change then it is presumed that it is in the producers' interest to hold prices constant.

The third feature (though this may be absent from Means's work) is that suppliers do intend to supply the demand which is forthcoming at the price which they set. This intention may be aided by the perception that average costs are approximately constant with respect to output. Firms may, of course, make mistakes and actual demand may diverge from that expected. Mistakes are generally absorbed by stock changes, but that does mean that subsequent output decisions are influenced by those mistakes and stock changes. It is assumed that for our purposes that mistakes over the level of demand are sufficiently small as to be ignored, though it is recognised that any discussion of the movement of the economy through time would need to pay due attention to the impact of stock changes.

Keynesian economics has often been associated with notions of price and/or wage rigidity. In the context of the Keynesian IS–LM approach, price flexibility was seen to lead back to full employment through the operation of the Pigou effect, so unemployment was associated with price inflexibility. In the literature associated with the so-called re-appraisal of Keynesian economics and the temporary equilibrium approach, the absence of the Walrasian auctioneer is said to lead to some price and wage inflexibility and rationing by the short side of the market. The question arises then as to how to characterise markets in which there is no such auctioneer. One route would be to follow Means and others and characterise such markets as quite different from atomistic competition. In particular, in product markets prices are seen as set by the producers. Another route, which has generally been followed in the temporary equilibrium literature, is to retain most elements of atomistic competition other than complete price flexibility.

These two routes are often inappropriately mixed. Malinvaud (1977: 9), for example, argues that '[t]he classical [*sic*] teaching, according to which prices quickly react to excess supplies or demands, is more and more inadequate for short-run macroeconomic analysis as we move into an ever-higher degree of organization of society'. He goes on to argue that '[t]he conclusion therefore emerges that short-term quantitative adjustments are much more apparent and influential than short-term price adjustments (*ibid.*: 10). This conclusion is based on empirical evidence on cost-plus pricing of, for example, Godley and Nordhaus (1972). Hence,

> [g]iven the short-run price rigidities that actually exist, the theory under consideration here is justified in assuming full price rigidity, i.e. in working with models in which prices and wage rates are exogenous. This is going to be a 'fix-price' theory according to the denomination proposed by J. Hicks. The denomination should, of course, not be taken literally since we do not mean that the prices will remain the same in the period under study as they did in the preceding period; we simply mean that their movement is 'autonomous'; it is not significantly influenced for our purposes by the formation of demands and supplies on which attention will concentrate. (Malinvaud 1977: 12; see Hicks 1974: 23 for similar sentiments.)

Malinvaud is then concerned to develop fix-price models in which any difference between supply and demand leads to the quantity traded being determined by the short side of the market (and then a consistency between what happens in the different markets).

It is clear that the authors we have considered in this chapter were not discussing fix-prices since price changes are explored within their model (and hence are not autonomous). Further, whether or not prices remain unchanged, the producers intend to supply whatever is demanded at the ruling price. Therefore there is no excess demand or supply, and hence no route by which the quantity traded is determined by the short side of the market.

It is clear that Keynes did not invoke price rigidity. One strand of the *General Theory* can be interpreted as the idea that even if product markets clear, labour markets do not always do so. This is reflected in the assertion of Keynes that the marginal product of labour and the real wage would be equal (his Classical Postulate I).[3] The obverse of this, price equal to marginal cost, provides equilibrium in the goods market in the sense that (atomistically competitive) firms are maximising profits and the supply of output has adjusted to the level of demand. Further the use of the equality between aggregate demand and aggregate supply schedules to provide the point of effective demand is another reflection of product markets clearing.

There is a clear difference between the effects of imposed price (or wage) rigidity and of price (or wage) constancy arising as a result of economic agents' decisions. In the first case, apart from a perceived need to explain the rigidity (Drazen 1980), there are usually unexploited gains from further trade. It then becomes difficult to see that the price rigidity can be sustained: the simple way of expressing this is to say that there will be pressures on price from excess demand or supply. In the second case, any decision on price (whether to hold it constant or to change it) is associated with other decisions. For example, with the implicit contract theory, wages and employment are decided upon simultaneously. Indeed in that context there arises the problem noted by Solow (1979), namely that wage constancy is associated with employment constancy rather than with employment variability, which had been the 'stylised fact' proclaimed by Keynesians adapting a wage-rigidity stance. In the case of product prices, Kalecki, Sweezy and Hall and Hitch all saw that price constancy in the face of demand movements could result from firms' own calculations, but that prices may well change in response to cost changes. But it is important to note that all of them appear to accept that firms adjust output to meet demand at the prevailing prices. Thus there is no suggestion here of price constancy leading to excess demand or supply (as would be the case with price rigidity, at least initially), but rather of output adjusting to meet demand.

The theories presented above differ to some degree over the responsiveness of price to costs. In the context of the 1930s this may not have been a crucial issue and so is not always explicitly dealt with. In the case of Sweezy, movement of the marginal cost curve within the gap in the marginal revenue curve would not lead to any price (or output) adjustment. Thus, over a range, profits absorb the effects of cost changes. For Hall and Hitch and for Kalecki, a cost change could be expected to lead to a proportionate price change. For Means, it could be inferred that large cost changes would lead to price changes but perhaps small cost changes would be absorbed.

It may be interesting to ask how a firm would alter price and output in response to variations in the demand which it faces. However, the answer to such a question can only be partial, for it does not address either the question of the origin of demand variation or that of the further repercussions of the price and output decisions. Those decisions will clearly have implications for income, wages and profits. At the aggregate level, there is then the question as to whether the wages and profits which result from a specific level of aggregate demand would themselves generate that level of demand. If it does, then there is macroeconomic equilibrium; if not, then there will be further changes to output and price.

The importance of the dichotomy drawn by Means between market prices and administered prices is that they arise from different market structures. This dichotomy is richer than the flex-price/fix-price one.[4] In particular, contemporary users of the flex-price/fix-price dichotomy have not drawn a sharp distinction between the differences in market structure for which the two types of price are relevant, but rather applied both types to essentially atomistically competitive markets. The dichotomy drawn by Means (and also that made by Kalecki) includes not only differences of the responsiveness of price to demand but also differences of market structure.

The price-inflexibility arguments have been illegitimately carried over from imperfect competition to a form of perfect competition. Price inflexibility in the face of demand change may arise with administered prices, that is, with the firms as price setters. This is translated into a market form in which firms are supposed to be price takers. The question is not whether price setters exist but rather who plays that role. The difficulty in identifying a price setter in perfect competition results in falling back on the device of an auctioneer. Imperfect competition clearly identifies the seller as the price setter (though there may be situations where that may not be so). The disinterested auctioneer is thereby replaced by price setters with specific interests, which will be pursued through the setting of prices (and other routes).

IV DIFFERENCES BETWEEN THE POST-KEYNESIAN APPROACHES

There has been a tendency to conflate the different post-Keynesian approaches to pricing. The reasons for this are understandable. For macroeconomic analysis, it is often sufficient to portray price as a mark-up over costs, without needing to specify the determinants of the mark-up or the precise definition of costs. The theories have the common elements of stressing the limited impact of demand (level or changes) on prices and, as we have argued above, the adjustment of output to satisfy demand. However, in other respects, there are some significant differences which we briefly explore in this section.

The major difference concerns the usefulness or otherwise of portraying firms as profit maximisers. This difference has two aspects. The first is whether the optimisation concept is useful in the context of price setting. Although Kalecki retained profit maximisation, he did argue that firms could not achieve maximisation with any degree of precision. Hall and Hitch did not specify the motivation of firms, and, as indicated above, they argued against the equality of marginal cost and marginal revenue. This division between those finding profit maximisation a useful device for modelling firm behaviour and those who reject (for a variety of reasons) notions of optimisation as useful in the understanding of human decision-making still continues.

The second aspect is less evident in the discussion above and relates to the relationship between short-term and long-term considerations. Hall and Hitch draw some attention to this and argue that orthodox treatment had played down, if not ignored, the relationship between demand in different time periods. Besides that consideration, the price set may influence the level of profits and thereby the finance available for investment and the growth of future demand. These linkages have been extensively explored by Eichner (1987), Harcourt and Kenyon (1976), Shapiro (1981), Wood (1975) and others (for further discussion see Sawyer 1992a). Amongst the authors considered here, Kalecki viewed the long period as a collection of successive short periods, and did not discuss the conflict between the short term and the long term. His approach could be summarised by saying that firms seek to maximise short-term profits, with investment decisions influenced by factors such as profits, output and capacity utilisation.

Means was more of a forerunner of those cited above, who view the management of firms as concerned with growth and the financing of investment. Barriers to entry provide some protection for incumbent firms and as a consequence

> management did not have to be primarily concerned with making the maximum amount of profit on each transaction or for the current pricing period (which covered a number of sequential transactions). Moreover, because the managers had no legal claim over corporate profits, they had no reason to try to maximize the corporation's profits in the 'long period'. . . . To carry out their growth strategy for the corporation, management adopted, Means argued, an administered price policy. (Lee 1990: 209.)

The above discussion can be briefly summarised by saying that Kalecki viewed producers as seeking as high a level of profits as possible in the short term, and then basing investment decisions on the profits generated. Means, in contrast, viewed pricing policy as being based on the growth requirements of the company.

V THE NATURE OF PRICES

There are a number of implicit, but nevertheless important, features of price in the Walrasian general equilibrium approach. Prices have an allocative function, and resources are only allocated by the price mechanism. Prices respond to excess demand or supply. In the

Walrasian tatonnement story, time is in effect suspended until the equilibrium price vector is discovered and then trading takes place. In much of Keynesian economics, the price response to excess supply has clearly been retained, whilst the allocative function of price has remained in the background. The importance of the post-Keynesian approaches to pricing is that each of the features of Walrasian general equilibrium mentioned above is denied.

The concept of excess demand was introduced in the context of perfect competition with economic agents facing parametric prices. The supply function does not have the same meaning under imperfect competition as under perfect competition. However, our interpretation of imperfect competition above is that producers will seek to operate on the demand curve facing them, and in that sense there is zero excess demand. Under perfect competition, the presence of excess supply or demand is clear evidence of disequilibrium in the sense that at least one side of the market is dissatisfied with that outcome. Under imperfect competition, the presence of excess capacity does not necessarily indicate disequilibrium so far as price and output decisions are concerned, in that there may be no forces at work at that level to reduce the extent of excess capacity. Producers have made decisions on prices and output (and thereby on capacity utilisation) which lead to the best outcome which they can achieve in the circumstances which they face (and in doing so collectively cause the economic environment to change). The level of capacity utilisation may be unsatisfactory but the producers can only respond to that by investment decisions (which is likely to introduce elements of instability in that high levels of capacity utilisation generate investment, thereby raising aggregate demand further). For a variety of reasons, producers may wish to have some degree of excess capacity (whether as a barrier against entry or as insurance against demand fluctuations and so on). This suggests that the presence of excess capacity may not generate pressures to lower prices (relative to costs). At a particular level of output there would be no tendency for prices to fall (relative to costs).

The movement of money wages is not a direct concern of this chapter, but let us assume that money wages fall under the impact of unemployment. Any impact on the real wage would depend on the firms' responses to the decline in labour costs: in the context of a closed economy, with a given level of demand, it would be expected that prices fall in line with wages, leaving the real wage unchanged.

Price changes may be associated with output changes, both resulting from changes in demand. In the approaches discussed above, the general expectation is that the major change will be in output with price change playing a minor role (from a given change in demand). As Robinson (1933: 72–3) pointed out, under imperfect competition it is even possible for prices to rise in the face of a decline in demand. Kalecki similarly noted that there were reasons for a rise in the price–cost margin as demand declined.

When producers (rather than a disinterested auctioneer) set prices then it would be expected that those prices would be set in the interests of the producers themselves. Thus the immediate function of price is to satisfy the objectives of the producers. Gerrard (1989) lists five roles of price: the conductive, positional, strategic, financial and allocative. All except the allocative function are derived from the use which the producers seek to make of price. For example, the financing role is derived from the producers seeking to set prices to generate finance for investment purposes. In contrast, the allocative role is only a by-product of price determination. In the Walrasian general equilibrium approach, the role of the auctioneer could be said to be dedicated to resource allocation and co-ordination of economic activity. The other side of this is that in the post-Keynesian approaches, economic co-ordination is undertaken in a variety of ways. This does not arise explicitly in the approaches to pricing discussed above, though

> [i]n conceiving of the corporate economy as a continuous monetary flow of economic activity that was co-ordinated by market and administered prices, by administrative co-ordination, and by rules and goals, Means sought to dispel the notion that the American economy operated as a cybernetic mechanism which automatically tended to eliminate underutilization of all economic resources, including labour, productive plant and natural resources. (Lee 1990: 220.)

VI CONCLUDING REMARKS

The four approaches to pricing originating from the 1930s discussed in this chapter should be seen as quite distinct contributions since there are significant differences between them. However, they do have a number of common features. They indicate an insensitivity of price to demand and demand changes, which may sometimes be usefully represented as a constancy of price. Since these approaches relate to conditions of imperfect competition, the consequences of any price constancy are quite different from those which arise from imposing price rigidity in the context of atomistic competition. Simply, the latter involves excess supply or demand, whereas the former results from the producers' decisions, with output adjusting to meet demand. More generally, these (and other) post-Keynesian approaches to pricing should be viewed as part of a quite separate paradigm of price determination and resource allocation.

NOTES

* An earlier version of this chapter was presented to the Post-Keynesian Economics Study Group in February 1989. I am grateful to the editors for comments on earlier drafts.

1. Our coverage does not claim to be comprehensive. In particular, the work of authors such as Andrews (e.g. 1949) have not been included. For discussion of the approach of Andrews, see Lee *et al.* (1986).
2. See also Samuels and Medema (1989) especially sections III and IV. Our information on Means's doctoral dissertation (1933) is drawn from that paper.
3. 'In contrast, Keynes' treatment of the labor demand function implies that the market for current output is clearing. The *General Theory* seems perfectly consistent on this point. Keynes implies throughout that prices, as contrasted with wages, adjust instantaneously, to bring the quantity demanded into line with the quantity supplied, the latter being fixed in the short run' (Grossman 1972: 28).

   'Far from assuming general price inflexibility, Keynes considered each sector of the economy separately. Indeed there is little doubt that Keynes regarded product prices as highly flexible – he frequently insisted in the *General Theory* that the real wage varied inversely with the level of employment in the short-run (which, given the assumption of a relatively stable *money* wage, implies flexible product prices)' (Brothwell 1975: 5).
4. Hicks linked the fix-price case with markets where prices were set by producers and the flex-price with 'speculative markets, in which prices are still determined by supply and demand' (Hicks 1974: 23). He argued that a theory was needed which took account of both types of markets. He saw the major difference between these markets as 'in the fixprice market . . . actual stocks may be greater, or may be less, than desired stocks; in the flexprice market . . . actual stocks are always equal to desired stocks – when the stocks of the traders are taken into account' (Hicks 1974: 25).

REFERENCES

Andrews, P.W.S., 1949, *Manufacturing Business*, Macmillan, London.

Brothwell, J.F., 1975, 'A Simple Keynesian Response to Leijonhufvud', *Bulletin of Economic Research*, 27.

Drazen, A., 1980, 'Recent Developments in Macroeconomic Disequilibrium Theory', *Econometrica*, 48.

Eichner, A.S., 1973, 'A Theory of the Determination of the Mark-up under Oligopoly', *Economic Journal*, 83, reprinted in Sawyer 1988.

Eichner, A.S., 1987, *The Macrodynamics of Advanced Market Economies*, M.E. Sharpe, Armonk, New York.

Gerrard, B., 1989, *Theory of the Capitalist Economy: Towards a Post-Classical Synthesis*, Basil Blackwell, Oxford.

Godley, W. and W. Nordhaus, 1972, 'Pricing in the Trade Cycle', *Economic Journal*, 82.

Grossman, H., 1972, 'Was Keynes a Keynesian?', *Journal of Economic Literature*, 10.
Hahn, F.H., 1978, 'On Non-Walrasian Equilibria', *Review of Economic Studies*, 45.
Hall, R. and C. Hitch, 1939, 'Price Theory and Business Behaviour', *Oxford Economic Papers*, no. 2, reprinted in Sawyer 1988.
Harcourt, G.C. and P. Kenyon, 1976, 'Pricing and the Investment Decision', *Kyklos*, 29, reprinted in Sawyer 1988.
Hicks, J., 1974, *The Crisis in Keynesian Economics*, Basil Blackwell, Oxford.
Kalecki, M., 1938, 'The Determinants of Distribution of the National Income', *Econometrica*, 6.
Kalecki, M., 1940, 'The Supply Curve of an Industry under Imperfect Competition', *Review of Economic Studies*, 7.
Kalecki, M., 1943, *Studies in Economic Dynamics*, Allen & Unwin, London.
Keynes, J.M., 1936, *The General Theory of Employment, Interest and Money*, Macmillan, London.
Kriesler, P., 1987, *Kalecki's Microanalysis: The Development of Kalecki's Analysis of Pricing and Distribution*, Cambridge University Press, Cambridge.
Lee, F., 1990, 'G.C. Means's Doctrine of Administered Prices', in P. Arestis and Y. Kitromilides, eds, *Theory and Policy in Political Economy*, Edward Elgar, Aldershot.
Lee, F. *et al.*, 1986, 'P.W.S. Andrews's Theory of Competitive Oligopoly: A New Interpretation', *British Review of Economic Issues*, 8.
Malinvaud, E., 1977, *The Theory of Unemployment Reconsidered*, Basil Blackwell, Oxford.
Means, G.C., 1933, 'The Corporate Revolution', manuscript of doctoral dissertation, Harvard University, Gardiner C. Means Papers, series I, Franklin D. Roosevelt Library.
Means, G.C., 1935, 'Industrial Prices and their Relative Flexibility', US Senate Document 13, 74th Congress, 1st Session, Washingdon, DC.
Means, G.C., 1936, 'Notes on Inflexible Prices', *American Economic Review*, 26, Supplement.
Means, G.C., 1972, 'The Administered-price Thesis Reconfirmed', *American Economic Review*, 62.
Okun, A., 1981, *Prices and Quantities: A Macroeconomic Analysis*, Basil Blackwell, Oxford.
Patinkin, D., 1951, 'Price Flexibility and Full Employment', in *Readings in Monetary Theory*, selected by a Committee of the American Economic Association, Blakiston, New York.
Robinson, J., 1933, *The Economics of Imperfect Competition*, Macmillan, London.
Robinson, J., 1977, 'What are the Questions?', *Journal of Economic Literature*, 15.
Samuels, W. and S.G. Medema, 1989, 'Gardiner C. Means's Institutional and Post-Keynesian Economics', *Review of Political Economy*, 1.
Sawyer, M., ed., 1988, *Post Keynesian Economics*, Edward Elgar, Aldershot.
Sawyer, M., 1992a, 'Prices and Pricing in the Post Keynesian and Kaleckian Traditions', in G. Mongiovi and C. Ruhl, eds, *Macroeconomic Theory: Diversity and Convergence*, Edward Elgar, Aldershot, forthcoming.

Sawyer, M., 1992b, 'The Relationship between Keynes's Macroeconomic Analysis and Theories of Imperfect Competition', in B. Gerrard and J. Hillard, eds, *The Philosophy and Economics of J.M. Keynes*, Edward Elgar, Aldershot, forthcoming.

Sawyer, M., 1992c, 'On Imperfect Competition and Unemployment', in A. del Monte, ed., *Recent Developments in Industrial Economics*, Macmillan, London, forthcoming.

Shapiro, N., 1981, 'Pricing and the Growth of the Firm', *Journal of Post Keynesian Economics*, 4.

Solow, R., 1979, 'Alternative Approaches to Macroeconomic Theory: a Partial View', *Canadian Journal of Economics*, 12.

Stigler, G., 1947, 'The Kinky Oligopoly Demand Curve and Rigid Prices', *Journal of Political Economy*, 55, reprinted in American Economic Association, *Readings in Price Theory*, Allen & Unwin, London, 1953 (page references refer to the reprint).

Sweezy, P., 1939, 'Conditions of Demand under Oligopoly', *Journal of Political Economy*, 47, reprinted in American Economic Association, *Readings in Price Theory*, Allen & Unwin, 1953 (page references refer to the reprint).

Targetti, F. and B. Kinda-Hass, 1982, 'Kalecki's Review of Keynes' *General Theory*', *Australian Economic Papers*, 21.

Wood, A., 1975, *A Theory of Profits*, Cambridge University Press, Cambridge.

6. Price and Monopoly in Kalecki's Theory

Jerzy Osiatyński*

I INTRODUCTION

Partly as a result of neo-classical criticism of Keynesian economics, it became popular in the early 1980s to explore the microeconomic foundations of macroeconomic theories. In the neo-classical general equilibrium theory, macroeconomic phenomena are only derivatives of the presumed microeconomic assumptions and interrelationships. In fact general equilibrium theory has no independent macroeconomic counterpart. In J.M. Keynes's *General Theory*, as well as in post-Keynesian economics, microeconomic relationships are not clearly defined. Rather they are derived by interpolating the macroeconomic inferences made by those theories. Kalecki's theory of capitalist economic growth differs from the above two approaches in that it contains clearly defined microeconomic foundations and a macroeconomic theory which is not a simple aggregation of those foundations.[1]

Following Chilosi (1989) and Kriesler (1987), Kalecki's microeconomic theory is understood here as his theory of pricing and national income distribution. His macroeconomic theory is here taken to mean his theory of investment and the determination of profits. This, along with the sectoral distribution of economic activity, determines the volume of total output and employment, and changes in them. Essentially, Kalecki's microeconomic theory postulates that, at less than full capacity utilisation, changes in effective demand and variable costs do not affect profit margins (unless there is a change in the degree of monopoly). In other words, *the relative shares of profits and wages in national income do not depend on the volume of output, and neither the volume of output nor profits depend on prices or relative shares in income*. This independence applies strictly only as long as saving out of wages and salaries is excluded, and in a closed economy. If these simplifying assumptions are abandoned, then the independence is only approximate.

Kalecki's theory of national income distribution is an integral part of his theory of capitalist reproduction. His study of the business cycle was the starting-point for this latter theory. The dynamics of a capitalist economy and its cyclical fluctuations were always the main topics of Kalecki's research.

Kalecki considered that the cyclical fluctuations of the capitalist economy as a whole are generated by fluctuations in the activity of private industrial enterprises. In his study of business cycles he divided up the income of the private sector into the earnings of workers (in his theoretical analysis this was more narrowly defined as manual workers' wages) and profits. Changes in those wages do not generate fluctuations in output and employment: those wages are themselves determined by fluctuations in output and employment ('workers spend what they earn'). Instead the source of cyclical fluctuations lies in changes in profits, since 'capitalists earn what they spend', and capitalists' expenditure on investment is cyclical. This starting-point delineates the scope and substance of Kalecki's theory of income distribution and the direction that he took in his research. We shall therefore present first the basic features of Kalecki's macroeconomic theory and only subsequently the four successive versions of the microeconomic basis of that theory.

II AN OUTLINE OF KALECKI'S MACROECONOMIC THEORY[2]

The theory of profits is the first element of Kalecki's macroeconomics. Its starting-point is the balance between output/income and expenditure in the national income accounts. If we deduct wages and salaries from the income side of the equation, and consumption out of wages and salaries from the other side of the equation, and we assume for the sake of simplicity that both deductions are equal, then gross after-tax profits, P, are equal to the sum of gross investment, I, the export surplus, E, the government's budget deficit, G, and capitalists' consumption, C_c:

$$P = I + E + G + C_c \tag{6.1}$$

The second element is the set of assumptions concerning consumption. Kalecki divides up the whole of consumption, C, into capitalists' consumption, C_c, and workers' consumption, C_w. Capitalists' consumption is made equal to the sum of a constant part, B_0, and a variable part which is proportionate to profits,

$$C_c = B_0 + \lambda(P), \qquad 0 < \lambda < 1 \tag{6.2}$$

Workers' consumption is equal to the sum of wages and salaries, W:

$$C_w = W \tag{6.3}$$

Moreover, since the share of workers' incomes, w, in total income, Y, is assumed to remain constant over the course of the business cycle, $W = w.Y$, $0 > w > 1$, the income of capitalists may be written as

$$P = (1 - w).Y$$

The third component is the theory of investment. According to Kalecki, investment, I, is a positive function of profits, P, and a negative function of the stock of capital, K:

$$I = m.P - n.K \qquad m, n > 0 \tag{6.4}$$

Since national income is the sum

$$Y = C + I + E + G \tag{6.5}$$

and profits are the sum

$$P = B_0 + I + E + G \tag{6.6}$$

the two equations combined give

$$Y = B_0 + \lambda(1 - w).Y + w.Y + I + E + G$$

or

$$Y = (B_0 + I + E + G)/(1 - \lambda)(1 - w) \tag{6.7}$$

hence

$$\Delta Y = (B_0 + I + E + G)/(1 - \lambda)(1 - w) \tag{6.7a}$$

Equation (6.7a) gives a multiplier analogous to the Keynesian income multiplier: $\Delta Y/\Delta(B_0 + I + E + G) = 1/(1 - \lambda)(1 - w)$. Dividing equation (6.6) by equation (6.7) we can see that this is also the share of profits in national income.

This multiplier differs from the Keynes–Kahn multiplier in that, apart from the coefficient λ, which expresses the share of consumption in profits, it also contains coefficient w, which represents the distribution of income between wages and profits. This is a consequence of Kalecki's conception of capitalism as a social system with only two classes in it.

A special feature of Kalecki's macroeconomic theory of investment determination, and hence also of his theories of capitalist profits and national income determination, lies in its formal independence from Kalecki's microeconomic assumptions about the determinants of prices and relative shares in national income. Let us therefore examine these assumptions more closely.

A Microeconomic Foundations I: Free but not Perfect Competition (1929–38)

Kalecki's first theoretical studies were based on a set of microeconomic assumptions that together give a model of an economy that is marked by free, but by no means perfect, competition. They consist of the following propositions:

- IA Prices are determined by the competitive mechanism of the market.
- IB Beyond a certain volume of output, the unit variable (marginal) cost curve rises with output (that is, it is U-shaped).
- IC Firms operate below full capacity levels of production.
- ID The relative share of wages in national income is given, without any clear explanation of the mechanism for determining the *absolute* level of real wages. (However, it is possible to conclude from various aspects of Kalecki's analysis that he considered that, as in classical economics or Marx's theory, this level is determined by socio-historical factors.)

Proposition IC distinguishes free from perfect competition. Less than full capacity utilisation means that market forces do not give rise to the perfectly competitive allocation of resources.

Furthermore, in accordance with empirical observations at that time, Kalecki assumed that over the course of the business cycle prices move pro-cyclically, and that money wages move similarly but more slowly. Therefore real wages change counter-cyclically. However, because employment varies with the level of output, Kalecki concluded that the share of real wages in national income is relatively constant.

Given these assumptions, and with the volume of output and

employment determined by his macroeconomic theory, a fall in real wages could not result in an increase in profits, which are determined by the level of effective demand. It would lead only to a fall in total output (in the case of a quantitative adjustment) or a reduction in the prices of wage goods (in the case of a price adjustment). Similarly, an increase in money wages would not reduce profits but increase output and employment (quantitative adjustment) or raise prices (price adjustment). Kalecki paid a great deal of attention at this time to explaining and justifying these conclusions (*MK* I).[3]

It is apparent from this that the interdependence between the microeconomic and the macroeconomic theories does not apply to prices (see propositions IB and IA above). At the same time, the conclusion that the relative shares of profits and wages in national income are independent of the levels of output and employment does not arise out of the microeconomic assumptions, but is a consequence of the ways in which money wages and prices change over the course of the business cycle. Although these fluctuations were confirmed at the time by empirical data, they had no satisfactory theoretical justification. It was not clear why changes in money wages, prices and employment must always offset each other.

B Microeconomic Foundations II: Imperfect Competition (1938–9)

Kalecki treated the assumption of free competition only as a first approximation. He was always aware of the importance of cartels, monopolist practices and oligopolistic competition. This was undoubtedly in line with the outlook of the Institute for the Study of Business Cycles and Prices, headed by Edward Lipiński, where Kalecki got his first permanent job studying the operations of cartels. In 1935, together with Ludwik Landau, he published a paper (*MK* VI) in the Institute about the way prices varied with, on the one hand, costs and, on the other hand, changes in industrial output. In this paper he called into question the notion of a rising variable cost curve. Soon afterwards, Kalecki rejected other tenets of the free competition model. In this he was certainly prompted by the discussions, in which he actively participated, at Piero Sraffa's seminar in Cambridge. Among other topics discussed there were the short-run cost curves of firms, as well as the work of Robinson (1933) and Chamberlin (1933) on imperfect competition. In 1938, Kalecki reformulated his theory of the business cycle, basing it on a model of imperfect competition instead of free competition.

The starting-point of the theory of imperfect competition was the microeconomic notion of a representative firm approaching a Marshallian short-period equilibrium. It consisted of the following propositions:

IIA Prices are determined by workings of imperfectly competitive markets.
IIB Unit variable costs are constant over the range of output up to the point of full capacity utilisation, after which they rise sharply, so that the firm's unit variable cost curve has the shape of a reversed 'L'.
IIC Firms operate below the level of full capacity utilisation.
IID Firms seek to maximise profits.

Given these assumptions, the respective share of wages and profits in national income are determined by the degree of monopoly. Following Lerner (1934), Kalecki (1939–40) defined this degree of monopoly, μ, as the ratio of price, p, to marginal cost, mc:

$$\mu = (p - mc)/p.$$

The profit-maximising firm's short-period equilibrium is at the point where its marginal cost is equal to its marginal revenue. The Lerner–Kalecki degree of monopoly is therefore equal to the inverse of the price elasticity of demand for the output of the firm. In view of this, strictly speaking it is not the degree of monopoly that determines the respective shares of wages and profits in the economy, but the price elasticity of demand.[4]

Was this really what Kalecki intended? This is not borne out by the way in which his microeconomic theory developed, nor by his early work on the theory of national income distribution, where he always refers to the degree of monopoly as the influence of cartels and monopolies, that is, the influence of the intensity of competition in markets, on income distribution. The degree of monopoly was supposed simply to measure (or reflect) that intensity.

In Kalecki's opinion, even at the peak of a boom, firms do not operate at full capacity. Assumptions IIB and IIC, which he retained in later versions of his microeconomic theory, lead to the conclusion that changes in demand are associated principally with quantitative adjustments. For their part, changes in prices reflect principally changes in the distribution of income between wages and profits (leaving aside the insignificant and indirect influence of changes in output on fixed costs, and hence on the relative share of wages and profits in national income).

This problem is essentially about what ultimately determines those relative shares in income: the degree of monopoly or the price elasticity of demand. Kalecki's new formulation led to other difficulties and confusions. If the marginal cost curve is U-shaped (proposition IB), then neo-classical economic analysis enables us to define the size of the firm and the industry. The 'equilibrium' of the firm, the industry, and even the economy as a whole, can also be determined in this way. But what determines the size of a firm, and its equilibrium, if its marginal cost curve is a reversed 'L' (proposition IIB)? The problem does not arise in Kalecki's theoretical system because, according to his macroeconomic theory, the size of the individual enterprise is determined by its access to capital, which is limited by the Principle of Increasing Risk. This in turn, jointly with profits, determines the level of investment (Kalecki 1971). In the neo-classical conceptual framework, this question is not so easily resolved while the almost horizontal marginal cost curve means that every equilibrium position is highly unstable.

As I have already mentioned, the starting-point for Kalecki's theory of income distribution is his microeconomic theory of the firm. He arrives at the theory of income distribution in the industry or the economy as a whole by aggregating the degree of monopoly in individual firms, weighted by their output. This method of aggregation is defective because using it makes the average degree of monopoly and the respective shares of wages and profits in income change every time there is a change in the structure of output[5] and that in turn depends on the structure of demand.

This formulation is also inadequate because it does not take sufficient account of changes in fixed costs. These must also have some effect on the degree of monopoly, and the relative shares of wages and profits in aggregate income. But changes in fixed costs are not necessarily affected by changes in the extent of competition in markets (Kriesler 1987: 42ff).

C Microeconomic Foundations III: The Theory of Oligopolistic Competition (1939–40)

In part under the influence of the criticism with which his theory of income distribution based on the degree of monopoly met, and in part because of developments in the analysis of monopolistic competition and his own empirical work on the relation of prices to costs in selected branches of British manufacturing, Kalecki (1939–40 and *MK* II) tried to rework his theory of income distribution. This time he sought to base it on the theory of oligopolistic competition. He took as his new starting-point not the representative firm but the industry. The new formulation was based on the following propositions:

IIIA Oligopolistic entrepreneurs set the prices of their products, taking into account the prices set by their competitors of the same or similar products.
IIIB The marginal cost curve of the firm is shaped like a reversed 'L'.
IIIC Firms operate below their full capacity.
IIID Entrepreneurs seek to maximise their profits by setting output at the point where their marginal cost equals their marginal revenue, under conditions of imperfect competition.

Under these assumptions, Kalecki arrived at his new concept of the degree of monopoly in such a way that it expresses the link between the distribution of income and the 'fundamental data' which arise out of the intensity of competition in the market. He did this by making a distinction between *shifts* in the demand curve for the product of a firm (or industry), which reflect changes in demand, and changes in market imperfections (that is, in the intensity of competition). The latter are reflected in changes in the *shape* of the demand curve (that is, the price elasticity of demand at different points along its length).

However, it is not possible to make this distinction between two sets of determinants of demand elasticity without some general theory of equilibrium in an oligopolistic economy. Kalecki did not undertake the task of creating such a theory and, to my knowledge, no one has successfully put one forward. Instead, Kalecki put forward a theory of partial equilibrium. He suggested that the extent of market imperfection, and hence also the degree of monopoly, was constant if the price elasticity of demand for the product of the firm in question was some function of the ratio of its price to the average price in the industry.

In fact this proposition is not valid. The demand curve for a firm's (or industry's) product depends on many factors, not only on the ratio of the given firm's price to the average in the industry. It also depends, for example, on the average price in other industries. Changes in relative prices in an industry generally lead to changes in the degree of monopoly.

Methodological difficulties also arise in defining an industry. Each firm's product must differ in some way from the products of other firms in the same industry because each producer must be able to fix a price that is different from those of his rivals. However, it cannot differ too much because, when fixing the price of his output, the oligopolist, if he is to be at all oligopolistic, must take into account the prices of the other producers. Therefore the marginal cost curves of the individual firms cannot differ too much. However, they should at the same time be independent of one another. In practice these contradictory criteria can only be reconciled by an arbitrary definition of the boundaries of an industry (Davidson 1959; Kriesler 1987: 61–4; Osiatyński 1986).

It is likely that Kalecki himself realised that this version of the microeconomic foundations of his theory was faulty. He never referred to it in his later publications, and he soon substituted a new formulation for it.

D Microeconomic Foundations IV: A New Approach to the Degree of Monopoly (1943–54–71)

Kalecki started off his new hypothesis from a distinction between services and manufacturing, whose prices were fixed by suppliers, and the primary industries, mining and agriculture, whose prices are demand-determined. Given a particular material-intensity of production, the distribution of national income between wages and profits is determined by the extent of competition in industrial production.

This version of the microeconomic foundation for his theory again starts with the notion of a representative firm. The microeconomics is based on the following assumptions:

IVA Oligopolistic entrepreneurs themselves set prices for their products, adding the gross profit margin to unit variable costs, and taking into account the prices set by their competitors for the same or similar products.

IVB The firm's marginal cost curve has the shape of a reversed 'L'.

IVC Firms operate below the level of production at which their capacity is fully utilised.

IVD 'In view of the uncertainties faced in the process of price fixing it will not be assumed that the firm attempts to maximise its profits in any precise sort of manner' (Kalecki 1954: 12).

The gross profit margin therefore depends not only on the elasticity of demand for a product, but also on the degree of concentration of production, on sales promotion through advertising and similar marketing strategies, on the extent and efficacy of open or tacit price agreements, on the power of trades unions, and so on. Kalecki called these factors the degree of monopoly. But this was no longer defined, as it was in, for example, the 1938 version of the microeconomics, as the ratio of the difference between the price and marginal cost, and the price. It was now a synoptic concept embracing all the factors influencing the price that the firm sets. Kalecki did not elaborate on the influence that the individual factors have on the derived price equations.

As far as 'the movement of the ratio of proceeds to prime cost in terms of changes in the degree of monopoly' was concerned, this was a matter for 'the economic historian who can contribute to such a study a more thorough knowledge of changing industrial conditions' (*ibid.*: 22).

The apparent vagueness in this version of Kalecki's microeconomics was criticised by many, including some of his students and some adherents of his theory (for example, Nuti 1970, Kaldor 1955). Cowling and Waterson (1976) and Sawyer (1982) proposed ways of dealing with this weakness in the theory. Their economic models postulate that oligopolists attempt to maximise profits over the short period (restoring proposition IIID in place of IVD). Three groups of factors determining the degree of monopoly can be distinguished in this way: (1) the degree of industrial concentration; (2) the intensity of open and tacit price agreements between firms; and (3) the elasticity of demand for a given firm's output. (However, these proposed solutions are not without their disadvantages; see Osiatyński 1986.)

Reservations were also expressed about Kalecki's aggregation procedure. This was because, in calculating average values and parameters in the price equation for the firm and the industry, the volume of its output is taken as the weighting for each firm's price equation. The average degree of monopoly in an industry or in the economy as a whole therefore depends also on the composition of production (Kriesler 1987: 66). Kalecki did subsequently introduce a revision to take account of changes in the structure of production. This was by adopting a constant product combination in his calculation of average degrees of monopoly. But then a problem arises with the introduction of new products which are not included in the constant product mix. Quite obviously the greater the structural changes and product innovations in the economy, the smaller is the cognitive value of this type of indicator.

A further problem arises in the empirical interpretation of changes in the degree of monopoly in recent years. All versions of Kalecki's theory of income distribution are based on the hypothesis that an increase in the concentration of production increases the extent of monopoly and thereby, *ceteris paribus*, increases profit margins and the share of gross profits in national income. However, the wave of industrial concentration that reached its climax between 1960 and 1975 did not produce an increase in the rate of profit in the merged enterprises. The enlarged corporations often reported declines in profitability in the short run, and were not significantly more profitable several years after they were combined than they had been previously (Cowling 1982, Buzzel 1984, Möller 1983).

III CONCLUDING REMARKS

If instead of the simplest of Kalecki's analytical models we introduce a model of an open economy with positive savings from wages and salaries, and with a part of overhead costs consisting of wages and salaries, then we can no longer maintain the elegant functional division between a microeconomic theory which explains relative shares in national income and, independently of this microeconomic theory, a macroeconomic theory which explains how the level of profits, output and employment are determined. Nevertheless, Kalecki's initial premise, that the key to explaining the distribution of income between wages and profits lies in entrepreneurs' price decisions, rather than changes in output, remains valid.

Although Kalecki's theory of income distribution does not explain the absolute level of wages and profits by reference to changes in the degree of competition in markets, it does explain changes in the relative shares of wages and profits. From the point of Kalecki's main purpose, which was to analyse the cyclical nature of capitalist reproduction, this is still a noteworthy result. In a world in which real wage reductions are widely recommended as a means of eliminating unemployment, Kalecki's theory allows us to examine the actual effects that such measures would have on the course of the business cycle.

In fact, Kalecki's theory, like that of Marx, is a macroeconomic theory of capitalist reproduction. Kalecki's theory was, however, different from the Marxian theory because the focus of his analysis was the mechanism of the business cycle. Moreover, unlike Marx's analysis, Kalecki's theory does not rely on the Law of Value and has a different microeconomic foundation: instead of a freely competitive economy, Kalecki has an oligopolistic economy.

There remain many formal shortcomings in the model; nevertheless, it can be used to show the ineffectiveness, and even harmfulness, of measures to combat unemployment such as cuts in real wages, recommended by neo-classical economics more than 50 years ago on the basis of assumptions of the IA and IB kind, and the principle of permanently full capacity utilisation in production. Once again these measures have zealous advocates, even though today nobody seriously questions the lack of realism of the assumptions on which they are based or the need to replace them with axioms of the IVA, IVB and IVC kind. Kalecki's analysis is a natural frame of reference for critics of this returning wave of neo-classical economics. This, among other things, explains the interest that has been observed in recent years in the microeconomic foundations of Kalecki's theory, and accounts for the many attempts to fill its gaps and correct its formal weaknesses.

NOTES

* This is a translation by J. Toporowski of a paper which was published in *Ekonomista* 1989 no. 3, shortly after its presentation, by the author, to the Post-Keynesian Economics Study Group.

1. I am only concerned here with the microeconomic foundations of Kalecki's theory of the dynamics of a capitalist economy. The microeconomics of socialist reproduction is discussed in Osiatyński (1988).
2. This formulation is based on Kalecki (1954).
3. Kalecki's *Collected Works* will be referred to as *MK*, followed by a volume number.
4. Attention was quickly drawn to this by Oscar Lange and other critics of Kalecki's theory. See *MK* II and Kriesler (1987: 26, 113–14).
5. Lange (1941) drew attention to this.

REFERENCES

Buzzel, R.D., 1984, 'Bringt Vertikale Integration Vorteile?', *Harvard Manager*, no. 1.

Chamberlin, E.H., 1933, *The Theory of Monopolistic Competition*, Harvard University Press, Cambridge, Mass.

Chilosi, A., 1989, 'Kalecki's Quest for the Micro-economic Foundations of his Macro-economic Theory', in M. Sebastiani, ed., 1989, *Kalecki's Relevance Today*, Macmillan, London.

Cowling, K., 1982, *Monopoly Capitalism*, Macmillan, London.

Cowling, K. and H. Waterson, 1976, 'Price–Cost Margins and Market Structure', *Economica*, 43.

Davidson, P., 1959, *Theories of Aggregate Income Distribution*, Rutgers University Press, New Jersey.

Kaldor, N., 1955, 'Alternative Theories of Distribution', *Review of Economic Studies*, 23(2), 83–100.

Kalecki, M., 1939–40, 'The Supply Curve of an Industry under Imperfect Competition', *Review of Economic Studies*, no. 2, and *MK* II.

Kalecki, M., 1954, *Theory of Economic Dynamics*, George Allen & Unwin, London.

Kalecki, M., 1971, 'Entrepreneurial Capital and Investment', in M. Kalecki, *Selected Essays on the Dynamics of the Capitalist Economy*, Cambridge University Press, Cambridge, and *MK* I.

Kalecki, M., (1990 and forthcoming), *Collected Works*, 7 vols, J. Osiatyński, ed., Oxford University Press, Oxford. (*MK* in text).

Kalecki, M. and L. Landau, 1935, 'Wahania cen i kosztów a wahania produkcji przemysłowej w Polsce (Fluctuations of Prices and Costs and of Industrial Output in Poland)', in M. Kalecki, *Dzieła*, vol. 6, Państwowe Wydawnictwo Ekonomiczne, Warszawa 1988, and in *MK* VI.

Kriesler, P., 1987, *Kalecki's Microanalysis: The Development of Kalecki's*

Analysis of Pricing and Distribution, Cambridge University Press, Cambridge.

Lange, O., 1941, 'Review of Kalecki's *Essays in the Theory of Economic Fluctuations*', *Journal of Political Economy*, 2.

Lerner, A.P., 1934, 'The Concept of Monopoly and the Measurement of Monopoly Power', *Review of Economic Studies*, 1.

Möller, W.P., 1983, *Der Erfolg von Unternehmenzusammenschussen*, Munich.

Nuti, M., 1970, 'Vulgar Economy in the Theory of Income Distribution', *De Economist*, 118.

Osiatyński, J., 1986, 'Kalecki's Theory of Economic Dynamics after Thirty Years', *Oeconomica Polona*, 1.

Osiatyński, J., 1988, *Michał Kalecki on a Socialist Economy*, Macmillan, London.

Robinson, J., 1933, *The Economics of Imperfect Competition*, Macmillan, London.

Sawyer, M.C., 1982, *Macro-economics in Question: The Keynesian-Monetarist Orthodoxies and the Kaleckian Alternative*, Wheatsheaf Books, Brighton.

7. Rentiers in Post-Keynesian Models

Amitava Krishna Dutt*

I INTRODUCTION

The rentier class has received a great deal of attention in the Marxian and post-Keynesian literature on distribution and accumulation. However, the implications of the existence of this class have not been systematically explored in terms of dynamic models of accumulation and distribution in the same way that the implication of the existence of capitalists and workers has been examined. Ricardo (1817) and other classical writers had examined models with three classes – capitalists, workers and landlords – but subsequent growth models, if they are concerned with classes at all, have dropped the third class. With the growing attention given to the rentier class, there appears to be a need to reintroduce it as a third class.

This chapter examines some dynamic post-Keynesian models of accumulation and distribution with a rentier class. To do so, in Section II the rentier class is defined and some introductory comments on its role in the economy are made; the main post-Keynesian ideas that are introduced into the models are discussed. Section III then develops a simple formal framework to analyse the dynamic role of the rentier class in the economy. The next two sections use this framework to examine two different models of distribution and accumulation. Finally, Section VI makes some concluding comments.

II RENTIERS AND POST-KEYNESIAN MODELS

Before we enter into formal analysis we should clarify what is understood in this chapter by the rentier class and by post-Keynesian models.

A The Rentier Class

The rentier class is defined as the class which obtains income from interest earnings on the loan of property held in the form of money. It can be distinguished from the class of workers, which earns wage income, and the class of capitalists, which earns profit income after wage and interest payments.

While Marx was primarily concerned with the appropriation of surplus value by the capitalist class he was also concerned (see Marx 1894) with the way this surplus was divided between the industrial and merchant capitalists, where the latter (rentiers in our terminology) lent to the former (capitalists in our terminology) to finance their productive operations, in return for which they received interest payments. Since Marx's time there has been discussion of the role of the rentier class in affecting the rate of interest and the rate of inflation, two factors which affect its economic fortunes. There has also been discussion of the role of the rentier class – which causes a leakage from the investible surplus – in imposing a brake on the rate of accumulation. Keynes (1936) recommended the euthanasia of the rentier, and post-Keynesians such as Weintraub (1958) and Davidson and Smolensky (1964) have conducted their macroeconomic analysis with a generally static three-class model which has a rentier class. Marxian writers have emphasised the antagonistic relations between industrial and financial capitalists (Bhaduri 1986)[1] and the role of the financial capitalists in affecting pricing, distribution and accumulation (Panico 1980, 1988; Pivetti 1985).

Our analysis will abstract from two important issues. First, we will not address the question of who exactly are the members of the class: are they coupon-clippers, poor widows, rich financiers and bankers, or parts of the working class? While this is an important question, the answer to it will depend on the particular institutional context of specific economies. The answer will also go some way towards deciding in which of the cases discussed below an economy finds itself, and it may also require some suitable modification of our analysis.[2] Second, we will narrow our analysis by distinguishing between the economic and political roles of the rentier class and focusing only on the former, in a precise sense discussed below. The analysis of the political role of the rentier class in the economy is far less clear and lends itself less easily to formal modelling; in any case, as we shall see, it is necessary to have a prior understanding of its economic role before we can embark on an analysis of its political role.

B Post-Keynesian Models

The economy in which the rentier resides will be one consistent with a post-Keynesian vision of the economy. Since the post-Keynesian vision of the economy is not a standardised one, it is useful briefly to discuss the central features of this vision in the way they are incorporated into our models, and to contrast it with some relevant features of neo-classical approach.[3] Four central post-Keynesian features characterise the economy modelled in the following sections.

The first feature is the importance of class distinctions. Following the classical writers, Marx and Kalecki, post-Keynesians have emphasised the importance of distinguishing between classes in their economic analysis. Our interest in the rentier class presupposes a view of the economy which emphasises classes. This emphasis on classes is a departure from the methodological individualism of neo-classical analysis.

Class analysis is relevant for our analysis in three separate ways. First, the role of 'class struggle' is important in determining the distribution of income. Here our approach follows Marx's theory of the rate of exploitation, or the rate of surplus value under capitalism, and Kalecki's (1971) theory regarding the role of class struggle in the determination of the mark-up rate. Second, following Marx, Kalecki (1971), Kaldor (1955–6) and Pasinetti (1963), we assume that the different classes have different saving propensities, so that income-distributional changes have an effect on the pattern of spending, saving and, hence, the rate of accumulation. Third, class struggle over what share each class receives of the economy's product can affect the rate of inflation.

The second feature is the importance of effective demand. This, of course, is a characteristic feature of Keynes's economic analysis, which finds a central role in all varieties of post-Keynesian analysis. As a result of this feature, demand forces are an important determinant of output (in some versions) and the rate of accumulation. We introduce this feature into the analysis using the now-famous desired accumulation function (see Robinson 1962). This can be contrasted to the neo-classical approach, where output and its rate of growth are supply-constrained, specifically, constrained by the supply of labour.

The third feature is the importance of uncertainty. The majority of post-Keynesian writers follow Keynes in emphasising that economic decision-makers make decisions in an uncertain environment. This recognition of the role of uncertainty has led to two different views on the usefulness of the equilibrium concept in economics. According to one view, since the economy is subject to inherent uncertainty and change, precise, formal modelling using equilibrium analysis becomes an impossibility. According to the other, in the presence of uncertainty individuals and groups resort to the use of rules of thumb and conventions, which leads to stable behaviour, and this behaviour lends itself to formal modelling. We follow the latter view and use equilibrium modelling to analyse the dynamic behaviour of the economy. This is not to imply that the equilibria are tranquil states; economic decision-makers still take uncertainty into account in deciding on their courses of action. Nor is it implied, as we shall see, that the equilibria are stable.

Some specific types of rules of thumb we will assume in our models are mark-up pricing, following Kalecki (1971), investment behaviour which makes investment depend on the rate of capacity utilisation, following Steindl (1952), and the wage-push behaviour of labour unions. These assumptions are contrasted with the optimising behaviour assumed in neo-classical theory, although with sufficient ingenuity one can provide optimisation underpinnings to any type of behaviour.

The final feature is the endogeneity of credit money in the economy. While traditional macroeconomic theory takes the supply of money to be exogenously given, as Chick (1986) points out, when the banking system has reached a sufficiently advanced stage, the additional demand for credit may be satisfied by the banking system, so that the supply of money becomes endogenous. Kaldor (1982), Weintraub (1978) and Moore (1988) have repeatedly stressed the endogeneity of credit money: banks operating with excess reserves will increase their loans at a given interest rate when there is a higher demand for loans; if they run out of reserves they will seek to increase their deposits, or borrow from the central bank. The central bank, as lender of last resort, will lend to the banks at the discount rate, over which banks set a mark-up when they fix their lending rates (Rousseas 1986, Moore 1988).

This view of the money supply process implies that the interest rate is a monetary phenomenon determined largely by central banking policy as opposed to its determination by the real forces of surplus (as in classical writers) or productivity and thrift (as in neo-classical theory). This monetary theory follows closely the writings of Marx and Keynes (see Panico 1988).

In addition to incorporating the ideas of many post-Keynesians this formulation of the theory of interest is very convenient for our purposes because it captures in a simple manner the 'power' of the rentier class. Since the rate of interest is determined by the discount rate of the central bank, we may assume that the rentier class can affect the determination of the interest rate by using its political power in affecting the level of the discount rate. By holding the interest rate to be given, we imply that the political power of the rentier class is given; we therefore confine our attention to changes in the economic power of the rentier class, as discussed below.

The general framework we develop in the next section builds on these four central post-Keynesian features,[4] adding more specific assumptions where necessary for analytical simplicity.

III THE GENERAL FRAMEWORK

The models to be discussed in the next two sections have some common features, which formalise the characteristics of the post-Keynesian vision as discussed above. This section discusses the assumptions which collectively describe this general framework. The assumptions may be classified into four groups.

First, we make some background assumptions. The economy is a closed one in which the government does not engage in fiscal activity. It produces only one good, using a fixed-coefficients technology and two 'factors' of production, labour and capital goods. Second, we make a set of assumptions regarding the three classes in the economy: workers, rentiers and capitalists. Workers provide labour and earn wage income. We assume that they do not save, so that their income is *only* from wages. The supply of labour is unlimited owing to the existence of a reserve army. Rentiers only hold bank deposits, denominated in terms of money, and earn interest income. They save a constant fraction of their income, s_r. Finally, capitalists earn the surplus income above the wage and interest payments. They own the firms – either through the ownership of stocks or directly – and the firms pay them the entire profits.[5] They save a constant fraction of their income, s_c.

Third, we make a set of assumptions regarding the behaviour of two other groups, banks and firms, at a point in time. For simplicity, we think in terms of a representative bank and a representative firm. The bank takes deposits from the rentier class. For simplicity, we assume that there are no costs to banking other than the cost of borrowing, and that the mark-up rate in banking is zero. This implies that the bank will borrow from the rentiers and lend to the firms at the same rate, which is the given interest rate, i. Firms borrow only for financing their fixed capital; we abstract from working capital costs. The credit supply is endogenous at this interest rate, as described above.

The firm, which produces and sells, has to make pricing, production and investment decisions. At a point in time it faces a given money wage, W, and has a historically-given mark-up, z, on prime costs, so that the price is given by

$$P = (1 + z)Wa_0 \tag{7.1}$$

where a_0 is the given labour–output ratio. Regarding production decisions, if there is sufficient demand for its product to produce at full capacity, it will do so, and output will be determined by its given stock of capital, K, and the given (minimum) capital–output ratio. If there is insufficient demand for full-capacity production, the firm will produce according to demand and experience excess capacity. Regarding investment plans, the firm's desired level of investment depends positively on the rate of profit and the utilisation of capacity, and negatively on the real rate of interest. We formalise this with the equation

$$g^I = \alpha + \beta u + \tau(r - i + P^*) \tag{7.2}$$

where g^I is the planned level of investment as a ratio of the stock of capital, u the level of capacity utilisation as measured by X/K where X is the level of output and K the level of capital stock, r the rate of profit, and variables with stars denote time rates of growth of the variables. For simplicity the actual rate of inflation and the expected rate are assumed to be equal.

Our final set of assumptions describe how the economy moves over time. Regarding the wage, we assume that labour unions have a desired or targeted real wage which depends on the relative power of the workers *vis-à-vis* the firms. If the actual real wage is lower than the desired one, the money wage will rise over time according to the equation

$$W^* = \Theta[V_w - V] \tag{7.3}$$

where V_w is the real wage desired by unions, $V = W/P$, and $\Theta > 0$ a speed of adjustment constant.

Regarding the price, we should distinguish between the cases of excess and full capacity. If excess capacity prevails, output will adjust to demand, as already assumed, so that there is no excess demand in the economy. In this case we assume that the firm has a desired markup which depends on the degree of industrial concentration and on the interest rate (since interest payments have to be paid from mark-up income) and which pushes up the price whenever the actual mark-up is less than the desired mark-up. A particular mark-up, from equation (7.1), implies a particular desired real wage, so that this adjustment story can be written in the simple form

$$P^* = \pi[V - V_f] \tag{7.4}$$

where V_f is the desired real wage firms wish to pay, depending on their desired mark-up, and $\pi > 0$ is a speed of adjustment constant. When full capacity utilisation prevails, however, excess demand may prevail in the economy at the historically-given price. In this case we assume that the investment plans of firms (as a fraction of existing capital stock), g^I, cannot be realised, and actual investment is given by the rate of saving as a ratio of capital, g. In this case the rate of price increase will be given by the strength of excess demand in the economy, so that

$$P^* = \mu[g^I - g] \tag{7.5}$$

where $\mu > 0$ is the (constant) speed of adjustment and the term within brackets measures the extent of excess demand.

Regarding the stock of capital, we assume away depreciation, so that the increase in the stock of capital is given by the actual rate of capital accumulation. In the case of excess capacity, since demand equals output, this is given by planned investment and saving, so that

$$K^* = g^I \tag{7.6}$$

In the case of full capacity utilisation, since planned investment and saving are not necessarily equal, it is given by savings, so that

$$K^* = g \tag{7.7}$$

Finally, the stock of wealth of the rentier class, D, grows according to their rate of saving, so that

$$\mathrm{d}D/\mathrm{d}t = s_r iD$$

which implies that

$$D^* = s_r i \tag{7.8}$$

The formal structure of our framework is then as follows. At a point in time which we will call the short run, we take as given P, W, K and D. Our assumptions will then determine how these four state variables will move over time in the long run, and we may analyse how the system evolves over time. We will examine these dynamics by examining the behaviour of V, the real wage, and $\delta = D/PK$, the wealth of the rentier class as a fraction of the stock of capital, using the relations

$$V^* = W^* - P^* \tag{7.9}$$

and

$$\delta^* = D^* - P^* - K^* \tag{7.10}$$

We now turn to a discussion of the two cases, of excess and full capacity, in turn.

IV THE CASE OF EXCESS CAPACITY

Assuming that the economy always exhibits excess capacity we discuss, successively, the behaviour of the economy in the short run and in the long run, and the effects of a rise in the interest rate.

A The Short Run

Given K, W, P and D, in the short run, output adjusts to clear the market. Supply–demand balance requires

$$X = Va_0X + (1 - s_c)[(1 - Va_0)X - i(D/P)] + (1 - s_r)iD/P + I \tag{7.11}$$

where X is the level of output, I the level of planned investment, and where the other symbols have already been defined. Dividing through by K this short-run equilibrium condition becomes

$$u = Va_0u + (1 - s_c)[(1 - Va_0)u - i\delta] + (1 - s_r)i\delta + g^I \tag{7.12}$$

For the determination of g^I we assume a special case of (7.2), where

$$g^I = \alpha + \beta u - \tau(i - P^*) \tag{7.2'}$$

where for simplicity we have dropped the rate of profit, r.[6] Given V and δ, equation (7.4) solves for P^*, and by substituting (7.2′) into (7.10) we can then solve for the short-run equilibrium value of u, given by

$$u = \{\alpha + (s_c - s_r)i\delta - \tau[i - \pi(V - V_f)]\}/[s_c(1 - Va_0) - \beta] \tag{7.13}$$

We assume that the parameters of the model ensure that the equilibrium satisfies $u > 0$ and that $u < 1/a_1$, which guarantees the existence of excess capacity. Note that $u > 0$ ensures that $1 > Va_0$, which ensures positive profits. We assume that the dynamic process which takes the economy to equilibrium is given by

$$du/dt = \Sigma[g^I - s_c(1 - Va_0)u - (s_c - s_r)i\delta] \qquad (7.14)$$

where $\Sigma > 0$ is a speed of adjustment constant and the term within square brackets measures excess demand in the goods market. Substituting from (7.2′) it follows that the short-run equilibrium is stable if

$$s_c(1 - Va_0) > \beta$$

or that saving is more responsive to changes in the rate of capacity utilisation than is investment, a standard stability requirement in macroeconomic models. We assume that this condition is satisfied.

B The Long Run

In the long run we assume that, in addition to movements in W, P, K and D according to equations (7.3), (7.4), (7.6) and (7.8), V_w depends on the state of slack in the labour market. This last assumption captures the fact that the relative power of labour unions is likely to be weaker when labour markets are slacker, and the short-run fixity and long-run variability captures the notion that changes in relative power are likely to be slow. Since a rise in capacity utilisation is accompanied by a fall in the unemployment rate, we assume that

$$V_w = V_w(u) \qquad (7.15)$$

where $V_w' > 0$, but 'small' in the sense to be discussed below. All this happens with the short-run equilibrium always being satisfied.

The dynamics in the long run can be examined by considering the movement of V and δ over time. Equations (7.3), (7.4), (7.6), (7.8), (7.9), (7.10) and (7.15) imply

$$V^* = [\Theta V_w(u) + \pi V_f] - (\Theta + \pi)V \qquad (7.16)$$

$$\delta^* = (s_r + \tau)i - (1 + \tau)\pi(V - V_f) - \alpha - \beta u \qquad (7.17)$$

Since u, determined in (7.13), depends also on V and δ, we obtain a dynamic system of the form

$$V^* = \phi(V,\delta) \qquad (7.18)$$

$$\delta^* = \sigma(V,\delta) \tag{7.19}$$

where the partial derivatives are given by

$$\phi_v = -\Theta\{1 - V_w'[(\tau\pi + s_c a_0 u)/(s_c(1 - Va_0) - \beta)]\} - \pi \tag{7.20}$$

$$\phi_\delta = \Theta V_w'(s_c - s_r)i/[s_c(1 - Va_0) - \beta] \tag{7.21}$$

$$\sigma_v = -(1 + \tau)\pi - \beta[\tau\pi + s_c a_0 u]/[s_c(1 - Va_0) - \beta] \tag{7.22}$$

$$\sigma_\delta = -\beta(s_c - s_r)i/[s_c(1 - Va_0) - \beta] \tag{7.23}$$

The signs of ϕ_v and σ_v are unambiguously negative, provided that V_w' is 'small' as assumed, and the conditions for the existence of stability of short-run equilibrium are satisfied. The sense in which V_w' is assumed to be small can be clarified as follows: it should be small enough to keep the term within curly brackets in (7.20) positive. The intuitive meanings of these derivatives are as follows. The rise in the real wage redistributes income towards workers, raises the aggregate consumption demand and hence the rate of capacity utilisation, and also raises the gap between the real wage firms pay and what they want to pay and hence the rate of inflation. Both these tendencies raise the rate of investment and further increase the rate of capacity utilisation. As long as the effect of this on the desired real wage of workers, V_w, is not greater than the increase in V itself – and this is the sense in which we assume V_w' to be small – V^* will fall, explaining the sign of ϕ_v. The higher level of inflation and accumulation which result from the increase in V explain the sign of σ_v.

The signs of ϕ_δ and σ_δ, however, are seen from (7.21) and (7.23) to depend on the sign of $s_c - s_r$. The effect of a rise in δ – the share of the rentier class in total capital – depends on whether capitalists or rentiers have a higher propensity to save. If s_c exceeds s_r, the redistribution of income due to a rise in δ increases consumption demand, the level of capacity utilisation and hence the rate of investment. The rise in the rate of capacity utilisation raises the real wage desired by workers and thus raises V^*, explaining the sign of ϕ_δ. The increase in the rate of accumulation reduces δ^*, explaining the sign of σ_δ. If, on the other hand, s_c is less than s_r, so that the rise in δ reduces aggregate demand, the signs of these derivatives will be reversed.

When $s_c > s_r$, the trace of the dynamic system, $\phi_v + \sigma_\delta < 0$, and the determinant, $\phi_v\sigma_\delta - \phi_\delta\sigma_v > 0$, so that the sufficient conditions of (local) stability of the long-run equilibrium are satisfied. However, when $s_c <$

s_r, while the trace is still negative, the determinant has a negative sign, violating the stability condition; the long-run equilibrium becomes a saddlepoint. All this can be shown in the phase diagrams of Figure 7.1. The case of $s_c > s_r$ is portrayed in Figure 7.1(a). Since $\phi_v < 0$ and $\phi_\delta > 0$ the $V^* = 0$ curve has a positive slope, and since $\sigma_\delta < 0$ and $\sigma_v < 0$, the $\delta^* = 0$ curve has a negative slope. With the horizontal and vertical arrows as shown (since $\phi_v < 0$ and $\sigma_\delta < 0$), the long-run equilibrium is a stable one. The case of $s_c < s_r$ is shown in Figure 7.1(b). Since $\phi_v < 0$ and $\phi_\delta < 0$, the $V^* = 0$ line has a positive slope, and since $\sigma_\delta < 0$ and $\sigma_v > 0$ the $\delta^* = 0$ line has a negative slope. With the horizontal and vertical arrows as shown, the long-run equilibrium is seen to be a saddlepoint. Depending on whether the initial δ happens to lie above or below the separatrix *SS*, the importance of the rentier class in the economy will (at least after a point) continuously increase or diminish (asymptotically). The zone below the separatrix can be called the zone of rentier elimination and the zone above it that of rentier domination. In the zone of rentier elimination the economic importance (as measured by δ) falls over time and the system implies their 'euthanasia'. Along such a path V increases and δ falls, so that u increases. Since by (7.4) a higher V is also associated with a higher rate of inflation, equation (7.2′) shows that along this path the rate of accumulation increases over time. Thus the decline of the rentier class is accompanied by an improving distribution of income (increasing V) and rising rate of accumulation (increasing g^I). In the zone of rentier domination the rise in δ implies the rise in the economic importance of the rentier class, but a fall in V reflects a worsening distribution of income. Along this path the rate of accumulation falls over time.[7]

C Effects of a Change in the Interest Rate

In considering the effects of changes in the interest rate it is necessary to inquire whether it is plausible to expect the desired mark-up of firms to depend on the rate of interest. Since interest payments must be made from mark-up income, it is plausible that the firms will wish to raise their desired mark-up when the interest rate increases. This relationship can be depicted by the equation

$$V_f = V_f(i) \tag{7.24}$$

Making this assumption we consider the short-run and long-run effects of a change in the interest rate. In short-run equilibrium u is given by (7.13). Differentiation with respect to i, using (7.24), yields

Figure 7.1

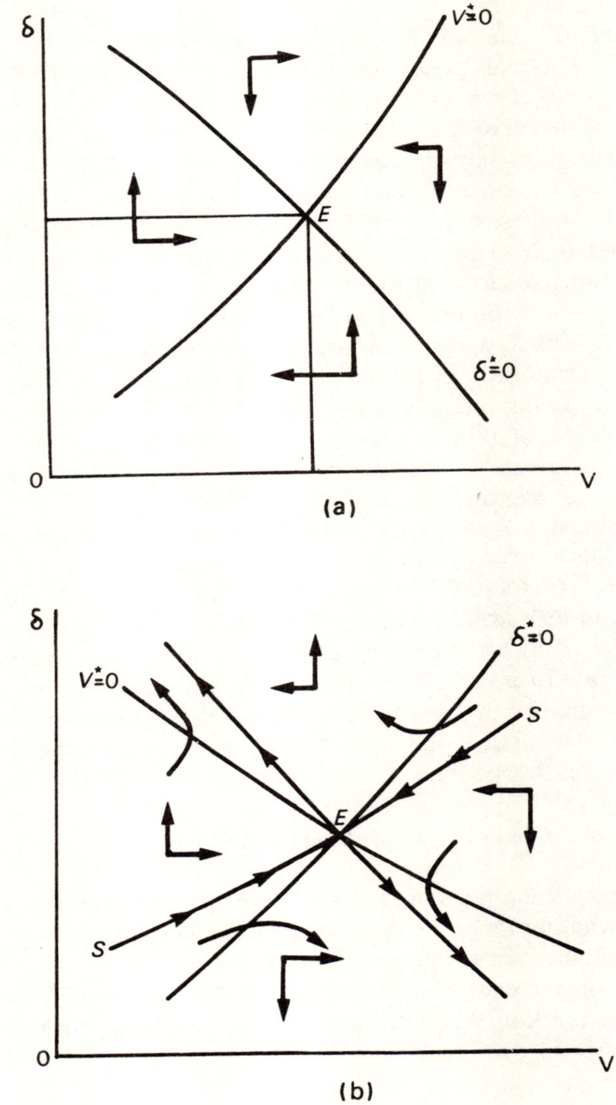

$$du/di = (s_c - s_r)\delta - \tau(1 + \pi V_f')$$

The first term shows the consumption effect of a redistribution between capitalists and rentiers: it will be positive if $s_c > s_r$, so that rentiers have a higher propensity to consume and the rise in the interest rate increases aggregate demand. The second term is negative if $-\pi V_f' < 1$, which ensures that a rise in i increases the rate of inflation by less than the increase in i so that the real interest rate rises. Since $\pi < 1$, $-V_f' < 1$ will ensure this; we assume that this condition is satisfied. All this implies that in the short run, if $s_r > s_c$, an increase in i will reduce capacity utilisation, while if $s_c > s_r$ the result will depend on the relative strength of the two effects, which depend on τ and δ.

In the long run the effects can be considered by examining shifts in the $V^* = 0$ and $\delta^* = 0$ curves of Figure 7.1. Regarding the $V^* = 0$ curve, the easiest case to consider is that in which, for simplicity, $V_w' = 0$. This implies, from equation (7.16), that the $V^* = 0$ curve becomes vertical at the value given by

$$V = (\Theta V_w + \pi V_f)/(\Theta + \pi)$$

where V_w is the fixed level of the targeted real wage. The increase in i, by reducing V_f, will shift this curve to the left. When V_w depends on u matters get more complicated. In this case, at a given V and δ on the $V^* = 0$ curve, an increase in i will affect u and thus affect V_w. For instance, if $s_c < s_r$ the increase in i will, as discussed before, reduce u and therefore reduce V_w. Since both V_w and V_f fall the right-hand side of (7.16) falls, so that, to set it equal to zero again, given a 'small' V_w', V has to be reduced. Thus the $V^* = 0$ curve, as in the simple case, will be pushed to the left. If $s_c > s_r$ the increase in i, as seen above, could increase or reduce u for given V and δ, so that it could increase or reduce V_w as well. Thus an increase in i may increase V_w and reduce V_f, rendering the effect on the right-hand side of (7.16) uncertain. Consequently, especially with a large enough Θ or V_w', the $V^* = 0$ curve could conceivably move to the right when i increases. To make the following analysis as simple as possible we assume in the following discussion that $V_w' = 0$, so that the $V^* = 0$ curve is vertical and will move to the left when i increases.

Now consider the effect on the $\delta^* = 0$ curve. Equations (7.13) and (7.24) can be substituted into (7.17) and δ^* can be set equal to zero to obtain

$$(s_r i - P^*)[s_c(1 - Va_0) - \beta] - \alpha s_c(1 - Va_0) + \tau(i - P^*)s_c(1 - Va_0) - \beta(s_c - s_r)i\delta = 0$$

Differentiation holding V constant yields

$$\mathrm{d}\delta/\mathrm{d}i = [1/\beta(s_c - s_r)i]\{(s_r + \pi V_f')[s_c(1 - Va_0) - \beta] + \tau(1 + \pi V_f')s_c(1 - Va_0) - \beta(s_c - s_r)\delta\}$$

which shows that the $\delta^* = 0$ curve can move up or down when i increases.

If $s_c > s_r$, the denominator of the expression is positive, and in the numerator the second and third terms are unambiguously positive and negative, respectively, and the first term can take either sign. If V_f' is small in absolute value the inflationary effect (which reduces the real value of deposits) will be weak and $\mathrm{d}\delta/\mathrm{d}i > i$ is possible, so that the curve moves upwards; but with a higher absolute value of V_f' the first term of the numerator can turn negative, and cause the curve to move downwards. The new long-run equilibrium will imply a lower V and the effect on δ cannot in general be determined.

If $s_c < s_r$ the denominator will be negative. In the numerator the last term will be positive, the second will remain positive and the first terms can take either sign. With a small absolute size of V_f', $\mathrm{d}\delta/\mathrm{d}i < 0$ seems most likely, so that the $\delta^* = 0$ curve moves down. Figure 7.2 shows the case in which this happens and the separatrix also moves to the right, so that the rise in the interest rate can shift the economy from the region of rentier elimination to one of rentier domination. This analysis should also tell us that this result is not inevitable, since with a large absolute value for V_f', the $V^* = 0$ curve can move by a large amount to the left and the $\delta^* = 0$ curve can move down by a small amount or in fact move up (especially with small β and τ) so that the separatrix can move upwards, *enlarging* the zone of rentier elimination. The reason for this somewhat counter-intuitive result is that the rise in the interest rate can increase the rate of inflation sufficiently to erode the real wealth of the rentier class over time, resulting in their eventual elimination despite their higher incomes.

V THE CASE OF FULL CAPACITY UTILISATION

Next we turn to the case in which demand is high enough to take the economy to full capacity utilisation. As in the previous case we consider, in turn, the behaviour of the economy in the short run, the long run, and when the interest rate changes.[8]

Figure 7.2

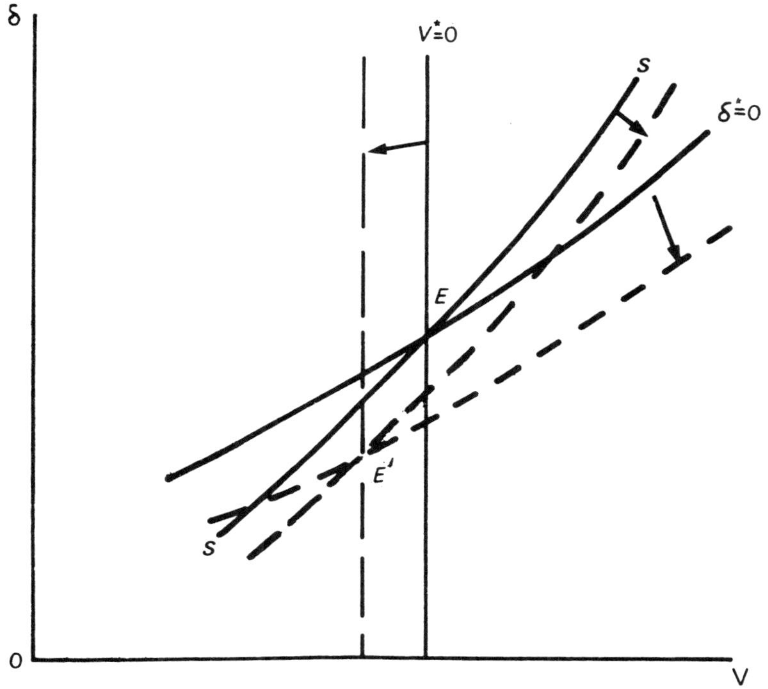

A The Short Run

In the short run W, P, K and D, and therefore V and δ, are given. Output is determined at this point in time from K and the capital–output ratio a_1, and the rate of profit from

$$r = [(1 - Va_0)/a_1] \tag{7.25}$$

As discussed above, with full capacity utilisation, so that $u = 1/a_1$, demand plans cannot be fulfilled. We assume that desired investment plans are given by[9]

$$g^I = \alpha + \tau(r - i + P^*) \tag{7.2''}$$

The actual rate of accumulation is given by the actual saving of the capitalists and rentiers, as stated in (7.7). This implies that

$$S = s_c[rK - i(D/P)] + s_r iD/P$$

where S is real saving. Dividing through by K, and using (7.25), this implies

$$g = s_c[(1 - Va_0)/a_1] + (s_r - s_c)\, i\delta. \qquad (7.26)$$

B The Long Run

Over time W, P, K and D change according to the equations (7.3), (7.5), (7.7) and (7.8), respectively. For simplicity – unlike the previous section – we assume that V_w is fixed. The dynamics of the system can be examined by analysing the dynamics of V and δ as given by (7.9) and (7.10). Substituting from equations (7.2″), (7.3), (7.5), (7.7), (7.8), (7.4), (7.25) and (7.26), equations (7.9) and (7.10) can be written as

$$V^* = m^0 - m_1 V + m_2\delta \qquad (7.27)$$

and

$$\delta^* = n^0 + n_1 V - n_2\delta \qquad (7.28)$$

where

$$\begin{aligned} m^0 &= \tau\mu i/(1 - \tau\mu) + \Theta V_w - [a_1\alpha - (s_c - \tau)]\mu/(1 - \tau\mu)a_1 \\ m_1 &= \Theta + (s_c - \tau)\,(a_0/a_1)[\tau\mu/(1 - \tau\mu)] \\ m_2 &= (s_r - s_c)i\mu/(1 - \tau\mu) \\ n^0 &= [s_r + \tau\mu/(1 - \tau\mu)]i \\ &\quad - [\alpha\mu a_1 + \tau\mu + s_c(1 - \mu(1 + \tau))]/(1 - \tau\mu)a_1 \\ n_1 &= [\tau\mu + s_c(1 - \mu(1 + \tau))]a_0/a_1(1 - \tau\mu) \\ n_2 &= (s_r - s_c)i[1 - \mu(1 + \tau)]/(1 - \tau\mu) \end{aligned}$$

The stability of this system depends on the properties of its Jacobian, J. Local stability requires that its trace,

$$\begin{aligned} tr(J) &= -(s_r - s_c)i[1 - \mu(1 + \tau)]/(1 - \tau\mu) \\ &\quad - [\Theta + \mu(s_c - \tau)(a_0/a_1)\tau\mu/(1 - \tau\mu)] \end{aligned} \qquad (7.29)$$

is negative and its determinant,

$$det(J) = [(s_r - s_c)i/(1 - \tau\mu)]\{\Theta[1 - \mu(1 + \tau)] - [\mu/(1 - \tau\mu)](a_0/a_1)[(s_c(1 - \tau) + \tau)^2(1 - \mu(1 + \tau)) + \tau\mu]\} \quad (7.30)$$

is positive.

We assume that μ and τ (parameters denoting the speeds of inflation and investment response, respectively) are small enough to satisfy the condition

$$1 - \mu(1 + \tau) > 0 \quad (7.31)$$

which ensures that inflation does not 'blow up', ruling out a hyper-inflationary tendency in the economy. We also assume that

$$s_c > \tau \quad (7.32)$$

which states that capitalist saving is more responsive to variations in the rate of profit than is investment, a standard stability requirement for macroeconomic models.

If $s_r > s_c$, so that the rentiers have a higher propensity to save than the capitalists, (7.29) shows that $tr(J)$ is necessarily negative. However (7.30) shows that $det(J)$ may be of either sign. If Θ is 'large' compared to μ so that the first term within the curly brackets dominates, we have $det(J) > 0$, and the system will be locally stable. The dynamics in this case can be portrayed by Figure 7.3: the economy will move to a long-run equilibrium given by S. If, on the other hand, Θ is 'small' compared to μ so that the second term within curly brackets in (7.30) dominates, we have $det(J) < 0$. The dynamics in this case is shown by Figure 7.4. The long-run equilibrium is a saddlepoint: depending on which side of the separatrix the economy starts from, it will either experience rentier domination or rentier annihilation.

If $s_r < s_c$, so that the rentiers have a lower propensity to save than the capitalists, $tr(J)$ can take any sign. Since the term outside the curly brackets in (7.30) is now negative, the implication of the relative sizes of Θ and μ is now reversed. If Θ is now 'small' in the sense of the previous paragraph, $det(J) > 0$. The situation is as shown in Figure 7.5: the economy will experience cyclical fluctuations; whether or not these oscillations will be damped depends on the $tr(J)$. If Θ is 'large', $det(J) < 0$ and the situation will be as depicted in Figure 7.6: we again have a saddlepoint equilibrium.

We have taken the real wage to be an indicator of income distribution, and it is therefore obvious how the distribution of income changes

Figure 7.3

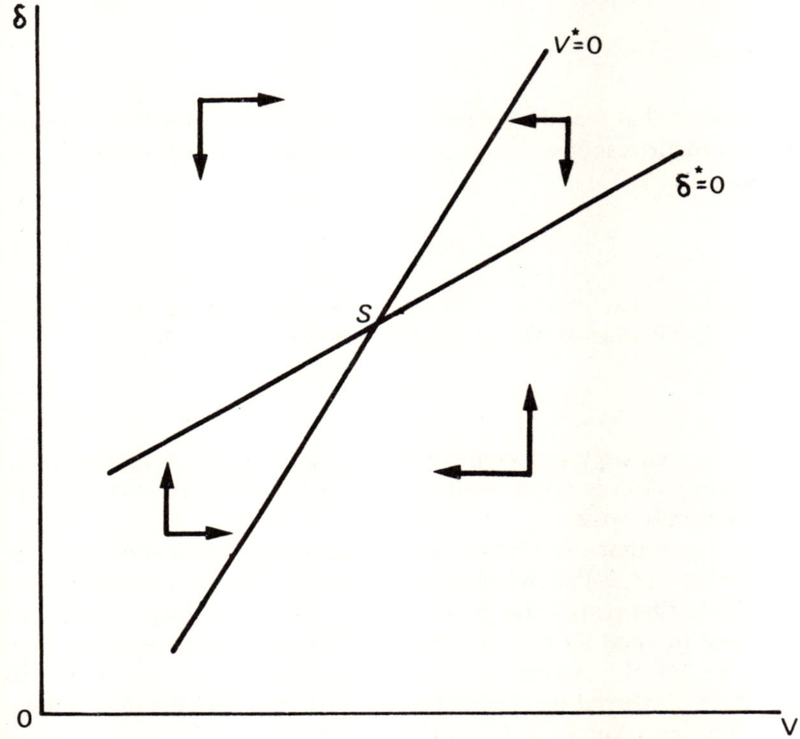

along any path in these figures. The behaviour of the rate of accumulation, our other indicator of the state of the economy, however, cannot be so easily determined when the economy moves along any particular path. To do so we may introduce into the figures iso-growth lines (not drawn), given by the equation

$$\delta = [g' - (s_c/a_1)]/(s_r - s_c)i + [a_0 s_c/a_1(s_r - s_c)i]V \qquad (7.33)$$

which is derived from (7.26), and where g' is any given level of accumulation. If $s_r > s_c$, for instance, this curve will have a constant positive slope, and higher levels of g' will imply curves further up and to the left. If we superimpose such a map in (say) Figure 7.4, we can say (for instance) that if we start from a high δ and low V the economy will initially experience an improvement in income distribution and a

Figure 7.4

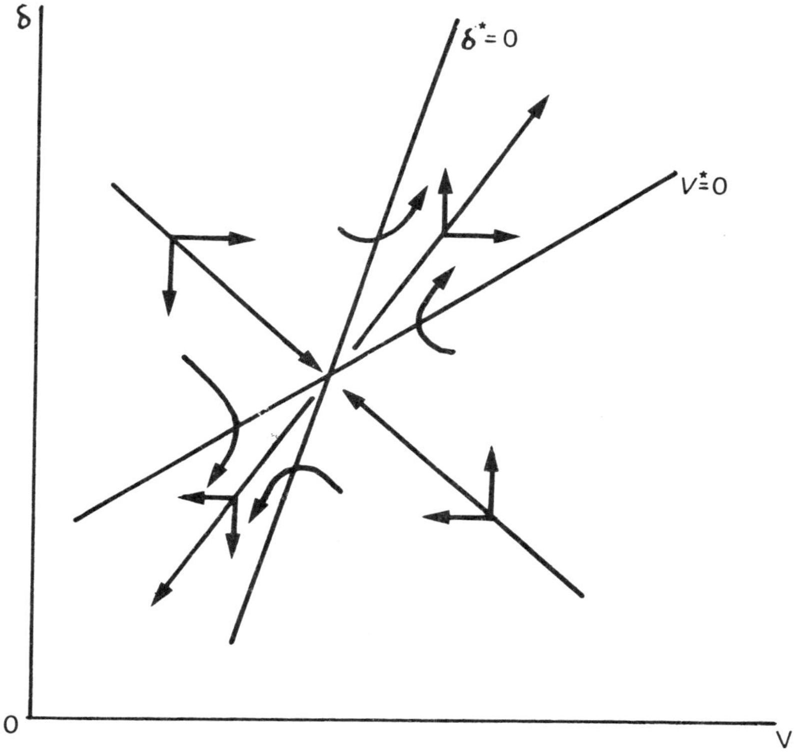

reduction in its rate of accumulation. Depending on which side of the separatrix it starts, it will then eventually experience a rising or falling V. If it happens to start below the separatrix, it will soon cross the $V^* = 0$ line and the economy will begin to experience a falling V. This worsens the distribution of income, but begins to counteract the retarding effect on the rate of accumulation of the fall in δ. The behaviour of the growth rate will depend on whether the economy's path (determined, among other things, by the speed of adjustment parameters for wages, Θ) has a slope higher or lower than that of the isogrowth lines (which, as we saw earlier, is independent of the speeds of adjustment coefficients).

C Effects of a Change in the Interest Rate

The effects of a change in the interest rate depend on whether s_r exceeds

Figure 7.5

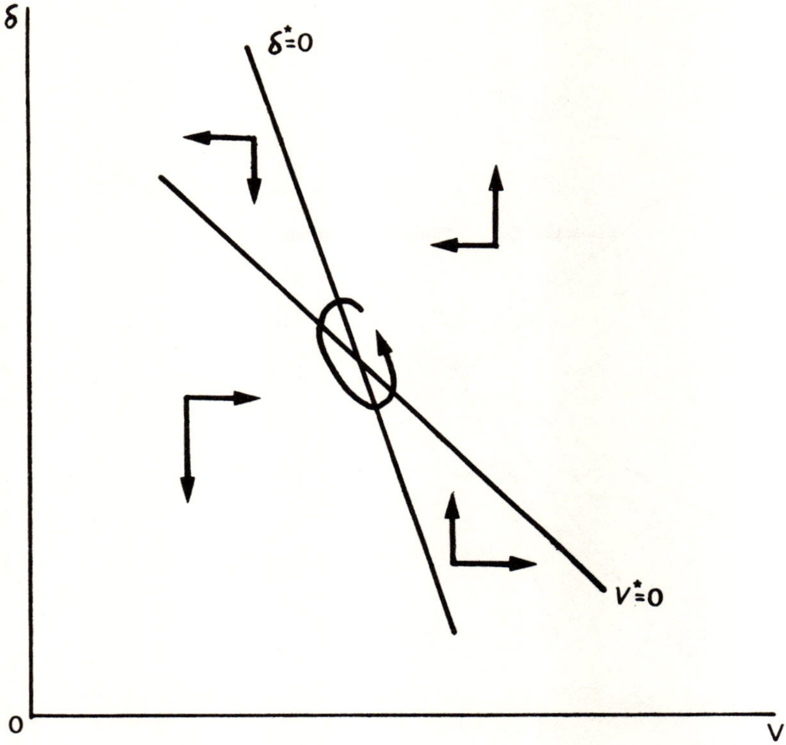

or is less than s_c. For ease of exposition we will consider primarily the case of $s_r > s_c$ with the stable interior long-run equilibrium, relegating the discussion of other cases to a few scattered remarks.

In the short run, with V and δ given, we find that

$$\mathrm{d}g/\mathrm{d}i = (s_r - s_c)\delta \tag{7.34}$$

$$\mathrm{d}g^I/\mathrm{d}i = -\tau \tag{7.35}$$

$$\mathrm{d}P^*/\mathrm{d}i = -\mu[\tau + (s_r - s_c)\delta] \tag{7.36}$$

$$\mathrm{d}D^*/\mathrm{d}i = s_r \tag{7.37}$$

which show that a rise in the interest rate increases the rate of

Figure 7.6

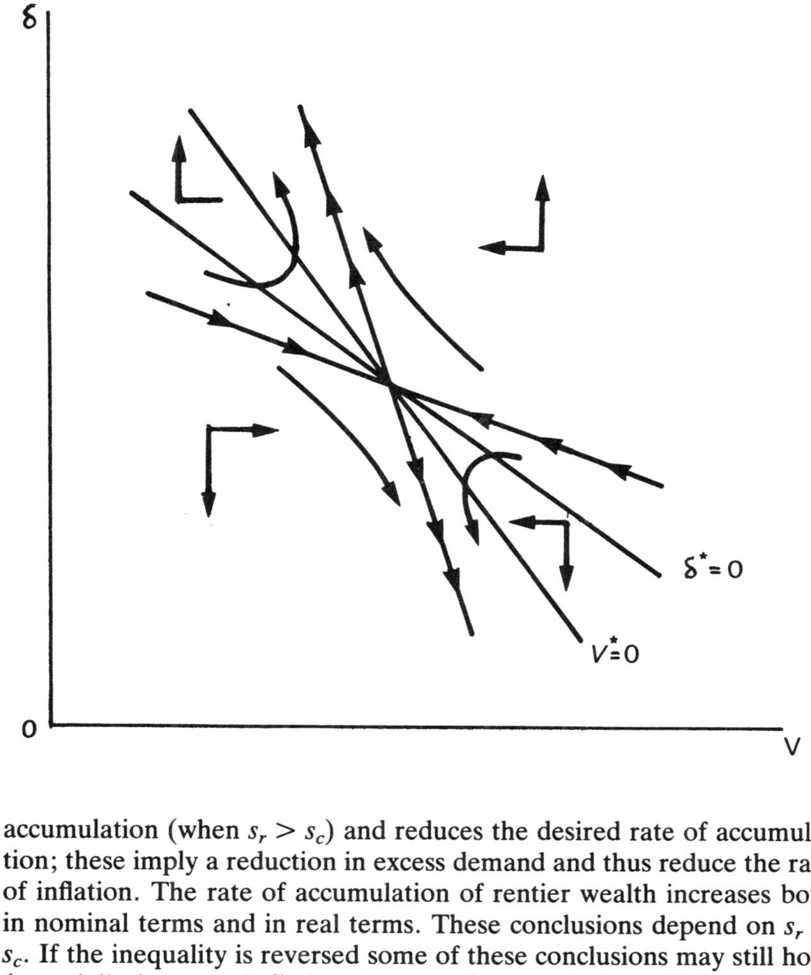

accumulation (when $s_r > s_c$) and reduces the desired rate of accumulation; these imply a reduction in excess demand and thus reduce the rate of inflation. The rate of accumulation of rentier wealth increases both in nominal terms and in real terms. These conclusions depend on $s_r > s_c$. If the inequality is reversed some of these conclusions may still hold (especially for a small δ), but the rate of accumulation will fall with the interest rate with the redistribution of income from capitalists to rentiers, where the latter have a lower propensity to save and where saving determines the rate of accumulation. It is thus possible for the rate of inflation to rise if the reduction in saving is greater than the reduction in the desired rate of accumulation. Since the economy is at full capacity, the level of output and the rate of profit (gross of interest) will not be affected.

In the long run the effects in the stable case with $s_r > s_c$ can be analysed using Figure 7.3. From equation (7.27) it follows that the increase in i will imply a higher V^*, so that the $V^* = 0$ curve will shift to the right. From equation (7.28) it follows that the $\delta^* = 0$ curve will be rotated. At lower levels of δ, δ^* will increase at a given V and δ since the increase in the real asset accumulation of rentiers will exceed the increase in the overall rate of accumulation; the $\delta^* = 0$ line will therefore shift down. At high levels of δ this can no longer be guaranteed, and the relevant segment of the $\delta^* = 0$ line can shift up. If we confine attention to the case in which the initial long-run equilibrium happens to be where the $\delta^* = 0$ line shifts, the new long-run equilibrium values of δ and V will be higher than the ones at the previous long-run equilibrium. Thus the relative position of the rentier class improves and there is an improvement in the distribution of income. Since V is higher it follows from equation (7.3) that the rate of wage increase will be smaller and at long-run equilibrium, since $W^* = P^*$, so will the rate of inflation. From equation (7.8) it follows that D^* will be higher, and since at long-run equilibrium $D^* = P^* + K^*$, the higher D^* and lower P^* must imply a higher rate of accumulation. Thus in addition to improving the distribution of income the increase in the rate of interest will also raise the long-run equilibrium rate of accumulation. It should be remembered, of course, that had the initial long-run equilibrium occurred at a high δ at which the $\delta^* = 0$ line moved up, it could no longer be guaranteed that both δ and V would rise. As long as V rises, however, it will follow that there will be an improvement in the distribution of income and the rate of accumulation.

These favourable results do not necessarily occur when s_r is not greater than s_c, since, as we saw in our discussion of the short run, in this case the rise in the interest rate will not increase the rate of accumulation. The analysis becomes quite complicated since we are no longer assured that the economy arrives at a stable long-run equilibrium, and to examine the effects of changes in interest rates we will need to examine changes in the behaviour of the economy along specific trajectories. To illustrate one case in which the rate of accumulation does not improve with the rise in the interest rate we consider the simple case, not considered before, in which $s_r = s_c$. In this case it can be checked from equations (7.27) and (7.28) that both $V^* = 0$ and $\delta^* = 0$ lines will be vertical, as shown in Figure 7.7. If we start with a situation in which the interest rate is low, it is likely that the $V^* = 0$ line will be to the right of the $\delta^* = 0$ line (where we assume that both lines lie in the positive orthant). The dynamics of the case are shown in Figure 7.7(a), which implies that the economy will tend to its long-run equilibrium real wage given by the $V^* = 0$ line, and δ, even if it initially rises, will tend to zero and the rentier class will be annihilated. An increase in the rate of interest will now shift both $V^* = 0$ and $\delta^* = 0$ lines to the right, but equations (7.27) and (7.28) show that the latter will shift more than the former. A sufficient increase in the interest rate will bring about the situation shown in Figure 7.7(b), with the economy tending again to its long-run equilibrium real wage given by the $V^* = 0$ line, but δ will eventually increase over time, increasing the share of the rentier class in wealth over time. In this case, since $s_c = s_r$, changes in δ will have no effect on the rate of accumulation, which will be determined by the level of the real wage (together with other parameters). Since the economy may be converted from one which experiences a falling real wage (since the $V^* = 0$ line is to the left of the position at which the economy is) to one which experiences a rising real wage (with the $V^* = 0$ line having shifted to the right of where the economy is) it will be converted from an economy with a rising growth rate to one with a falling growth rate.

VI CONCLUSION

Our discussion of the role of the rentier class in post-Keynesian models has three important implications. First, the role of the rentier class in the economy depends on the structural characteristics of the economy. While this conclusion should not come as a surprise to those who do not believe in a single model for all seasons (and lands), our analysis, which has distinguished clearly between two different models – one with excess capacity and one with full capacity utilisation – shows exactly how economic structure affects the behaviour of the economy and the role of the rentier class in it. This implies, of course, that general conclusions regarding the role of the rentier class cannot be drawn from the two models analysed here. Its role in other types of economies – which do not have post-Keynesian features – will have to be carefully analysed using alternative models of accumulation, distribution and inflation.[10]

Second, the relative sizes of the saving propensities of the rentiers and capitalists are important in determining the role of the rentier class in the economy. This comes out most clearly in the model with excess capacity, although we have also seen that it is an important issue in the model with full capacity utilisation as well. For instance, in the former model, if the rentier class has a higher propensity to save than does the capitalist class, it will play a regressive role in the economy: its interests will be inversely related to the interests of higher accumulation and

Figure 7.7

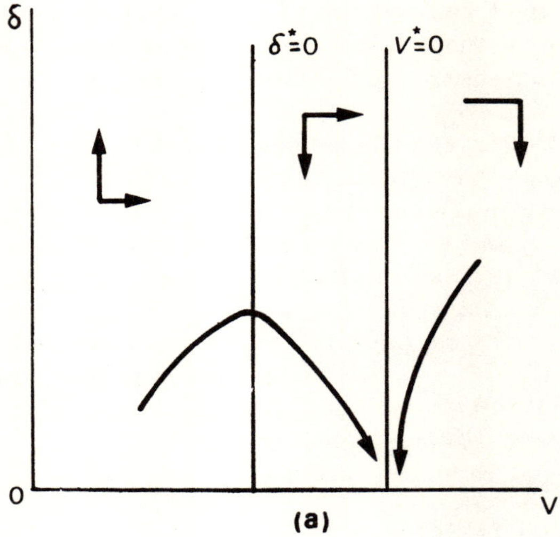

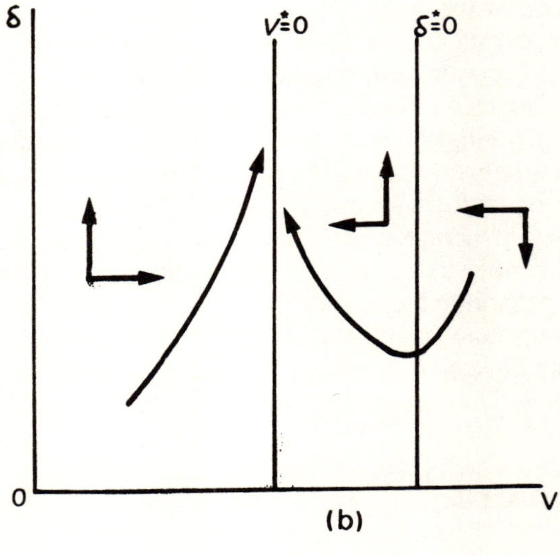

improved distribution. It is thus important to know, in a specific context, who the members of the rentier class are and what are their characteristics compared to those of members of other classes. Very little can, of course, be said *a priori*. However, it can be speculated, on the strength of our results of the excess capacity model, that if the rentier class is comprised of a few extremely rich individuals who are isolated from the pressures of consumerism, it is more likely to play a regressive role in the economy than if it is comprised of a large number of poorer individuals who share the characteristics of the working classes.

Third, the degree of wage flexibility in the economy is an important parameter in determining the role of the rentier class. The degree of wage flexibility has entered our models in two different senses. In one sense, it has entered as determining the response of the desired wage of workers to changes in the state of the labour market, that is, as determining the magnitude of V_w'. The excess capacity model implies that if the rentier class has a higher propensity to save than the capitalist class, then the greater the degree of wage flexibility in this sense, the greater will be the deleterious effects of rentier domination: the rise in the rentier share in wealth will cause larger reductions in the real wage desired by workers and exacerbate the slump. This seems to confirm the fears of post-Keynesians regarding the possible destabilising effects of wage flexibility.[11] In another sense, the degree of flexibility has entered as a determinant of the rate at which the money wage changes in response to gaps between the desired real wage of workers and the actual real wage. The model of full capacity utilisation shows that this parameter, Θ, determines the stability of the long-run equilibrium, but it does so in a way which depends on the relative size of the saving propensities of the rentiers and the capitalists. We have shown that when s_r is greater than s_c greater wage flexibility in this sense results in the stability of the economic system, whereas when s_r is smaller than s_c greater wage stability is destabilising. Thus, again, post-Keynesian worries about greater wage stability are not unfounded, but they are not always justified.

We conclude by noting that these results have been derived using rather simple and specific models of accumulation and distribution. First, even if we confine our attention to post-Keynesian models, our models have abstracted from several important issues which have been emphasised in post-Keynesian writing. Specifically, the role of debt in affecting the investment plans of firms, and the role of banks in changing the interest rate (through a change in their mark-ups) when the debt position of borrowers changes, have been ignored. These and other complications, however, can be introduced into the models we have considered without much difficulty. Second, as we have mentioned earlier, we have examined only the *economic* role of the rentier class, by examining changes in the share of rentier wealth in the total capital of the economy, and ignored its *political* role by holding the interest rate to be exogenous. We have discussed the effects of exogenous changes in the interest rate, and these can be interpreted as changes in its political power (although we have found that it is not always in the interests of the class to want to raise the interest rate). It is conceptually a simple matter to endogenise the political power of the class, for instance by making the interest rate depend – in the long run – on the economic power of the rentier class, thereby extending the models of this chapter.

NOTES

* The material on which this chapter is based was presented on 16 February 1990, at the Conference of the Post-Keynesian Study Group. I am grateful to the participants of the conference, and to Victoria Chick and Philip Arestis, for their comments and encouragement.

1. See also Bhaduri (1983) for a discussion of the relation between productive and unproductive investment; for some purposes we could interpret capitalists as making productive investment and the rentiers as making unproductive investment. Unproductive investment, of course, includes other types of activity, such as speculation, which are not undertaken by the rentier class as we have defined it.
2. For the case in which workers are also rentiers, see Dutt and Amadeo (1989).
3. For a survey of the post-Keynesian literature in the broad way in which it is defined here, see Hamouda and Harcourt (1988).
4. Although we have discussed the four features separately, they are not independent. For instance, the importance of uncertainty and the endogeneity of credit money are often viewed as important features on which the existence of the desired accumulation function depends.
5. The existence of undistributed profits would not change the nature of the analysis if firms saved a constant fraction of profits. We do not examine the market for stocks explicitly, and do not distinguish between stock prices and the price of capital goods. This simplifies our analysis considerably, and allows us to abstract from capital gains and speculative bubbles.
6. In this model this is not too much of a simplification, since it can be shown that

   $$r = [z/(1 + z)]u$$

   so that, given z, the effects of a change in r are captured by changes in u, which is an argument in the investment function. In the long run, since z changes with V, r and u no longer move proportionately.
7. For a further discussion of these results, and for a less formal discussion of this model, see Dutt (1989a). This model draws on Rowthorn (1981) and Dutt (1984, 1987).
8. For a brief, self-contained, exposition of the formal structure and dynamics of the model, see Dutt (1989b). This model draws on Marglin (1984).

9. The βu term of (7.2) has been absorbed in the constant term α.
10. See Dutt (1990) for a discussion of some alternative models, although without a rentier class.
11. See Dutt (1986–7) for such fears, and for references to the literature.

REFERENCES

Bhaduri, A., 1981, 'Class Relations and the Pattern of Accumulation in an Agrarian Economy', *Cambridge Journal of Economics*, 5(1), 33–46.

Bhaduri, A., 1983, *The Economic Structure of Backward Agriculture*, Academic Press, London.

Bhaduri, A., 1986, *Macroeconomics: The Dynamics of Commodity Production*, M.E. Sharpe, Armonk.

Chick, V., 1986, 'The Evolution of the Banking System and the Theory of Saving, Investment and Interest', *Economies et Sociétés* (Cahiers de l'ISMEA, Série Monnaie et Production), 3, 111–26.

Davidson, P. and E. Smolensky, 1964, *Aggregate Supply and Demand Analysis*, Harper & Row, New York.

Dutt, A.K., 1984, 'Stagnation, Income Distribution and Monopoly Power', *Cambridge Journal of Economics*, 8(1), 25–40.

Dutt, A.K., 1986–7, 'Wage Rigidity and Unemployment: the Diagrammatics of Two Views', *Journal of Post Keynesian Economics*, 9(2), 279–90.

Dutt, A.K., 1987, 'Alternative Closures Again: Comment on "Growth, distribution and inflation" ', *Cambridge Journal of Economics*, 11(1), 75–82.

Dutt, A.K., 1989a, 'The Role of the Rentier Class in a Model of Accumulation, Distribution and Inflation', mimeo, Department of Economics, University of Notre Dame.

Dutt, A.K., 1989b, 'Accumulation, Distribution and Inflation in a Marxian–Post Keynesian Model with a Rentier Class', *Review of Radical Political Economics*, 21(3), 18–26.

Dutt, A.K., 1990, *Growth, Distribution and Uneven Development*, Cambridge University Press, Cambridge.

Dutt, A.K. and E.J. Amadeo, 1989, 'A Post Keynesian Model of Growth, Interest and Money', mimeo, Department of Economics, University of Notre Dame.

Hamouda, O. and G.C. Harcourt, 1988, 'Post Keynesianism: from Criticism to Coherence?', *Bulletin of Economic Research*, 40(1), 1–33.

Kaldor, N., 1955–6, 'Alternative Theories of Distribution', *Review of Economic Studies*, 23(2), 83–100.

Kaldor, N., 1982, *The Scourge of Monetarism*, Oxford University Press, Oxford.

Kalecki, M., 1971, *Selected Essays on the Dynamics of the Capitalist Economy*, Cambridge University Press, Cambridge.

Keynes, J.M., 1936, *The General Theory of Employment, Interest and Money*, Macmillan, London.

Marglin, S.A., 1984, 'Growth, Distribution and Inflation: a Centennial Synthesis', *Cambridge Journal of Economics*, 8(2), 115–44.

Marx, K., 1894, *Capital*, vol. 3, 1981 reprint, Vintage, New York.

Moore, B.J., 1988, *Horizontalists and Verticalists: The Macroeconomics of Credit Money*, Cambridge University Press, Cambridge.

Panico, C., 1980, 'Marx's Analysis of the Relationship Between the Rate of Interest and the Rate of Profits', *Cambridge Journal of Economics*, 4(4), 363–87.

Panico, C., 1988, *Interest and Profit in the Theories of Value and Distribution*, Macmillan, London/St Martin's Press, New York.

Pasinetti, L., 1963, 'The Rate of Profit and the Rate of Economic Growth', *Review of Economic Studies*, 29, 267–79.

Pivetti, M., 1985, 'On the Monetary Explanation of Distribution', *Political Economy. The Surplus Approach*, 1(2), 73–103.

Ricardo, D., 1817, *Principles of Political Economy and Taxation*, in P. Sraffa, ed., 1951, *Works and Correspondence of David Ricardo*, vol. I, Cambridge University Press, Cambridge.

Robinson, J., 1962, *Essays in the Theory of Economic Growth*, Macmillan, London.

Rousseas, S., 1986, *Post Keynesian Monetary Theory*, M.E. Sharpe, Armonk.

Rowthorn, R., 1981, 'Demand, Real Wages and Economic Growth', *Thames Papers in Political Economy*, Autumn.

Steindl, J., 1952, *Maturity and Stagnation in American Capitalism*, Basil Blackwell, Oxford.

Taylor, L., 1983, *Structuralist Macroeconomics*, Basic Books, New York.

Weintraub, S., 1958, *An Approach to the Theory of Income Distribution*, Chilton, Philadelphia.

Weintraub, S., 1978, *Keynes, Keynesians and the Monetarists*, University of Pennsylvania Press, Philadelphia.

8. A Post-Keynesian Approach to the Incidence of Taxation

Richard Damania and Douglas Mair

I INTRODUCTION

The term 'the incidence of a tax' means rather different things to neo-classical and post-Keynesian economists. To a neo-classicist, the 'incidence of a tax' refers to the effects of a given policy instrument on the distribution of private real incomes, viewed from either the sources of income side or the uses of income side. Incidence is concerned with changes in relative rather than in absolute prices. The use of macro-economic policy instruments to alter the level of aggregate private incomes is a separate issue from the use of tax policy to change the distribution of a given level of private income. The post-Keynesian approach differs significantly by arguing that the macroeconomic effects of broad-based taxes cannot be ignored. In this chapter we shall argue that the differences between neo-classical and post-Keynesian approaches to tax incidence are more fundamental than simply the inclusion or exclusion of macroeconomic effects. There are, in our view, certain fundamental problems which neo-classical theory fails to address but which we think can be dealt with more satisfactorily from a post-Keynesian standpoint. After reviewing some of the general problems of neo-classical theory, we present a post-Keynesian model which derives from Kalecki (1937) and Asimakopulos and Burbidge (1974). We extend this model to incorporate a property tax and a poll tax and analyse the effects of substituting a poll tax for a property tax. Our reason for analysing this particular combination is that in 1990 the UK government did in fact make this very substitution. In response to long-standing and deep-seated dissatisfaction with the domestic property tax (or rates), the government replaced rates in 1990 with a per capita community charge (or poll tax). The poll tax has proved to be as unpopular as rates and concern among Conservative members of parliament for the electoral consequences of fighting the next general election on the issue of the poll tax was a major factor leading to Mrs Thatcher's replacement as Prime Minister in November 1990.

II A CRITIQUE OF TAX INCIDENCE IN NEO-CLASSICAL THEORY

In neo-classical models of tax incidence, the standard assumptions are that markets are either purely competitive or monopolistic; aggregate supplies of labour and capital are fixed; and the analysis of tax changes is carried out in a world in which savings and investment are completely insensitive to tax-induced changes in rates of return. Neo-classical models derive in the main from the Harberger (1962) general equilibrium models and have these basic assumptions: fixed factor supplies (thus dispensing with the need to consider the effects on savings, investment and growth); perfect factor markets; closed economic systems; linear homogeneous production functions; homogeneous marginal propensities; and no fixed-money assets.

As Mieszkowski (1969) has stated: 'modern [neo-classical] general equilibrium theory is based on the marginal productivity theory of income distribution which assumes that firms choose factor proportions so as to minimise costs and set commodity prices at profit maximising levels'. By postulating profit-maximising behaviour by firms, neo-classical theory precludes the possibility of short-run shifting of a tax such as the corporation tax or the business property tax: neither price nor marginal cost are affected by the tax, so no price or output adjustment will be made. There are two features of the neo-classical model which are fundamental in determining the parameters of tax incidence. These are, first, the theory of income distribution and, second, the theory of effective demand, savings and investment. In the Harberger model, both theories ensure that the economy is at full employment, so that total income is constant and incidence is thus a question of relative price effects. But if it can be shown that full employment cannot be guaranteed by the system, or that either or both of its supporting theories are deficient, then total income can no longer be assumed to be constant. Incidence theory will then have to deal with situations of potentially variable aggregate demand.

Marginal productivity theory has the great attraction of permitting the construction of a general equilibrium model, but at a very great cost. The general equilibrium system excludes time, uncertainty, economies of scale, business cycles and involuntary unemployment and has no logical place for money. Lydall (1979) concludes that neo-classical distribution theory provides no clear predictions about the factor distribution of income and he considers the Walrasian general equilibrium model to be empirically empty and theoretically unsatisfactory. Trussler (1982) has demonstrated that marginal productivity theory is only coherent as a theory of income distribution for individual sectors in a highly disaggregated Walrasian economy characterised by perfect competition. It cannot logically be used in analyses of the Harberger type where the sectors under consideration are large and the factors of production, particularly capital, heterogeneous. Marginal productivity theory only applies under conditions of full employment; there is no detailed neo-classical theory for dealing with income distribution in an economy experiencing other than temporary unemployment.

In neo-classical economics, the mechanism for attaining a full employment level of output is the equalisation of desired savings with desired investment via a rate of interest which clears the capital market. Problems arise when disequilibrium savings occur, as a result of the average propensity to save being too high in relation to the desired level of investment. This means that private consumption must be lower than the desired level, so that total income is lower than the full employment level by the amount of this deficiency in demand. Thus, if taxes do affect the choice between savings and consumption, but not the level of desired investment, then aggregate demand and supply effects must be brought into incidence analysis. But neo-classical incidence theory specifically excludes macro-policy effects as having no relevance for incidence analysis. In neo-classical models, the possibility of taxes influencing savings-consumption choices is guarded against by the assumption of homogeneous marginal propensities to consume which prevents income redistribution from affecting the savings-consumption choice.

A second, and more important, possible reason for the deviation from full employment concerns the internal logic of neo-classical models. It is possible that the interest rate mechanism does not function to equate savings and investment, which may be equalised through some other mechanism but not at a level consistent with full employment. Eatwell (1979) has pointed out that the essential requirement of neo-classical macro-theory is the existence of an elastic demand schedule for investment, and Eatwell (1976) and Garegnani (1970) have shown that no such schedule can be constructed, except in a one-commodity economy. The rate of interest as a mechanism for achieving full employment equalisation of saving and investment is invalid. This means that investment is endogenous with respect to income distribution and output in the short run. Investment plans come first and the required savings, which can only come from profits or wages, are then produced through the working of the economy. These savings can only be produced from profit and wages incomes. This implies that investment plans will have a major influence on income distribution through changes in absolute (not relative) prices, output and aggregate demand. There is no reason, according to Eatwell and Garegnani, why the level of output that emerges from this process should be the full employment level. The upshot of this critique is that neo-classical tax incidence models can be used to produce results through an internally consistent process only under the specific conditions of perfect competition and disaggregated markets with single products. Any deviation from these assumptions means that neo-classical models do not produce correct results.

A striking feature of the neo-classical tax incidence literature is its neglect of the public sector. This omission is not wholly surprising because general equilibrium models describe perfectly competitive auction markets, while much of the allocative decision-making in the public sector is guided by political rather than by market forces. However, in a recent development of the basic Harberger framework, Henderson (1985) has explicitly introduced the public sector into the standard two-sector general equilibrium model, but in such a way as to preclude any qualitative predictions of tax shifting.

General equilibrium models also assume that the stock of capital is fixed and that its supply is exogenously determined. To overcome this problem, Brueckner (1981) has developed a model in which capital is endogenously determined as an intermediate good in the production process. While this represents a useful development of the basic two-sector model, the incidence of a tax on capital cannot be discerned from the Brueckner model. Also, it would appear that 'capital' in this model is merely an intermediate good rather than the durable, malleable asset of conventional general equilibrium models. The conclusions of the Brueckner model are inextricably linked to the assumed structure of the economy and, hence, incidence depends crucially on that structure.

The fundamental conclusion of the Harberger model that a uniform factor tax is borne by factor owners has endured despite numerous theoretical developments and modifications to the basic model. This is not surprising because, given the basic assumptions of the model, a tax can only be shifted by reducing the supply of the taxed activity. A general tax on a fixed factor such as land or capital is a clear case where the taxed activity cannot be varied, and hence the entire burden is borne by the factor owners. In the Harberger model and its derivatives, factor supplies are not allowed to vary and, therefore, the shifting of a general tax is precluded by definition. Feldstein (1974) has analysed the conditions under which this conclusion holds and has shown that even if factor supplies are fixed, considerations of risk and uncertainty may lead to partial shifting of a general factor tax. Feldstein's analysis is based on the more restrictive one-sector neo-classical model. However, he does suggest that the long-run incidence of a tax will reflect a combination of risk-induced portfolio changes and the long-period marginal productivity changes resulting from changes in the stock of capital. A shortcoming of the Feldstein model lies in its failure to incorporate risk into the long-run analysis, but this is unlikely to alter the fundamental results that a uniform factor tax can be shifted in the long run. Feldstein's analysis demonstrates the sensitivity of Harberger-type models to plausible and minor changes in their assumptions. General equilibrium conclusions depend crucially on the assumptions of fixed factor supplies and of certainty. This emphasises the need to attempt to analyse incidence in the context of a growing economy with variable factor supplies.

The 'dynamic' incidence of a tax is primarily an investigation of its effects on the level of savings and the growth rate in the economy. While there is no single well-defined approach to dynamic incidence, much of the literature is based on conventional neo-classical growth models in which factor supplies are allowed to vary and the emphasis is on the interdependence between changes in the supplies of labour and capital. Typically, labour is treated as a primary factor of production, while the stock of capital is assumed to depend on savings out of capital income. The dependence of capital accumulation on past labour supply and savings implies that taxes affect the growth path of the economy through their impact on the supply of labour and aggregate savings.

Following Atkinson and Stiglitz (1980), the dynamic incidence of a general property tax can be analysed within the Solow (1956) one-sector neo-classical growth model. In this model a property tax is equivalent to a tax on the stock of capital. Since all assets earn the same rate of return, a tax on capital and a levy on capital income are also equivalent. Also, since there is only one commodity in the model, there can be no partial taxes, such as a differential property tax. The most controversial aspect of this dynamic incidence literature is the assumed form of the savings function and the conclusions are highly sensitive to the form of the function that is assumed. More generally, by confining attention to steady state growth, the analysis abstracts from important features of the economy such as uncertainty, 'animal spirits' or disequilibrium. To incorporate these features it becomes necessary to include an investment function and this, in turn, gives rise to the Harrod instability problem.

Harberger introduced a monopolistic corporate sector into his general equilibrium tax incidence model and concluded that tax incidence under alternative forms of competition 'differs in only minute detail' from the competitive case. Harberger's analysis of monopoly is technically flawed and misleading and a number of studies, such as Anderson and Ballentine (1976), Atkinson and Stiglitz (1980) and Davidson and Martin (1985), have attempted to extend and modify the basic two-sector model to allow for imperfect competition and oligopoly. It has frequently been asserted that tax incidence can be arrayed along a spectrum between the polar cases of monopoly and perfect competition. The papers cited above reveal that this assertion is highly misleading. In the Davidson–Martin model, for example, a general factor tax under oligopolistic competition raises after-tax profits – a result that can never arise under the polar extremes of monopoly or perfect competition.

Atkinson and Stiglitz analyse the incidence of a capital tax in a model where one sector of the economy is assumed to be monopolistically competitive and is imbedded in the standard general equilibrium framework. Adapting the Atkinson and Stiglitz model to accommodate a property tax generates the result that capital bears the full burden of a uniform property tax in an imperfectly competitive economy. Again, this result is not surprising because the introduction of a monopolistic sector does little to alter the basic shifting mechanism of the standard neo-classical model. A tax in this framework can only be shifted by varying the supply of the taxed product or factor. Given the Atkinson–Stiglitz assumption that the supply of capital is fixed and fully employed, a uniform tax on capital is necessarily borne by its owners. The Atkinson–Stiglitz results depend crucially on the assumed form of the utility function and little generality can be claimed for them.

The essential feature of oligopoly is interdependence and it is this which gives rise to problems in identifying the incidence of taxes in oligopolistic markets. The work of Martin and Davidson has revealed that the mechanisms of tax shifting in oligopolistic markets differ fundamentally from those under either monopoly or perfect competition. The Davidson–Martin model assumes two sectors, one perfectly competitive, the other oligopolistic: also firm behaviour in the oligopolistic sector is governed by non-Cournot tacit collusion in the form of output quotas. Consider first a uniform capital tax in the Davidson–Martin model. A uniform capital tax which lowers net returns also serves to reduce the incentive to cheat by raising the present value of future losses from retaliation. This permits the cartel to restrict output further and, as a result, profits and prices rise. This shifting conclusion contrasts with the conventional neo-classical result that a uniform capital tax is borne by the owners of capital. However the Davidson–Martin model is incomplete in several important respects. Its conclusions depend on the assumed form of the supergame and it ignores important informational problems in detecting cheating. However the results do suggest that group interdependence plays a crucial role in determining the degree of tax shifting in highly concentrated markets.

While the introduction of market imperfection represents a useful extension to the standard general equilibrium framework, the models discussed above are all characteristic of the neo-classical paradigm. Thus they assume that resources are fully employed, that factor markets are perfect, that production functions are linearly homogeneous and that there is instantaneous price adjustment. Considerations of risk, variable factor supplies, growth and firm interdependence all serve to invalidate the basic neo-classical result that a uniform factor tax is borne by its owners. We argue, therefore, that general equilibrium models are highly sensitive to minor modifications and that their results are consequently misleading.

More fundamentally, it can be argued that the neo-classical conception of 'capital' as a malleable asset is invalid, thereby vitiating any conclusions based on neo-classical general equilibrium models. As Steedman (1986) has demonstrated, even if some plausible interpretation can be given to the assumption of a given aggregate value of capital, and he argues that this is open to reasonable doubt, the 2 × 2 general equilibrium model with given supplies of labour and 'capital' will not yield the standard set of tax incidence theorems. We end this section by indicating our agreement with Steedman's conclusion that all is not well in general equilibrium tax incidence theory and offer the rest of this chapter as a modest contribution towards what may be done to construct a more useful theory.

III A POST-KEYNESIAN MODEL OF TAX INCIDENCE

The above section has identified serious points of difficulty with the neo-classical general-equilibrium approach to tax incidence. We now present a post-Keynesian model of tax incidence and exemplify its operation with reference to the substitution of a poll tax for a property tax. Our starting-point is Kalecki's 1937 paper, 'A Theory of Commodity, Income and Capital Taxation'. Kalecki recognised something which had totally eluded Keynes: that the *General Theory* provided a new basis for inquiry into the problems of taxation. As Rothschild (1961) was to write:

> But what causes the main income shares to be what they are is a question which Keynes did not attack. On the whole, he seems to have accepted the traditional marginal productivity approach without realising that with his new theory about the determinants of employment he had undermined the foundations of the old micro-economic distribution theory. For aggregate demand determines factor employment and incomes and the distribution of these incomes in turn influences the level and structure of aggregate demand. The Keynesian theory thus provided a challenge for reconsideration of the distribution problem.

Kalecki's analysis of the influence of various taxes on effective demand led him 'to quite unexpected results, which may be of practical importance'. In particular, he concluded that capital taxation was the best way to stimulate business and reduce unemployment although he doubted if it would ever be applied on a large enough scale to achieve that end. Kalecki's short-period model was extended and developed by Asimakopulos and Burbidge. Their model identifies the effects on workers, rentiers and capitalists of substitutions between taxes on profits, consumption, rentiers' income and wages or of balanced changes in taxes and the level of government spending, by examining the resulting changes in after-tax profits, rentiers' consumption, the after-tax real wage rate, price and the level of output (or employment).

The analysis focuses on situations of short-period equilibrium where desired saving equals net investment. Both the distribution of income and its level are determined by this equilibrium condition. Savings are done by capitalists in the form of retained profits and by rentiers who receive a fraction, B, of profits and save a fraction, s_r. For simplicity, the model assumes that workers do no saving, but all that is really required is for the MPS of workers to be less than that of rentiers or capitalists. In order to obtain the equilibrium level of savings in response to a tax change, profits must change; that is, an increase in profits necessitates either an increase in prices or in employment (and hence output). The competitive version of the model is closed by taking output (and employment) as given and allowing price to vary. The oligopolistic version assumes prices are fixed, but that employment and output vary.

Asimakopulos and Burbidge derive two equations to determine the effects of tax changes. For short-period equilibrium in which the goverment's budget is balanced:

$$(1 - t_f)\pi^*[(1 - B) + s_r(1 - t_r)B] = p(I - D) \qquad (8.1)$$

where

t_f = tax rate on profits
π^* = profits in real terms, that is, money profits, π, divided by p
p = factor cost price of output
B = proportion of after-tax profits paid to rentiers
s_r = propensity to save of rentiers
t_r = tax rate on rentiers' incomes
I = total planned gross investment in real terms
D = total depreciation in real terms

Equation (8.1) shows that after-tax profits in real terms are a function of net investment, the retention ratio $(1 - B)$, the tax rate on rentiers' incomes and rentiers' propensity to save. The second equation relates the mark-up and employment to pre-tax profits:

$$(k/1 + k)a.L = \pi^* + D \tag{8.2}$$

where

k = average mark-up over prime costs
a = average output per worker
L = total level of employment

In the case where the government's budget is assumed to be in balance in each period, the short-period equilibrium distribution of income between profits and wages is determined by the requirement that desired private saving be equal to the intended level of investment. Equations (8.1) and (8.2) are used to estimate the incidence of tax changes. Take, for example, a situation in which there is an increase in the tax on profits, no change in the tax on consumption, (t_c), or rentiers' income and the tax on wages is a dependent variable. Consider the term for net investment, $(I - D)$, on the right-hand side of (8.1). This is assumed to be given for the period under consideration and since on the left-hand side of (8.1) the terms $(1 - B)$ and $s_r(1 - t_r)B$ are unchanged, it follows that after-tax profits in real terms, $(1 - t_f)\pi^*$, are also unchanged. Rentiers' consumption, $(1 - s_r)(1 - t_r)(1 - t_f) B\pi/p(1 + t_c)$ which is a function of after-tax profits, is also unchanged. Workers' consumption in real terms is also unchanged since it is equal to the difference between the unchanged amount available for consumption and unchanged rentiers' consumption. Since profits before tax in real terms must be higher, it can be seen from equation (8.2) that the mark-up is higher owing to higher market prices. This is because, under full employment, output is fixed; thus an increase in demand leads to an increase in both price and mark-up. The pre-tax real wage rate must, therefore, be lower, but the tax rate on wages, which is a dependent variable, is also lower, fully compensating for the change.

This result contrasts with the orthodox neo-classical conclusion that the burden of an increase in corporation tax in the short period is on profits. This is because neo-classical theory assumes that the real wage is determined in the labour market as part of a process ensuring full employment. When the tax rate on profits is increased and the government spends the proceeds in a distributionally neutral manner, the real wage is unchanged. Pre-tax profits must be unchanged since output, employment and the wage bill are constant. The burden of the tax will be solely on profits. Private investment and capitalists' consumption, which are dependent variables, will be lower as a result of the tax and will be replaced by government expenditure. By contrast, in the Asimakopulos–Burbidge model, investment is assumed to be an independent variable in the short period and, along with the savings propensities of rentiers and capitalists, determines the short-period equilibrium distribution of income. After-tax profits are determined by the requirement that, in equilibrium, savings must be in the desired relation to income and equal to investment. The real wage takes on the value consistent with this level of profits and is determined by conditions in the commodity market.

IV WHO PAYS THE POLL TAX?

We now proceed to show how we adapt the Kalecki–Asimakopulos–Burbidge model described above to accommodate, first, a poll tax and, second, a property tax before discussing the differential incidence effects of substituting a poll tax for a property tax. For simplicity we assume that total tax revenue is made up of either a poll tax or a property tax on rentiers and workers and, throughout, a property tax on business.

A Incidence of the Poll Tax

The aggregate tax schedule of government in real terms is given by:

$$PT = PT_r + PT_w + BPT \qquad (8.3)$$

where

PT = total tax revenue
PT_r = poll tax paid by rentiers
PT_w = poll tax paid by workers
BPT = property tax paid by business

Let firms' net profits, NP, be defined as:

$$NP = \pi^* - BPT \tag{8.4}$$

Since firms retain a fraction $(1 - B)$ of profits, retained earnings, π_r, are given as:

$$\pi_r = (1 - B)(\pi^* - BPT) \tag{8.5}$$

and distributed profits are given as:

$$B(\pi^* - BPT) \tag{8.6}$$

Since rentiers pay the poll tax, net rentier income is given as:

$$Y_r = B(\pi^* - BPT) - PT_r \tag{8.7}$$

In addition, rentiers save a proportion, s_r, of their net incomes:

$$S_r = s_r[B(\pi^* - BPT) - PT_r] \tag{8.8}$$

By assumption, workers do no saving so that *aggregate savings* is the sum of equations (8.5) and (8.8). Thus:

$$S = s_r[B(\pi^* - BPT) - PT_r] + (1 - B)(\pi^* - BPT) \tag{8.9}$$

In Keynesian equilibrium, with a balanced budget assumed for convenience, aggregate savings, S, must equal net investment $(I - D)$. Rearranging (8.9) yields:

$$S = (\pi^* - BPT)[s_r(B - PT_r) + (1 - B)] = (I - D) \tag{8.10}$$

Rearranging (8.10) defines *equilibrium real gross profits*, π^*, as:

$$\pi^* = (I - D)/[s_r(B - PT_r) + (1 - B)] + BPT \tag{8.11}$$

From (8.11), it follows that:

$$d\pi^*/dBPT > 0; \quad d\pi^*/dPT_r > 0; \quad d\pi^*/dPT_w = 0$$

From (8.10), *equilibrium net profits*, NP, are given as:

$$NP = (\pi^* - BPT) = (I - D)/[s_r(B - PT_r) + (1 - B)] \quad (8.12)$$

From (8.12), it follows that:

$$dNP/dBPT = 0; \quad dNP/dPT_r > 0; \quad dNP/dPT_w = 0$$

Rearranging (8.10), we find *rentiers' net income* $[(\pi^* - BPT)(B - PT_r)]$ as:

$$Y_r = (\pi^* - BPT)(B - PT_r) = (I - D) - (\pi^* - BPT)(1 - B) \quad (8.13)$$

Rentiers' consumption, C_r, is a fraction $(1 - s_r)$ of rentiers' net income:

$$C_r = (1 - s_r)Y_r = [(I - D) - (\pi^* - BPT)][1 - B)(1 - s_r)]/s_r \quad (8.14)$$

It follows from (8.14) that:

$$dC_r/dBP_T = (dNP/dBPT).(dC_r/dNP)$$

Also from (8.14), it can be seen that:

$$dC_r/dNP = -(1 - B) < 0$$

and from above we know that $dNP/dBPT = 0$.
Hence:

$$\begin{aligned} dC_r/dBPT &= \underset{(=0)}{(dNP/dBPT)}.\underset{(<0)}{(dC_r/dNP)} = 0; \\ dC_r/dPT_r &= \underset{(>0)}{(dC_r/dPT_r)}.\underset{(<0)}{(dC_rd/NP)} < 0 \\ dC_r/dPT_w &= \underset{(=0)}{(dNP/dPT_w)}.\underset{(<0)}{(dC_r/dNP)} = 0 \end{aligned}$$

From Asimakopulos and Burbidge (p. 271), we take the 'income side' output identity:

$$Y/p = wL/p + \pi^* + D + t_cC \quad (8.15)$$

where

Y = nominal income
w = wage rate

Rearranging (8.15) yields:

$$\pi^* = Y/p - wL/p - D - t_cC \tag{8.16}$$

From (8.11), we have:

$$\pi^* = (I - D)/[s_r(B - PT_r) + (1 - B)] + BPT \tag{8.11}$$

Equating (8.16) and (8.11) and rearranging, we define *equilibrium net wages* as:

$$C_w = wL/p - PT_w = Y/p - D - t_cC - (I - D)/[s_r(B - PT_r) + (1 - B)] - BPT - PT_w \tag{8.17}$$

It follows from (8.17) that under *oligopoly*, where p is assumed fixed:

$$\begin{aligned} dC_w/dBPT &= (dp/dBPT).(dC_w/dp) = 0 \\ dC_w/dPT_r &= (dp/dPT_r).(dC_w/dp) = 0 \\ dC_w/dPT_w &< 0 \end{aligned}$$

$dp/dBPT = 0$ and $dp/dPT_r = 0$ under oligopoly.

In contrast, under *perfect competition*, p is flexible. Thus in general:

$$dp/dPT_i\ (= d\pi^*/dPT_i).(dp/d\pi^*), \text{ where } PT_i = PT_r;\ PT_w \tag{8.18}$$

It follows from (8.18) that under *perfect competition*:

$$\begin{aligned} dp/dPT_i &= \underset{(>0)}{(d\pi^*/dPT_i)}.\underset{(>0)}{(dp/d\pi^*)}.\underset{(<0)}{(dC_w/dp)} < 0; \\ dC_w/dPT_r &= \underset{(>0)}{(d\pi^*/dPT_r)}.\underset{(>0)}{(dp/d\pi^*)}.\underset{(<0)}{(dC_w/dp)} < 0; \\ &\text{and } dC_w/dPT_w < 0 \end{aligned}$$

The results obtained from equations (8.11), (8.12), (8.17) and (8.18) are shown in Tables 8.1, 8.2 and 8.3 below. Table 8.1 shows the short-period effects of balanced increases in taxes and government expenditure under conditions of oligopoly and Table 8.2 shows the same effects under conditions of perfect competition. In Tables 8.1 and 8.2, an increase in government expenditure (ΔG) is financed in turn by an increase in business property taxes (ΔBPT), rentiers' poll taxes (ΔPT_r) and workers' poll taxes (ΔPT_w), holding the other two taxes unchanged. The principal difference between the two tables is in the effect on workers' real wages (or consumption). Under oligopolistic conditions, workers' consumption will only fall when ΔG is being financed by an increase in workers' poll taxes (ΔPT_w); whereas under perfect competition, workers' consumption will fall irrespective of which poll tax is being increased to finance ΔG. This result arises because by assumption, under perfect competition, the economy is at its full employment level but prices are flexible. An increase in demand will lead to an increase in price (that is, mark-up), thus resulting in a fall in workers' real wages. Under oligopoly, where price is assumed fixed but output is flexible, the fall in workers' real wages (after tax) happens only when ΔG is being financed by an increase in workers' poll taxes.

Table 8.3 shows the differential incidence effects of making substitutions between the poll taxes on rentiers and workers and the business property tax. To illustrate what is happening, look at the result given in row (b) of Table 8.3. Here the business property tax is being

Table 8.1 Short-period effects of balanced increases in taxes and government expenditure (G), Oligopoly

	Profits π^*	*Net profits* ($\pi^* - BPT$)	*Rentiers' consumption* C_r	*Workers' consumption* C_w	*Employment/ output*
(a) $\Delta BPT = \Delta G > 0$; $\Delta PT_r = \Delta PT_w = 0$	+	0	0	0	+
(b) $\Delta PT_r = \Delta G > 0$; $\Delta BPT = \Delta PT_w = 0$	+	+	−	0	+
(c) $\Delta PT_w = \Delta G > 0$; $\Delta BPT = \Delta PT_r = 0$	0	0	0	−	0

Table 8.2 Short-period effects of balanced increases in taxes and government expenditure (G), Perfect Competition

	Profits π^*	*Net profits* $(\pi^* - BPT)$	*Rentiers' consumption* C_r	*Workers' consumption* C_w	*Employment/ output*
(a) $\Delta BPT = \Delta G > 0$; $\Delta PT_r = \Delta PT_w = 0$	+	0	0	–	0
(b) $\Delta PT_r = \Delta G > 0$; $\Delta BPT = \Delta PT_w = 0$	+	+	–	–	0
(c) $\Delta PT_w = \Delta G > 0$; $\Delta BPT = \Delta PT_r = 0$	0	0	0	–	0

Table 8.3 Short-period differential incidence effects of balanced changes in poll tax and business property tax, Oligopoly

	Profits π^*	*Net profits* $(\pi^* - BPT)$	*Rentiers' consumption* C_r	*Workers' consumption* C_w	*Employment/ output*
(a) $\Delta BPT > 0$; $\Delta PT_w < 0$; $\Delta PT_r = 0$	+	0	0	+	+
(b) $\Delta BPT > 0$; $\Delta PT_r < 0$; $\Delta PT_w = 0$	+	–	+	0	+
(c) $\Delta PT_r > 0$; $\Delta PT_w < 0$; $\Delta BPT = 0$	+	+	–	–	+

increased and is offset by a reduction in the poll tax on rentiers; workers' poll tax is unchanged. An increase in the business property tax, *BPT*, leads to a decline in retained profits and to a fall in distributed profits and hence to a fall in rentiers' savings. The total decrease in savings is given by $[(1 - B)BPT + s_rB(BPT)]$. But the reduction in PT_r raises rentiers' savings by s_rPT_r. Now if $[(1 - B)BPT + s_rB(BPT)] > s_rPT_r$, then aggregate savings must decline and profits must rise to restore savings to their original level. Thus:

$$s_r - PT_r - [(1 - B)BPT + s_rB(BPT)] = s_rPT_r - BPT[(1 - B) + s_rB].$$

But we know that $PT_r = BPT$, so that therefore $BPT[s_r - (1 - B) + s_rB] < 0$. Therefore the decline in savings by businesses exceeds the increase in savings by rentiers, so that profits must rise in order to restore savings to their equilibrium level.

B Incidence of a Property Tax

Having analysed the incidence of the poll tax, we now proceed to analyse the property tax. Mair (1984) has incorporated a property tax into the Asimakopulos–Burbidge model by means of the following additional assumptions. Two categories of tenure are identified – renting and owner-occupation; and two classes of individuals – workers and rentiers – rent or own residential property. All landlords are rentiers. If landlords' non-property income is wholly from investment, then their property income is supplementary to their investment income. If their non-property income is from employment, then their property income is supplementary to their wage income. All owner-occupiers are rentiers. Property income is equal to the imputed income from property. All property is in private ownership: all rentals are market rentals and the assessed value of property is a true measure of market rental. There is a single rate of property tax.

We repeat the analysis of equations (8.3) to (8.18) but substitute a domestic property tax on rentiers (DPT_r) for the rentiers' poll tax (PT_r) and a domestic property tax on workers (DPT_w) for the workers' poll tax (PT_w). We show the short-period differential incidence effects of substituting the poll tax for the domestic property tax in Table 8.4. The important row is row (d) where we show the result of increasing the poll tax and reducing the domestic property tax. In so doing, we make the assumption that this change lowers the tax burden on rentiers and raises the amount of tax paid by workers; that is, $PT_r < DPT_r$ and $PT_w > DPT_w$. (Figures on the gains and losses by band of household income in the UK in 1984/5 of the substitution of a Community Charge (or poll tax) for rates (domestic property tax) show that the gains accrue in the upper income groups where rentier income is concentrated. See *Paying for Local Government*, London: HMSO 1986, Cmnd 9714, Tables F3, F4 and F5 and Figures F6 and F7.) The lower tax burden on rentiers raises savings and, as a result, profits fall to restore the equilibrium savings level. The fall in profits in turn induces a reduction in output and employment. Alternatively, the argument is that the reduced tax burden on rentiers raises consumption by less than the increase in rentiers' net income; that is, the marginal propensity to save of rentiers, $s_r > 0$. At the same time, the higher poll tax levied on workers lowers their consumption by the full amount of the tax; that is, the marginal propensity to save of workers, $s_w = 0$. Thus aggregate demand falls and profits decline. This result holds as long as $s_w < s_r$.

Table 8.4 Short-period differential incidence effects of substituting poll tax for domestic property tax, Oligopoly

	Profits π^*	*Net profits* $(\pi^* - BPT)$	*Rentiers' consumption* C_r	*Workers' consumption* C_w	*Employment/ output*
(a) $\Delta BPT > 0$; $\Delta DPT < 0$	+	−	+	+	+
(b) $\Delta PT_r > 0$; $\Delta DPT < 0$	+	+	−	+	+
(c) $\Delta PT_w > 0$; $\Delta DPT < 0$	−	−	+	−	−
(d) $\Delta(PT_r + PT_w) > 0$; $\Delta DPT < 0$ (where $PT_r < DPT_r$ and $PT_w > DPT_w$)	−	−	+	−	−

V CONCLUSION

There is widespread recognition that tax incidence theory is in some disarray. Atkinson and Stiglitz, for example, write:

> The general equilibrium analysis of tax incidence has to date been undertaken largely independently of the literature on macroeconomics. Thus, competitive equilibrium models, with all markets clearing, have been used to investigate the incidence of different taxes, whereas a quite separate literature, using aggregate demand/monetary models, has examined the

> implications of taxes for the level of employment and the rate of inflation. In other areas of economics, this gap has been narrowed . . . but in public finance the separation has persisted much longer. (1980: 222.)

It is somewhat ironic that, despite having recognised the micro–macro lacuna in the neo-classical literature, Atkinson and Stiglitz relegate their reference to Kalecki and Asimakopulos and Burbidge to a footnote. Other leading public finance scholars have also expressed their frustration with neo-classical tax incidence theory. Thus Richard Musgrave:

> While recognising the admirable contribution to the theory of incidence rendered by Harberger's analysis of the corporation tax and Mieszkowski's application thereof to the property tax, I must insist that the local consistency or beauty of such models is no proof that they describe what in fact happens. The assumptions of profit maximisation and perfect capital mobility are useful, and the economist's problem would be simplified if the world in fact met these assumptions. But the Creator's concern with the happiness of economists might not have sufficed to arrange things this way. Seeing the operation of markets as I do, I must allow for the implications of alternative assumptions. The problem then becomes one of empirical evidence and not merely of logical consistency. (1974: 226.)

What we have done in this chapter is to consider the implications of 'alternative assumptions' and, as Kalecki surmised over 50 years ago, we have come up with some 'unexpected results'. Whether these results have any greater relevance for the 'solution of practical problems' is not an issue we have addressed in this chapter. The theory of tax incidence we have presented has the great advantage over its neo-classical competitor of fully compatible micro- and macro- elements. It can operate comfortably under conditions of less than full employment and under oligopolistic market structures. It is based on a theory of income distribution which is empirically testable and which has in fact been tested by Reynolds (1984).

The question we raised in Section IV is – who pays the poll tax? The answer is – as it must inevitably be – it all depends. It all depends on what accommodating changes government makes to its own expenditures or to other taxes anent a change in the poll tax. These changes are worked through with respect to the changes in profits which must take place to allow a restoration of the equilibrium relationship between savings and net investment, noting that this need not necessarily be a full-employment equilibrium. If the example which we consider corresponds most closely to the actual situation in the UK, the substitution of a poll tax for a domestic property tax will result in a fall in workers' consumption, that is, workers' real incomes, if workers are assumed to do no saving. Profits, output and employment will also fall, although there will be an increase in rentiers' consumption.

The discussion in the UK since 1986, when the government announced its intention to replace the local property tax with a local poll tax, has concentrated mainly on the distributional and administrative implications of the reform. While the government has stressed the need to control the aggregate level of local authority spending and has imposed limits on the amounts which local authorities are permitted to raise through local taxes, there has been no recognition of the macroeconomic effects of the substitution of the poll tax for the property tax. In part this is a consequence of the conventional neo-classical approach to tax incidence which is to emphasise relative price and income changes within a given level of aggregate income. However, even if thought had been given to the macroeconomic effects of the reform, we doubt that neo-classical analytical techniques are sufficiently robust for the purpose. What is required is an analytical approach which explicitly recognises the feedbacks between changes in the distribution of income and the aggregate level of income. In this chapter we have shown how a Kaleckian approach allows a fuller appreciation of the macroeconomic effects of tax reforms.

REFERENCES

Anderson, R. and J.G. Ballentine, 1976, 'The Incidence and Excess Burden of a Profits Tax under Imperfect Competition', *Public Finance*, 31(2), 159–76.

Asimakopulos, A. and J. Burbidge, 1974, 'The Short Period Incidence of Taxation', *Economic Journal*, 84, 267–88.

Atkinson, A.B. and J.E. Stiglitz, 1980, *Lectures on Public Economics*, McGraw-Hill, London.

Brueckner, J.K., 1981, 'Labour Mobility and the Incidence of the Residential Property Tax', *Journal of Urban Economics*, 10, 173–82.

Davidson, C. and L.W. Martin, 1985, 'General Equilibrium Tax Incidence Under Imperfect Competition', *Journal of Political Economy*, 93(6), 1212–23.

Eatwell, J., 1976, 'A Simple Framework for the Analysis of Taxation, Distribution and Effective Demand', mimeo, Department of Economics, Cambridge University.

Eatwell, J., 1979, *Theories of Value, Output and Employment*, Thames Papers in Political Economy, Thames Polytechnic, London.

Feldstein, M.S., 1974, 'Tax Incidence in a Growing Economy with Variable Factor Supply', *Quarterly Journal of Economics*, 88, 551–73.

Garegnani, P., 1970, 'Heterogeneous Capital, the Production Function and the Theory of Income Distribution', *Review of Economic Studies*, 37, 407–36.

Harberger, A.C., 1962, 'The Incidence of the Corporation Income Tax', *Journal of Political Economy*, 93(2), 248–64.
Henderson, J.V., 1985, 'The Tiebout Model: Bring Back the Entrepreneurs', *Journal of Political Economy*, 70, 215–40.
Kalecki, M., 1937, 'A Theory of Commodity, Income and Capital Taxation', *Economic Journal*, 47, 444–50.
Lydall, H., 1979, *A Theory of Income Distribution*, Clarendon Press, Oxford.
Mair, D., 1984, 'Towards a Kaleckian Theory of the Short Period Incidence of the Property Tax', *Government and Policy*, 2, 117–34.
Mieszkowski, P.M., 1969, 'Tax Incidence Theory: The Effects of Taxes on the Distribution of Income', *Journal of Economic Literature*, 7, 1103–24.
Musgrave, R.A., 1974, 'Is the Property Tax on Housing Regressive?', *American Economic Review, Papers and Proceedings*, 64, 222–9.
Reynolds, P.J., 1984, 'An Empirical Analysis of the Degree of Monopoly Theory of Distribution', *Bulletin of Economic Research*, 36(1), 59–84.
Rothschild, K.W., 1961, 'Some Recent Contributions to a Macroeconomic Theory of Income Distribution', *Scottish Journal of Political Economy*, October, 173–99.
Solow, R.M., 1956, 'A Contribution to the Theory of Economic Growth', *Quarterly Journal of Economics*, 70, 65–94.
Steedman, I., 1986, 'Produced Inputs and Tax Incidence Theory', *Public Finance*, 31(3), 331–49.
Trussler, S., 1982, 'Regional and Inter-Regional Fiscal Incidence; Theory, Methodology and Applications', unpublished PhD thesis, University of Cambridge.

9. Vertical Integration, Planning and the Market

Paul Auerbach

I THE THEORETICAL CONTEXT

One of the most important and, it seems, never-ending debates in economics and political economy is over the roles and the relative virtues of the plan versus the market. Here I argue that, paradoxically, the view of the evolution of the industrial structure originating from Friedrich Engels and followed up by John Kenneth Galbraith and the Monopoly Capital tradition has much in common with the pure free market approach emerging from such economists as Ronald Coase. Both believe, from opposing perspectives, that it is possible to separate in a mechanistic way the notions of 'market' and 'plan'. I believe that such a separation is artificial. In truth, well-developed markets often result from careful planning, and meaningful planning cannot exist without markets for the making of rational calculations. These propositions can be demonstrated in the context of the substantive history of capitalist industrial development in the twentieth century, and specifically with consideration of the emergence of the multinational firm.

For Engels, the emergence of giant firms under capitalism in the 1890s had *already* replaced market relations and the law of value with a form of planning. Within the giant firm there already existed, according to Engels, 'islands' of pure planning which were isolated from market forces. As such, these spheres of planning would serve as models for the future socialist society. The creation of socialism in the form of 'one big factory' from this advanced form of capitalism would be a simple task. Another authority of great influence whose views reinforced the Engels vision was Yurii Larin, who wrote of the great successes in planning the whole economy to be seen in Germany during the First World War.

Thus, from Engels a vision of socialism emerged embodying a particular view of tendencies within capitalism, and from Larin came an incorrect analysis of the war economy of Germany. These perceptions had a profound influence on the policies pursued by Soviet Russia in the period of War Communism, and by the USSR during the command-administrative system instituted during the first Five Year Plan (Auerbach *et al*. 1988). Parallel views on the development of capitalism can be found at a much later stage in the West in, for instance, the famous book by John Kenneth Galbraith, *The New Industrial State* (1967; see also Auerbach 1984).

The underlying principles of Galbraith's book may be used to summarise the essential principles of the planning school:

1. The first principle of the planning school is the belief that the emergence of twentieth-century technologies dictates that the growth of giant firms will inevitably lead to the swallowing up of small firms in the economy. Galbraith's central example of the modern giant firm in the 1960s was the American car manufacturer General Motors.
2. The second principle is that these giant firms such as General Motors have achieved total *control* over their environment: they control the market through monopoly power, they control consumers through advertising, and they control their financial environment because they can finance new investment from profits, without having to obey the dictates of the financial markets. In the Finance Capital variants of this theory, the web of connections with banks and other financial institutions is crucial.
3. The conclusion drawn by Galbraith and the planning school is the notion that capitalism in its most advanced manifestations such as General Motors has surmounted the use of markets and uses instead a sophisticated form of planning: the market has already been replaced by the plan in the most advanced stages of capitalism (Auerbach *et al*. 1988).

The fundamental fallacy to be found in the ideas of these believers in planning, Engels and Galbraith, is the notion that we can separate the question of planning from the presence of market relations. But this same fallacy can be seen in writings from the opposite perspective – from conservative believers in the free market. The article by Ronald Coase, 'The Nature of the Firm' (1937), is one of the most influential of the past half-century in Anglo-Saxon economics. Almost all present-day discussions surrounding the firm and the level of vertical integration emanate from this piece. It suffers from the same fallacy as that contained in the works of the planning school of Engels and Galbraith – the notion that the question of planning can be separated from the presence of markets. I will summarise Coase's argument with a representative passage:

> the operation of the market costs something and by forming an organisation and allowing some authority (an 'entrepreneur') to direct the resources, certain marketing costs are saved. The entrepreneur has to carry out his function at less cost, taking into account the fact that he may get factors of production at a lower price than the market transactions which he superseded, *because it is always possible to revert to the open market if he fails to do this*. (Emphasis added.)

The last part of the above passage has been emphasised because it is crucial to the critique presented here. For Nobel Prize winner Kenneth Arrow as well, 'organizations are a means of achieving the benefit of collective action in situations in which the price system fails' (1973: 33). But is it really coherent to speak of a price system prior to a discussion of the nature of the organisations that generate this system?

It may seem that Coase's central point, that is to say, that firms are formed when the benefits of using the market are exceeded by the costs, is close to tautology. But in fact the argument is far from being trivial. On the contrary, it is a powerful way of structuring our analysis of business and its evolution: the market and the price mechanism exist, and exist ubiquitously – why then are there firms? It is like overhearing a twenty-fifth-century conversation between robots who want to know why *homines sapientes* exist(ed). The question here is not just one of history, but of conceptual priority: can a rich array of markets exist without organisations to generate them?

Historically, the evolution and development of markets – of their extent and their depth – has been contingent on the actions pursued by traders. The presumption from orthodox theory of the ubiquitous existence of 'things' with well-defined boundaries called markets is unfounded. Markets are in fact not *things* but behavioural relations between economic actors. The boundaries of a market cannot be specified independently of the behaviour of the participants in that market, as is demanded in orthodox theory: the boundaries of a market – qualitative, spacial and temporal – are inherently bound up with the behaviour of the participants involved in that market (Auerbach 1988: Ch. 3, and 1990). Firms have been *at the same time* devices for the avoidance of the market mechanism *as well as* for its extension. The option of avoiding internal organisation by the use of the market is only possible if *other* entities, such as firms, have been organised in sufficient depth for a 'market' to appear for the service at hand.

A one-sided approach, a presupposition of the existence of markets and the failure to see the role of firms in the *making* of markets informs Coase's analysis and that of his followers. It further distorts their treatment of the extent of the firm and the approach to vertical integration. Here is a representative quotation from Coase on the subject:

> Changes like the telephone and telegraph which tend to reduce the cost of organising spacially will tend to increase the size of firm [unless, as Coase suggests in a footnote, they have an even greater effect in reducing the cost of using the price mechanism]. *All changes which improve managerial technique will tend to increase the size of firm*. (Coase 1937, emphasis added.)

Note that in Coase's analysis, 'markets' are fully in place, so that increases in managerial technique will substitute for *already existing markets*. There is no place in this analysis for the possibility that improvements in managerial technique which are of special benefit to relatively smaller entities (such as inexpensive desktop computers) might cause the *creation* of markets *where none had heretofore existed*, and vertical dis-integration.

II VERTICAL INTEGRATION AND PLANNING

The level of vertical integration would seem to be a fruitful indicator of the extent to which a capitalist firm or an economy as a whole is 'planned', as opposed to using a market mechanism. The most readily available measure of vertical integration for the whole economy is value added/sales.

An economy which is completely vertically integrated – which consists totally of 'planned' entities which make everything for themselves – has a ratio equal to unity. This measure is in many ways not wholly adequate.[1] First, in some contexts, the use of the measure will violate one sense of our intuitive notion of what it means for a firm's activities to be 'planned': contemporary tendencies in the direction of the buying-in of technically integrated facilities in the chemical industry and of the purchase by firms of complete computer-integrated manufacturing systems from outside suppliers[2] will *lower* our chosen measure of planning. Furthermore, when the index is derived from census data, it will only measure vertical integration *within* establishments; increased integration associated with multi-plant operation will not be accounted for.

Of even greater significance is the apparent contemporary growth in quasi-integration between firms. It is widely believed in the West that

Japanese industrial success, especially in inventory and quality control, is in a substantial way related to the tight co-ordination maintained by manufacturers (such as Toyota) with independently owned suppliers (see Abegglen and Stalk 1985). The growth and popularisation of this remarkable form of administrative co-ordination, however, will not register as an increase in our 'planning' index of vertical integration. While guidance and co-ordination from dominant firms over independently owned suppliers has always existed in the West (a prominent example being that offered by the UK retailer Marks and Spencer to its food and textile suppliers), in recent years many western firms claim to have greatly extended their use of co-ordination with supplying firms, and some examples of this phenomenon will be given below.

The problem being posed here is as follows. Throughout the twentieth century giant firms have grown and continued to develop the tools and techniques of business calculation and control. Furthermore, they have widened their conception of the range and scope of the tasks – from the control of primary inputs going into the product to all aspects of its marketing – which have to be co-ordinated. The expansion of the scope and the ambitions of the contemporary firm can be seen in the increasing fashion for the concept of 'design': firms from the very preliminary stages of the development of a product are making strenuous efforts to link the product's development with its marketing potential. It is no longer acceptable to treat these functions of the firm in isolation (Lorenz 1989).

All of these factors would seem conducive to the evolution of the economy in the direction predicted by Friedrich Engels, who thought that capitalism was evolving in the direction of 'one big factory' and of John Kenneth Galbraith, who believed we are observing the emergence of a 'new industrial state' in which would emerge large spheres of self-contained co-ordination and planning. And yet while vertical integration, our measure of planning, increased substantially from the 1880s to the 1920s, since the 1920s in the US on available statistical indicators *there has been no rise in vertical integration*. This is our paradox.

We have indicated above some of the reservations one must have about the use of this measure of planning. And yet, notwithstanding all questions we may have about our interpretation of this measure, we see about us, even at the end of the twentieth century, no tendency for the world economy to be dominated by giant, fully vertically integrated, 'planned' companies. I believe that the reason there has remained an apparent balance between the market and planning in the most advanced industrial economies is that there is a much more complex relationship between these two concepts, the market and the plan, than is commonly recognised. For the planning school of Engels and Galbraith, the growing sophistication of management in capitalist firms should have meant a decline in the rich variety of markets and small businesses which have existed under capitalism. For the followers of Coase, rich markets always exist as an alternative to planning; planning will only exist under capitalism when, *for some specific reason*, a market fails to appear.

But the real situation is more complicated. The aggressive, innovative *planning* by the Japanese steel producers in the 1960s and 1970s transformed the world steel industry. Before the Japanese intervention, the world steel industry consisted of large national firms with monopoly power of the Galbraith type. But planning by Japanese steel producers in co-operation with the Japanese government transformed the world-wide industry into one in which no firm or group of firms had substantial market power: even the shipment of steel across the Pacific Ocean ceased to be an obstacle to the Japanese industry as a result of their innovations, and the subsequent emulation of the aggressive behaviour of the Japanese producers by others around the world has transformed the industry. Steel has now become a simple market-type commodity, like wheat or cotton.

This development of a market in steel resulted from the increased level of sophistication of planning by producers. This is a common result: improved planning by capitalist firms often does not increase the level of planning in the whole economy, but paradoxically, *may enhance the markets* for these goods. Thus, on the page opposite the aforementioned article by Lorenz in the *Financial Times*, we find a discussion of the emergence of a new 'market' for Facilities Management – there now exists a rich array of outside contractors who can be hired by firms to manage, for instance, their computer facilities for them. This market emerges from the exercise of planning decisions made by two groups of participants, the firms offering these services and the firms using them. The latter have made a management planning decision to calculate precisely the opportunity cost of 'do-it-yourself' in this sector of their business. These disparate planning decisions then permit vertical disintegration on the part of the firms hiring these services (Bradshaw 1989). In other cases, a more precise calculation of these opportunity costs by purchasers may result in a widening of the domain of the market: General Motors of Europe claims that substantial savings resulted from the global sourcing of inputs – a movement away from the xenophobic prejudice (especially among German engineers) that only local suppliers were to be trusted (Treece *et al.* 1990).

There is such a fashion for the concept of 'the market' at present that it is important to note that there are certain things which must be done explicitly in a planned way. Among very large firms, the extension of the business planning horizon has implied that innovation must be co-ordinated to take into consideration a progressively broader range of supply and demand-based complementarities. In order to create the compact disc system, for instance, Philips had to co-ordinate research between its electronics and optical divisions (as well as with Sony). Within its electronics division, vertical co-ordination of research had to proceed so that integrated circuits appropriate to the system could be developed. On the demand side, the Philips record division (which is part of Polydor) not only had to develop new processes for the production of these discs, but had to devise a world-wide strategy for the marketing and repertoire of these discs, all of which had to be timed and co-ordinated with the production and sale of the players themselves. In the absence of the 'visible hand' of the Philips management in the genesis of this product, its emergence from a 'market' of producers would have taken decades. Subsequently, such severe competition has emerged world-wide in the market for compact disc players that this product, too, is now sold much like a commodity such as steel.

The precise nature of the advantages accruing to large, integrated firms still awaits satisfactory theoretical development. An orthodox approach of the Coase–Williamson type (Williamson 1975) emphasises that some form of integration will take place when there are difficulties in the writing of complex contracts between separate firms. This static, transactional approach to firm behaviour puts no special emphasis on the advantages which accrue to internalised planning when we examine production and, especially, innovation (for example, the compact disc) from a dynamic, 'flow-through' perspective.[3] Thus successful Japanese firms in the computer and telecommunications industries seem to believe that the future belongs to those firms who are fully integrated in a backwards direction to the production and development of the seed corn (or as they would say, the rice) of the electronics industry – the semiconductor. (See Lewis *et al.* 1989 and Neff *et al.* 1989.)

Another possible advantage of this form of integration is in even stronger contradiction to a notion of the invariant superiority of market-based relationships: a frequently proffered explanation for the ravaging of US merchant semiconductor producers by integrated Japanese electronics manufacturers in the 1970s and 1980s has been that, through cross-subsidisation, and because of their links to financial institutions as members of Japan's *keiretsu* or business groups, the Japanese firms were able to maintain levels of semiconductor research and development even during periods of trough in the market, an option not open to the (more specialised) US semiconductor manufacturers. If a free market for capital (one where there is an 'arm's-length' relationship between firms and their sources of capital, as in the US) does indeed possess a tendency towards myopia or 'short-termism', the long-term planning perspective and therefore the investment policies of these integrated and diversified Japanese firms, with their administrative links to financial institutions, may prove to have been more efficacious than those which could have emerged from the workings of a free capital market (see Auerbach 1988: Chs 7 and 9).

Planning by *governments* under capitalism can also promote the development of markets. As we have seen, there is a tendency in capitalist development towards commodification; that is, towards the development of product standardisation. Periodically, with the emergence of new technologies, difficulties arise in capitalism which block this inherent tendency to commodify production. In the 1890s in the US

> the market was flooded with competing types of electrical apparatus and chemical products peddled by the new companies, in addition to the plethora of machined goods and machinery itself. Since each company was concerned above all with promoting its own products, and devised unique means of evaluating their quality and performance, *comparison between competing products was difficult.* And since each manufacturer used its own specially machined parts, *replacement by those of another was virtually impossible.* (Noble 1979: 69–70, emphasis added.)

In the 1920s it was administrative action by the Department of Commerce under the future President Herbert Hoover and the trade associations which imposed uniformity of standards and specifications on machine tools and electrical equipment. It was this planned and co-ordinated activity – sometimes by firms working through trade associations, and at other times through the mediation of government – which created the prerequisites for market competition between firms producing commensurate commodities with uniform specifications. Thus *administered, planned action by central authorities made possible the development of markets and the commodification of these products*.

For any *individual* firm, the heterogeneity of performance specifications stood as an obstacle to expansion and development plans and thus to profitability, but only a central administrative body could plan and co-ordinate the conflicting interests of enterprises. At present, we may observe a titanic battle between two groups, one led by IBM and the other by AT&T, over the imposition of a uniform operating standard to permit different types of computers to share software applications and to 'talk' directly to one another. The impetus towards uniformity of standards comes from computer users, whose desire is for commodification – comparability and interchangeability – between the products they purchase, so that they are 'less reliant upon individual manufacturers of proprietary computer systems' (Kehoe 1989). In this case, it is clearly not in IBM's interests to impose standards that will tend to commodify the products of the computer industry, but it is being forced to accede to this demand by the actions of another giant, AT&T, with less of a vested interest in computer hardware. It seems unlikely however, that such a move towards standardisation and commodification could take place in the absence of action by one of the following: hegemonous giants such as IBM and AT&T, a governmental authority, or, least likely, a tight coalition made up solely of the lesser computer manufacturers. What seems well-nigh impossible to imagine is that this move towards standardisation could have emerged from the 'spontaneous' workings of the free market.

As we have shown, the richness and extent of markets are contingent on the kinds of planning decisions made by central administrative agencies and by individual firms. It is also true, however, that *successful planning by the capitalist firm has taken place in the context of market alternatives and an awareness of their existence. The organisation and direction of the firm, contrary to the ideas of Engels, have not become a purely 'technical' problem of administration*. Thus, in the course of the twentieth century, many giant corporations have used the multidivisional structure, in which divisions function as self-sufficient entities, in order to simulate *inside* the company the discipline of the market. Furthermore, as we have seen, 'best practice' in vertically integrated firms has progressively gone in the direction of judging internal purchases against free market alternatives whenever possible, thereby militating against the prejudice of the firm's engineers to 'do it yourself'.

Many innovative acts of planning, integration and co-ordination are themselves responses to competitive pressures to reduce costs and to pursue sales in new domains. A recent joint venture by Ford and Mazda to produce a 'world car' is just such an instance, with the car to be assembled in twelve locations for 90 different markets (Treece and Borrus 1990). This is not to deny, of course, that 'planning', in the form of vertical integration or of price-fixing agreements between firms, may in some contexts merely have an anti-competitive motivation: see the recent example of the response of British cement manufacturers to increasing international competitiveness (Leadbeater 1989).

Even the most recent triumphs of capitalist planning and co-ordination within and between enterprises, such as the famous Japanese 'just-in-time' system for the control of inventories, emerge from market pressures to minimise holding costs while retaining maximum flexibility to respond to changes in demand: 'just-in-time says you only make what you can sell' (Batchelor 1989; see also Abegglen and Stalk 1985, Ch. 5). Closer links with suppliers are taking place in many industries not only to control inventories, but to facilitate innovation:

> competition . . . has led vehicle manufacturers to place a greater reliance on their suppliers in an attempt to keep up with technology and keep costs down. Today the vehicle manufacturers are regarding their component suppliers as partners and are correspondingly involving them more closely in their business and at an earlier stage of new model development. Accompanying this has been a marked reduction in vehicle manufacturers' own in-house component producing facilities. (Way 1989.)

Note that this intensification in forward planning on the part of vehicle manufacturers will be accompanied by a *fall* in the observed level of vertical integration.

III PLANNING AND THE MULTINATIONAL FIRM

We may now explore these issues in the context of the emergence of the multinational firm.[4] The multinational enterprise has long been thought to pose particular difficulties for economic orthodoxy. Why indeed should such a phenomenon exist at all? In a world with a free flow of goods and capital and complete information, specialisation on the part of enterprises and countries would take place. There is little room in such a world for the sprawling, transnational entity.

A large literature has come forth to account for the existence of the multinational.[5] In the terms which are used to justify the existence of the firm itself, already familiar to us from Coase, the multinational only comes forth because of the presence of market imperfections – to preserve an inherent technological, managerial or marketing advantage that might be dissipated through, for instance, licensing. A strong prediction emerging from this 'internalisation' paradigm as exposited by (mainly) British economists is that multinational investment should be concentrated in high-technology sectors. Ironically, the strongest counter-example comes from Britain itself, the second greatest multinational investor, with its concentration on such low-technology sectors as tobacco, alcohol and food products.

The orthodox approach is irrelevant to the historical development of the multinational and emerges from a static perspective on the problem. At a given moment, a firm may face a choice between exporting and indulging in foreign direct investment. It is then relatively trivial to suggest that the greater the market imperfections, the more likely that the firm will internalise the production decision and indulge in a vertically integrated, foreign direct investment solution. When, in the extreme case, no local markets in the relevant services needed by the firm exist, the firm indulges in almost total vertical integration.

The fundamental problem with the internalisation approach is that it does not confront a central historical fact: the great expansion of multinational activity which took place after the Second World War was coincident with an explosion of trade and the lessening of market imperfections of all kinds – the stabilisation of the international monetary system, the introduction of the General Agreement on Tariffs and Trade (GATT) and a host of other measures. Those very conditions which have been conducive to an expansion of trade have also promoted the growth of multinational activity. *The development of the 'market' and the 'plan' have been complementary developments in the post-war world.*

The essential and implicit assumption embodied in the orthodox approach is that the firm, at any point in historical time, is making its calculations along the outer frontier of trade-offs between alternative methods of maximising wealth: no possibilities have escaped our Benthamite rational calculator, even in an international context. If the Benthamite firm is led in the direction of multinational activity because it is not confronted with suitably rich market alternatives, this 'market failure' results either from government interference or from one of the specific forms of this failure (such as the 'public good' aspects surrounding the dissipation of knowledge) legitimated in orthodox economic theory.

Such an approach leaves no room for the kind of systematic growth and development that have always characterised the world of international investment and trade, most especially in the post-war years. Continuous transformations in the skills and ambitions of managers to think in ever broader, more world-wide terms about possibilities for the manufacture and sale of the firm's products, the expanding facilities for transportation, communication and monitoring of these possibilities and the 'demonstration effect' of rivals in the international arena are of far more significance to long-run developments than any static decision on whether to 'use the market' or to invest directly in international facilities.

The orthodox tendency to view managerial activity in 'optimising' terms rather than in an historical, relativist perspective is coupled with a belief in the ubiquitous presence of rich markets in all goods and services whenever there is no governmental interference or any specific form of market failure. But rich markets may be absent for other reasons. In many goods and services, markets may be thin simply because of the relatively low level of economic development in the economic region concerned. The conventional approach to multinational investment is that such investment is the response of those firms able to 'internalise' these activities: the multinational was seen as a triumph of vertical integration.

Of course, it was no such thing. The vertical integration approach appeared to give a satisfactory explanation of a phenomenon at a particular historical moment: many post-war multinationals, especially those from the US, did function at exceptionally high levels of vertical integration, bringing with them their own, home-based resources even for marketing and finance. Vertical integration was a response to the fact that in the immediate post-war world, even in Western Europe, there were few domestic infrastructures – industrial, financial or in marketing – which American multinationals felt could fulfil their needs.

Vertical integration is not the magic 'key' to the multinational, as so many contemporary writers believe. I do not wish to be misunderstood on this point. There is, unquestionably, an important sense in which the multinational has continued to develop as a 'planned' entity. Sophisticated multinationals such as Ford and IBM have been progressing from the running of collections of 'truncated replicas' in Western Europe to planning, specialised and co-ordinated roles for its various subsidiaries as part of European and world-wide strategies. This is a fact of central significance for the UK as the country finds itself the host of specialised facilities which are merely a small part of the grand strategies of giant firms. The growth of international integration, however, has been tempered by the fashion emerging from Japanese firms for tight just-in-time inventory controls and quality monitoring of suppliers, which constrains the extent of geographical dispersion in many industries and demonstrates that growing sophistication within firms will not necessarily register as increases in cross-border production.

But there is a far more significant factor countervailing against the growth of cross-border vertical integration than the growth of just-in-time inventory systems: growing managerial sophistication has not been a phenomenon exclusive to the multinationals, but has affected all firms and institutions and therefore the 'markets' *which are created by* the activities of these firms and institutions. By the early 1970s, manufacturing and resource-based multinationals setting up in Western Europe had been followed by a 'second wave' of supporting companies such as component suppliers, advertising agencies and financial institutions (including such lesser manifestations as the growth of international factoring), which are of special interest to smaller, non-integrated firms. 'Do-it-yourself' activities become less of a necessity for multinational enterprises attempting to function at a world-class level, as they may purchase financial, marketing and other infrastructures around the world when it seems advantageous to do so. These rich economic infrastructures have progressively become more widely dispersed and are no longer the almost exclusive domain of the US, as they appeared to be in the immediate post-war period.

Thus, as can be seen in host countries such as Britain and even more dramatically in economies such as South Korea, the multinational has been the key device for the diffusion of managerial techniques (and of 'efficient' labour relations, a price often extracted by multinationals as a condition of entry), thereby accelerating the level of competition in the world economy. Indeed, the success with which Japanese multinationals have inculcated their own standards of quality control and punctual delivery to domestic suppliers may be one of the most significant side-effects of their investment in Britain.

The opposite line of causation also holds: not only does multinational activity promote competition, but an increasingly competitive environment has helped to engender multinational activity. In the inter-war period cartels, by cutting up the world into economic spheres of interest, inhibited not only international trade in the industries affected but international investment as well. In the post-war world, earlier phases of multinational activity, especially from the US, were often characterised by a 'product life cycle' model: once products had been fully exploited in the United States, they were fobbed off on the rest of the world. The present, more competitive environment encourages international investment, with firms' managements under pressure to think about simultaneous world-wide distribution and sales of new goods, either as uniform 'world products' or, more likely, as modified for the specific needs of national markets before any 'competitive advantages' are snapped up by rivals. It has been suggested that increasing competition promotes international investment in a more direct way: 'With stiff competition at home, American telephone companies see a move to fast growing Europe as an imperative. Says Robert D. Dalziel, vice-president for AT&T International Communications Services, "The only way to expand is outside of the US" ' (Riemer 1990).

Further pressures in this direction result from the 'supply side'. The first is the need to amortise as broadly and as quickly as possible the (ever-increasing) fixed costs of marketing new products in many industries. Secondly, there is the need for giant firms, once secure in the computer, telecommunications and car industries, to merge both within and across national boundaries and/or to make international cross-border links (such as joint ventures) to preserve or extend their technological, marketing or other capabilities in this atmosphere of greater international competitiveness. Thus we may read that

> The hectic pursuit of Jaguar by Ford and General Motors has been a startling admission by the world's two largest car makers of their failure to break into the exclusive upper reaches of the world's luxury car market . . . GM's and Ford's long-established leadership of the world motor industry is under threat as never before from their Japanese rivals. For two decades they have watched like giants with feet of clay, as the Japanese car makers have stolen trick after trick, inexorably eroding the US car makers' previously impregnable position. (Done 1989.)

There are thus two alternative approaches to multinational development: an orthodox one which emphasises the role of the multinational in surmounting market failure, and an evolutionist one in which the expansion of business horizons dictates that the developing richness and 'perfection' of markets is a process complementing multinational expansion rather than countervailing it.

An evolutionist approach perceives multinational development in ways which significantly contradict orthodoxy: first, the multinational is viewed in the context of complementary developments and not as an isolated phenomenon. Those very factors which are conducive to the developing richness of markets will also promote multinational expansion; second, as market imperfections lessen, as with the moves towards European integration in 1992, the orthodox approach logically must presume a tendency towards a lessening of multinational activity, at least from firms based within the Community. Indeed, a conundrum in the orthodox multinational literature is the fact that the Treaty of Rome of 1957 was followed by a significant expansion in intra-Community trade *and* investment, activities perceived as substitutes in orthodox thought. Contrarily, from the evolutionist perspective, it is predicted that international economic activity of all kinds – trade (including intra-industry trade, a result which stands in contradiction to orthodox theory (Greenaway 1988)), joint ventures and agreements and multinational investment – are likely to increase with growing integration. In many cases, the investment is merely intended as an 'opening' for exports in markets habituated to using local suppliers. In other cases international investment is promoted by the expansion of firms' geographical horizon and those very kinds of financial and legal uniformity emerging in the post-war era which have also engendered increases in international trade. Again, contrary to the orthodox perception of the multinational as evidence of 'the growing significance of hierarchical advantages' (Dunning 1983), the evolutionist perspective predicts an ever-increasing number of smaller, dis-integrated multinational firms alongside continuing developments in the sophistication of mature multinational firms.

IV CONCLUDING REMARKS

The multinational is often taken to represent the victory of the hierarchical over the market form of governance. But in fact it has emerged, as we have seen, along with a growth of so-called market relations. Those very conditions which have been conducive to an expansion of trade have also promoted the growth of multinational activity.

Not only does marketisation often emerge out of acts of planning, but the forms which planning takes in modern capitalist firms can only be understood in the context of the market environment which exists externally to the firm: this market environment has a crucial effect on the formation of the internal structure of the firm and on its procedures for decision-making. Engels's notion of the existence of a regime of autonomous planning inside the firm, quite separate from the domain of the market, is in sharp contrast to the substantive economic history of the twentieth century.

There is thus a subtle relationship, a dialectical one, if you please, between the development of markets under capitalism and the evolution of planning, where planning is seen to emanate both from the firm and from centralised bodies such as national governments. Both 'market' and 'plan' exist together, at the same time complementing each other and functioning as conflicting modes of operation. Any attempt to understand either of these modes of governance in isolation from the other is doomed to failure.

NOTES

1. Detailed treatment of the problems concerning the measurement and conceptualisation of vertical integration is to be found in Auerbach 1988: Ch. 8.
2. Such systems are still in their infancy – see Edquist and Jacobsson 1988.
3. An illuminating discussion of dynamic, sequential models compared with static, simultaneous ones may be found in Skott 1990.
4. These issues are explored more fully in Auerbach 1989.
5. See Dunning 1988 for a summary and bibliography of this literature.

REFERENCES

Abegglen, J.C. and G. Stalk, 1985, *Kaisha: The Japanese Corporation*, Basic Books, New York.

Arestis, P. and Y. Kitromilides, eds, 1990, *Theory and Policy in Political Economy*, Edward Elgar, Aldershot.

Arrow, K., 1973, *The Limits of Organization*, W.W. Norton, New York.

Auerbach, P., 1984, 'On the Theory of Social Democracy', *British Review of Economic Issues* 14, Spring, 83–92.

Auerbach, P., 1988, *Competition*, Basil Blackwell, Oxford.

Auerbach, P., 1989, 'Multinationals in the British Economy', in Green, 1989, ed., *The Restructuring of the U.K. Economy*, Harvester, London.

Auerbach, P., 1990, 'Market Structure and Firm Behaviour: An Empty Box?', in P. Arestis and Y. Kitromilides, eds, 1990, *Theory and Policy in Political Economy*, Edward Elgar, Aldershot.

Auerbach, P., M. Desai and A. Shamsavari, 1988, 'The Dialectic of Plan and Market', *New Left Review* 170, July/August, 61–78.

Batchelor, C., 1989, 'You Only Make What You Can Sell', *Financial Times*, 14 November.

Bradshaw, D., 1989, 'One's Burden is Another's Profit', *Financial Times*, 27 October.

Casson, M., ed., 1983, *The Growth of International Business*, Allen & Unwin, London.

Coase, R., 1937, 'The Nature of the Firm', *Economica*, New Series, 4, 386–405.

Done, K., 1989, 'Desperate for the Luxury Cachet', *Financial Times*, 3 November.

Dunning, J., 1983, 'Changes in the Level and Structure of International Production: the Last One Hundred Years', in Casson, M., ed., 1983, *The Growth of International Business*, Allen & Unwin, London.

Dunning, J., 1988, *Explaining International Production*, Unwin Hyman, London.

Dunning, J. and P. Robson, eds, 1988, *Multinationals and the European Community*, Basil Blackwell, Oxford.

Edquist, C. and S. Jacobsson, 1988, *Flexible Automation*, Basil Blackwell, Oxford.

Galbraith, J.K., 1967, *The New Industrial State*, Signet Books, New York.

Green, F., ed., 1989, *The Restructuring of the U.K. Economy*, Harvester, London.

Greenaway, D., 1988, 'Intra-Industry Trade, Intra-Firm Trade and European Integration: Evidence, Gains and Policy Aspects', in Dunning and Robson, eds, 1988.

Kehoe, L., 1989, 'AT&T Introduces Upgraded Unix System', *Financial Times*, 1 November.

Leadbeater, C., 1989, 'Breaking Up What Was Set in Concrete', *Financial Times*, 22 December.

Lewis, G. *et al.*, 1989, 'Computers: Japan Comes on Strong', *Business Week*, 23 October.

Lorenz, C., 1989, 'Unleashing the Potential of Design', *Financial Times*, 27 October.

Neff, R. *et al.*, 1989, 'Why NEC Has U.S. Companies "Shaking in their Boots" ', *Business Week*, 26 March.
Noble, D., 1979, *America By Design*, Oxford University Press, Oxford.
Riemer, B., 1990, 'The New Rush to Europe', *Business Week*, 26 March.
Skott, P., 1990, 'An Essay on Keynes and General Equilibrium Theory', in Arestis and Kitromilides, eds, 1990.
Treece, J. and A. Borrus, 1990, 'How Ford and Mazda Shared the Driver's Seat', *Business Week*, 26 March.
Treece, J. *et al.*, 1990, 'Is Another Smith Headed for the Top at GM?', *Business Week*, 26 March.
Way, A., 1989, 'Manufacturers Treading the Path to Partnership', *Financial Times*, World Car Industry Supplement, 13 September.
Williamson, O., 1975, *Markets and Hierarchies*, Collier-Macmillan, New York.

10. Macroeconomic Policy Co-ordination and Commodity Input Prices

Peter Reynolds*

I INTRODUCTION

The purpose of this chapter is to explore some issues concerned with the international co-ordination of macroeconomic policies. There is now a considerable body of literature on the theory of macroeconomic policy interdependence and a growing collection of empirical studies directed at evaluating potential benefits from co-ordination. It is certainly possible to specify a multi-country model which can be used to show that there are potential benefits to be gained from policy co-ordination, though the extent of such gains is less clear-cut empirically. At a policy level there is debate about what reforms, if any, should be made to the international monetary system so as to benefit from the potential gains and thereby improve world welfare.

Although this chapter begins by reviewing some of the important features and conclusions drawn from this literature, it is argued that, since the conclusions are sensitive to the underlying model of the world economy, this represents a serious qualification. Consequently, Section III outlines a post-Keynesian perception of the structure of the world economy, emphasising some of the important differences between the industrial countries and the producers of primary products. Key features of the interaction between these two main sectors are elucidated in Section IV. This leads to the inescapable conclusion that increased synchronisation of the industrial economies has actually contributed to the inflationary and recessionary tendencies of the last two decades.

II THEORY AND EVIDENCE ON MACROECONOMIC POLICY CO-ORDINATION

Co-operation, co-ordination, convergence and synchronisation are terms commonly used when referring to international aspects of macroeconomic policy, but unfortunately, not only are they not always clearly defined, they are also sometimes defined or used in different ways. In what follows we attempt to use the first three of these terms in a way consistent with Artis and Ostry (1986), deriving from Wallich (1984). Co-operation is used as a generic term which may refer to anything from the exchange of information at one extreme to a formal agreement at the other. Macroeconomic policy co-ordination occurs where 'individual national policies are significantly modified by reason of the recognition of international interdependence' (Artis and Ostry 1986: 21). This would appear also to be consistent with the definition that 'countries modify their economic policies in what is intended to be a mutually beneficial manner, taking account of international economic linkages' (Group of 30 1988).[1, 2] 'Convergence', which may refer to either policies or performance, makes little sense unless it is specified which particular measure of policy stance or indicator of performance is being referred to. Policies or performance indicators are convergent if they are 'becoming more similar' (*ibid.*) or divergent if they are becoming less similar. Hence policy co-ordination may, in principle at least, involve using certain policy instruments in either a similar or dissimilar way and may lead to certain economic performance indicators either converging or diverging. Synchronisation means occurring at the same time. In this chapter we use the term in a very specific sense, to refer to the situation where a particular economic variable – usually the level of industrial production – follows a very similar time-path in two or more different countries. In what follows, it is advocated that governments co-ordinate their policies in such a way as to reduce the degree to which the expansionary phases of their respective business cycles are synchronised.

A The Theoretical Case for Co-ordination

A popular way of expressing the theoretical basis on which the case for co-ordination is predicated is to use the analytical framework set out by Hamada (1974, 1985).[3] Adopting a two-country model, each country is assumed to have two macroeconomic targets, say, internal and external balance, linked by a quadratic objective function. Each country has one policy instrument, typically the domestic money supply, and, because of international interdependence, each country's welfare is affected both by the level of its own money supply and that of its trading partner. For each country a reaction function is derived, indicating its response to any value taken by the other country's money supply, so that Nash and Stackelberg equilibria can be obtained. The Nash equilibrium represents the level at which each country would set its policy instrument, under the assumption that the two countries behave independently of each other.[4] This is shown to be Pareto inferior to a set of possibilities which exist along a contract curve representing a locus of tangencies of the two welfare functions. Since it is assumed that positions on the contract curve can be achieved by co-ordinating economic policies, the model predicts that macroeconomic policy co-ordination can increase welfare in both countries.

This conclusion is predicated on the assumptions of well-defined welfare functions and most importantly that the decision-makers have full knowledge of the structure of the world economy, although the full import of this assumption is sometimes slightly disguised by referring instead to policy-makers not agreeing on the true model.[5]

B The Importance of Model Structure

The key features of the world model which are most important are the 'policy spillovers' from one country to another. Indeed, if the economic policy decisions of one country had no effect whatsoever on its trading partners, then the case for co-ordinating national economic policies would entirely evaporate. Although this is fully acknowledged by participants in the debate, it might be considered surprising that the precise form of the international linkages often receives cavalier treatment.

A major contributor to the literature on co-ordination states quite categorically, 'There are three transmission mechanisms by which events in one economy can affect another' (Hughes-Hallett 1989: 185). First, real-income linkages occur because of the effect on a country's exports of a change in the level of demand in one of its trading partners. It is this effect that is fundamental to the 'international Keynesian' perspective on economic policy. If trading partners expand their economies together, they will each demand increasing quantities of imports from the other, so that neither country experiences the balance of payments difficulties that would result from unilateral expansionary action. Second, monetary effects occur both as a result of financing balance of payments changes with less than perfectly flexible exchange rates and, perhaps more significantly, as a result of international capital flows in response to actual and anticipated differentials in interest and exchange rates. Finally, there are relative price adjustments, transmitted through movements in the terms of trade.

Many writers, including Currie (1990), acknowledge that since the international linkages are many and complex, models which focus on only one or two of these may be quite inadequate or even misleading as a basis for policy recommendations. It is our belief that a particular transmission mechanism, or group of mechanisms, has been underrated to the detriment of policy advice. Where policy co-ordination has contributed to the synchronisation of the business cycles of the industrial nations, this has had adverse effects on the prices of primary commodities and the purchasing power of commodity producers. The adverse effects of such co-ordination have been further compounded by the impact of interest rate changes on the ability of developing countries to meet debt repayments, with further repercussions on purchasing power. There have been consequent adverse feedback effects on the demand for industrial products, exacerbating individual countries' business cycles and imparting both an inflationary and a stagnationary bias to the world economy.

C Forms of Policy Co-ordination

Following Cooper (1985), we identify three broad forms of economic policy co-ordination. Co-ordination may take the form of setting up a rule-based regime, so that national governments act independently within a set of rules designed such that the independent welfare-maximising decisions lead to an outcome superior to the Cournot–Nash position. Or a supranational organisation may be established, responsible for complete policy co-ordination. Finally, a less rigid arrangement is the use of economic summits.

The record of economic summits is not very encouraging. In reviewing their achievements over the early 1980s, Artis and Ostry conclude:

> The summit meetings served to reinforce and fortify the confidence of individual member countries in broadly shared diagnoses of the problem and appropriate prescriptions for domestic policy. This process of providing mutual intellectual, moral and political support resulted in the adoption of a planned policy of macroeconomic synchronisation, 'engineered' institutionally by means of the OECD/summit nexus. (1986: 44–5.)

Judged by their past record, the effect of economic summits appears to be to encourage a form of economic policy co-ordination which serves to exacerbate one of the underlying sources of instability.

Proposals for rule-based regimes tend to focus mainly on the exchange rate. Since the exchange-rate effects of monetary policy are amongst the most obvious and transparent instances of policy spillover, this is perhaps not surprising. Although it is beyond our scope to consider individual proposals in detail, we note that a crucial ingredient missing from current discussions, which was central to the plans that Keynes was advocating in the early 1940s but notably absent from the Bretton Woods agreement, is an international agency responsible for the stability of commodity prices. One of the main problems associated with the operation of international commodity agreements (ICAs) in the post-war period is that they have been under-funded.[6] Once again a return to the ideas of Keynes and Kaldor may be insightful. A properly funded commodity buffer stock scheme, for example as proposed by Kaldor (1983), financed by the issue of special drawing rights (SDRs), would direct funds to the countries most in need of them, help to reduce one of the main sources of world instability and improve the chances of success of a return to a more orderly system of world exchange rates.

D Empirical Studies

Empirical evaluation of the gains from policy co-ordination has been largely via the use of simulation exercises using macroeconometric models. As the gains from policy co-ordination depend on the structure of the economic model being considered, it is not surprising that results have been varied, though as Hughes-Hallett observes, 'The conclusion which emerges from the empirical work in this area is that these gains are small' (1989: 206). A particularly important contribution by Frankel and Rockett (1988) explicitly considers the possibility that policy-makers do not agree on the true model. For a simulation based on the United States and 'Europe' (which is taken as shorthand for the non-US OECD), the authors consider the effects of policy co-ordination using ten major econometric models. As policy-makers in the two countries may each believe in any of the ten models, there are one hundred possible combinations of belief. However, since the 'true' model could also be any one of the ten, there are one thousand possible outcomes. Frankel and Rockett find that the United States gains from co-ordination in 546 cases and 'Europe' gains in 539 cases.[7]

Lack of knowledge about the precise international linkages must seriously qualify the claim that there are significant gains to be had from policy co-ordination when such claims are based on theoretical models of known structure. The claim is even more fallible in situations where the assumed model ignores certain types of interaction between OECD countries and the rest of the world. The rest of this chapter adopts a theoretical perspective which highlights such interactions.

III AN ALTERNATIVE THEORETICAL PERSPECTIVE

The perspective adopted here falls clearly in the tradition of economics usually associated with the names of Kalecki, Keynes and Kaldor and referred to as post-Keynesian economics. We adopt the distinction widely attributed to Kalecki, whereby changes in the prices of most industrial goods are largely cost-determined, whereas in the primary sector prices respond more directly to changes in demand (Kalecki 1943, 1954, 1971). A similar distinction has been made by many other economists, including Kaldor (1976, 1983), who argued that fluctuations in the production of industrial products lead to fluctuations in commodity prices and also that fluctuations in the prices of primary commodities are a serious source of both inflationary and recessionary tendencies in the world economy.[8, 9]

The distinction between these two broad types of price formation to a certain extent parallels attempts to model the world economy in terms of two major sectors, variously referred to as North and South, Core and Periphery or Centre and Periphery.[10] Although the core–periphery distinction in some ways parallels the division of the world into advanced, industrialised countries and less developed economies, the correspondence is not precise. Less developed countries (LDCs) are not the only producers of primary products and the periphery includes the newly industrialised countries. Some LDCs are also important producers of industrial products. In fact, developed countries account for almost a half of the world supply of primary products. Nonetheless, the relationship is very asymmetrical in that LDCs' share of world trade in manufactures is approximately 15 per cent, whereas about 85 per cent of their export earnings come from primary products (Thirlwall 1989: Ch. 14). This high degree of specialisation on the part of primary producers leaves them very susceptible to fluctuations in primary product prices, especially as many of their products are produced under conditions of fairly inelastic short-run supply so that prices are very responsive to fluctuations in demand.

There are other important aspects of the interdependence between these two sectors. The less developed countries, including primary product producers, tend to be amongst the world's debtor nations, with debts often denominated in terms of US dollars. Debt repayments must therefore be financed out of foreign exchange earnings, deriving principally from commodity exports. Changes in interest rates affect the debt repayment capacity of LDCs dramatically. In fact, it has been estimated (van Wijnbergen 1985) that a 1 per cent increase in interest rates will have an effect on the income of LDCs sufficient to offset the effect of a 1 per cent rise in centre countries' industrial production. If the industrial countries, which are the principal powers responsible for setting world interest rates, use high interest rates as an economic policy instrument at times when overall world industrial demand is low, then LDCs can be faced with big increases in debt repayments at a time when demand for their principal products and their sources of finance are at their lowest. This is not an insignificant factor in explaining the debt crisis of the early 1980s. A further consequence, which has adverse effects on the major industrial economies, is that LDCs' export earnings resulting from receipts of revenues from primary commodities may be diverted from effective demand for industrial goods to debt repayments. The overall impact on industrial-sector effective demand then depends on the effects on effective demand of these debt repayments – on whether they lead to increased liquid asset holdings within the financial circulation or whether they re-enter the industrial circulation as real demand for produced goods.

The final aspect of international interdependence which we consider is the relationship between the rates of expansion of industrial production in individual countries and the rate of growth of world industrial production as a whole. If one accepts the hypotheses that the rate of growth of world output is significant in explaining variations in world commodity prices and that variations in world commodity prices, via their direct effect on input costs, are fundamental to the determination of domestic inflation rates, then it follows that inflationary pressures will be at their greatest when domestic expansion is accompanied by the expansion of world industrial production as a whole. Conversely, if reduced commodity prices, resulting from lower economic activity in the industrial countries (OECD) have adverse effects, via the income of primary producers, on industrial output in OECD then, once again, there is a case for reducing the depressing effect emanating from the OECD. Furthermore, high interest rates will have a dampening effect, so that synchronised recession, along with high interest rates, could have a self-reinforcing impact far more damaging on output in both world sectors than many economists would believe. In the model outlined here, restrictive monetary policies have very clear, definite, recessionary effects on real output. The greater the degree to which such policies are synchronised then the greater will be the recessionary impact.

IV THE KEY RELATIONSHIPS

In this section we focus on three key aspects of the interaction between industrial countries and primary producers in the world economy. The first aspect considered is the effect of the behaviour of primary commodity prices on both the rate of inflation in industrial countries and the level and rate of change of world industrial production. Second, we examine the way in which the cyclical pattern of world industrial production affects the behaviour of primary commodity prices. Third, we examine the extent to which changes in the degree of international macroeconomic synchronisation affect the cyclical pattern of world industrial production.

Since the first two relationships have been quite well established elsewhere, we briefly review the theory and evidence relating to them and examine some preliminary ideas and data pertaining to the third relationship.

A The Effect of Changes in World Commodity Prices on Inflation and Economic Activity in Industrial Countries

Kaldor (1976) explained the concurrent existence of inflation and recession in the world economy in terms of the interaction between the primary and industrial sectors. If all prices were perfectly flexible then one might argue – from a neo-classical perspective – that the price mechanism would ensure that the terms of trade between primary and industrial producers would adjust to maintain balanced growth in the world economy. However, the industrial sector is not characterised by flex-price markets, and such balanced growth patently does not happen.

According to post-Keynesian economics, prices of industrial goods are determined by firms adding a mark-up to some measure of unit prime costs. There are various theories of mark-up determination, including Kalecki's (1943, 1954, 1971) theory of the degree of monopoly, Cowling and Waterson's (1976) theory of short-period profit maximisation under conditions of oligopolistic interdependence, and various theories whereby the mark-up is determined by firms' needs to generate internal funds for investment (Eichner 1973, 1976; Wood 1975).[11] It is a prediction of all these models that prices would adjust little or not at all in direct response to short-run changes in demand.

It is worth pointing out that although the inflexibility of industrial prices is entirely consistent with and indeed explained by post-Keynesian economic theory, it can also be explained within a more orthodox short-period profit-maximising framework of analysis. In an economy consisting of firms operating under conditions of imperfect competition, where each firm faces a downward-sloping demand curve, the existence of small menu costs may mean that the optimal response to a change in demand is to leave prices as they are.[12]

There is now a wealth of empirical evidence supporting the proposition that in the industrial sector of the world economy prices are determined by a mark-up on some form of unit prime costs or on normal costs, with fluctuations in demand being met mainly by output changes rather than price changes, particularly in the short run.[13] A consequence of this price inflexibility, pointed out by Kaldor (1976), is that any imbalance between the industrial and primary sectors is borne largely by adjustment in primary product prices. In fact, to the extent that primary product prices do not change, it is industrial-sector output that also bears some of the adjustment burden. Kaldor (1976) further argued that as a result of the asymmetry between the two sectors, any large fluctuations in commodity prices, whether in favour of or against primary producers, tend to have a dampening effect on industrial activity.

To put this into historical context, in 1976 Kaldor argued that the rapid expansion of world industrial production in the early post-war period was facilitated by land-saving technological change in agriculture but with various government schemes obviating serious price effects. It is certainly clear that the last two decades have been characterised by severe fluctuations in commodity prices combined with lower rates of expansion in economic activity.

Kaldor's analysis focuses on asymmetries in both the price and income effects resulting from a change in commodity prices. First, changes in world commodity prices have an asymmetrical effect on the terms of trade: a fall in commodity prices moves the terms of trade against primary producers, whereas a rise is less effective at moving them in their favour. This is because increases in commodity prices feed through as increases in industrial costs, which are marked up. Then *via* a process of real-wage resistance the higher prices get reflected as money-wage increases. Both of these processes may be less effective, or at least slower, in a downward direction, so that commodity price fluctuations have an inflationary bias.[14]

Second, there is an impact on effective demand which is asymmetrical also. Reductions in commodity prices lead to reduced real income for primary producers, which gets translated into reduced demand for industrial goods. Although this same process may work in reverse, large surpluses tend to be recycled relatively slowly.

In summary, commodity price increases contribute to inflation in industrial countries, with decreases tending to have a recessionary rather than disinflationary impact. It follows that a higher degree of fluctuation in commodity prices will be associated both with lower levels of economic activity (or at least lower rates of economic growth) and with a general inflationary bias.

Figure 10.1 shows the behaviour of various commodity price indices from 1960 to 1988. Increased volatility in all three indices is apparent from about 1971. Table 10.1 gives results from regressing the logarithm of the all-commodities price index against time for the two sub-periods 1960–71 and 1972–88. Fluctuations certainly appear to dominate the trend for the second sub-period. Table 10.2 reports estimates of the trend rate of growth of total industrial production (all industrial countries) for the two sub-periods and for the period 1960–88 as a whole. Although the index of industrial production is a little more volatile for the second sub-period, the increased volatility is much less pronounced than is the case for commodity prices. The rate of growth of industrial production has certainly been slower for the second sub-period, so that slower economic growth in the industrial countries does appear to be associated with greater variability of world commodity prices.

Figure 10.1 Commodity price changes, all, metals, agricultural raw materials (%)

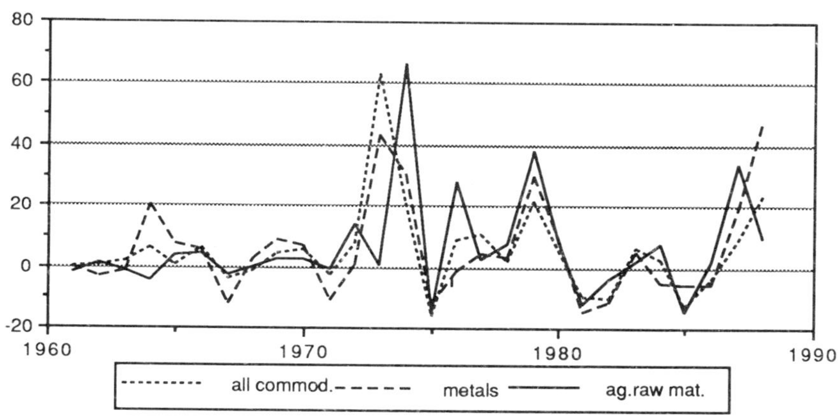

Beckerman (1985) and Beckerman and Jenkinson (1986) have also argued that the behaviour of world commodity prices has a significant impact on economic activity in industrial countries, but focusing

Table 10.1 World commodity prices, trend and deviation from trend

Regression of the logarithm of the all-commodities price index against time					
Period	*Constant (t ratio)*	*Coefficient (t ratio)*	$\bar{R}^2$	*SEE/Mean*	*Chow test*
1960–71	3.69 (236.39)	0.0150 (7.13)	0.82	0.0067	$F(2,25) = 11.3049$
1972–88	4.05 (21.01)	0.0267 (2.99)	0.33	0.0391	n.a.

primarily on the price rather than the income effects and without relying to the same extent on the asymmetry that is fundamental to Kaldor's analysis. Indeed, the key premise of Beckerman (1985) is that the reduced pressure on world commodity prices at the end of the 1970s and during the early 1980s played a fundamental role in reducing the rate of price inflation in the industrial countries during the same period. Beckerman and Jenkinson (1986) argue quite convincingly that the behaviour of world commodity prices is a very significant determinant of the domestic inflation rate for most industrialised countries and furthermore that any trade-off between unemployment and inflation that does exist is appropriately understood as a trade-off not at the level of individual countries but at the world level, occurring through commodity prices. Such a view is further substantiated by Grubb (1986). However, since violent fluctuations in the rate of price inflation are also a severe handicap to the smooth progress of industrial economies, the case for reducing commodity price instability follows just as strongly from the Beckerman analysis as it does from that of Kaldor.

Table 10.2 Growth of industrial production, all industrial countries

Regression of the logarithm of industrial production against time					
Period	*Constant (t ratio)*	*Coefficient (t ratio)*	$\bar{R}^2$	*SEE/Mean*	*Chow test*
1960–71	3.60 (264.96)	0.0573 (31.04)	0.99	0.0056	$F(2,25) = 74.4063$
1972–88	4.03 (105.78)	0.0218 (12.35)	0.90	0.0079	n.a.
1960–88	3.76 (125.32)	0.0347 (19.87)	0.93	0.1837	n.a.

B Changes in Industrial Production and World Commodity Prices

The relationship between changes in world industrial production and world commodity prices has been studied extensively.[15] A cursory glance at Figure 10.2 indicates that, to an extent at least, the series for industrial production and nominal commodity prices move together. Real and nominal commodity prices follow a similar pattern: as noted by Gilbert, 'a downward trend in nominal prices implies a markedly downward trend in real prices' (1990: 80). The much greater volatility in commodity prices since 1971 has already been alluded to and this is manifested in both the nominal and real indices. This is apparent even if we exclude the 1972–4 commodity prices boom. However, since it is less clear that this is associated with greater volatility in the series for industrial output, we consider other possible sources of instability in commodity prices for the post-1971 period. The first question to consider is whether the increased volatility in the 'All-Commodity' index is due to greater synchronisation in the behaviour of its constituents. As already indicated from Figure 10.1, the indices for metals and for agricultural raw materials do move quite closely together and, at least in the last two decades, with the all-commodities index. It is also clear that these indices taken separately show greater volatility since 1971, so that the greater volatility in the composite index is not merely due to the constituents starting to move together. The most

Figure 10.2 Changes in industrial production and commodity prices (%)

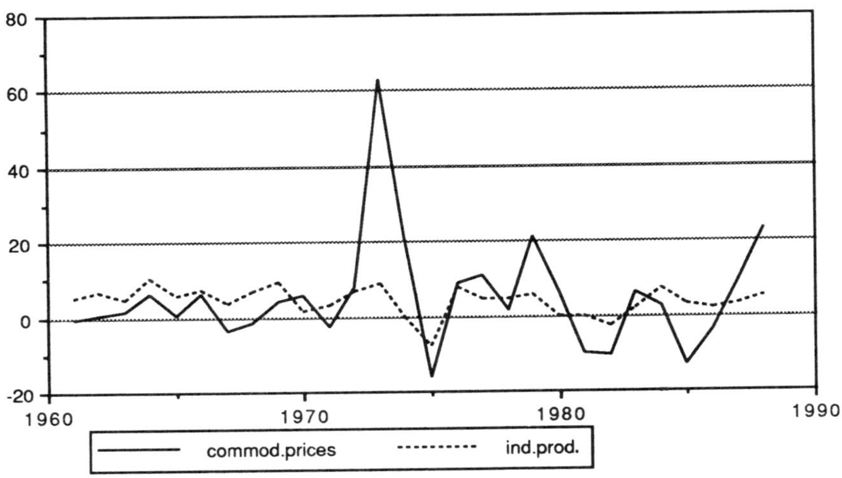

erratic index is that for beverages, shown alongside the indices for food and agricultural raw materials in Figure 10.3. This has certainly been influenced not only by various international commodity agreements (ICAs), but also by fluctuations in supply due to weather conditions.

Figure 10.3 Commodity price changes, food, beverages, agricultural raw materials (%)

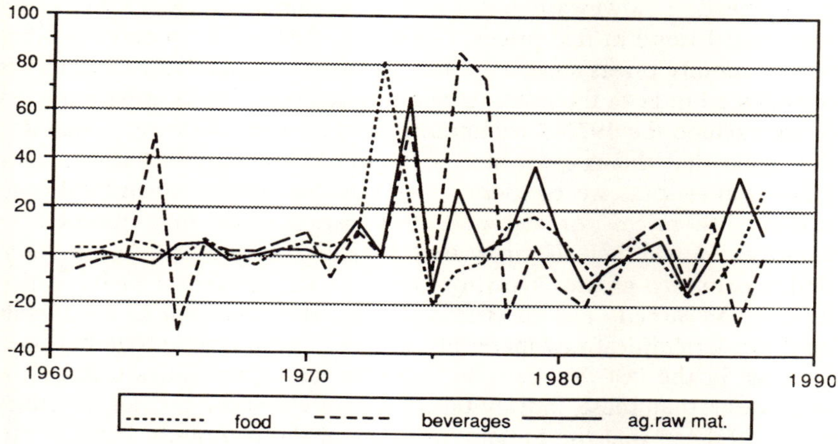

Changes in the dollar exchange rate have a clear inverse effect on both the nominal and real prices of primary commodities. This relationship has now been investigated extensively. Gilbert (1989) predicts from single- and multi-country models that the long-run elasticity of dollar commodity prices with respect to changes in the exchange rate of the dollar should lie between 0 and -1, though acknowledging that many econometric estimates exceed this. The discrepancy is ascribed to the use of an inappropriate exchange rate index and to the effects of LDC indebtedness.

A further source of increased volatility is that during the period of prolonged high world interest rates, industrial users of raw materials may be tempted to economise on stockholdings, so that fluctuations in industrial output will be reflected more directly in the prices of raw materials, rather than in stockholdings.

Sylos-Labini (1982) regressed the 'rate of variation' in agricultural raw material prices (excluding oil) on the 'rate of variation' in industrial production for the periods 1958–71 and 1972–80. His results, which were published without any diagnostic statistics, are reproduced in Table

10.3, along with our own equations, which are derived from regressing the change in the logarithm of the IMF price index of all commodities on the change in the logarithm of world industrial production, covering the period 1961–88. Our study indicates that there is a structural break in the relationship occurring at approximately 1971–2, and at least for the latter period changes in industrial production exert a significant contemporaneous effect on commodity prices. Gilbert (1990) estimates two equations for non-oil commodity prices, both equations including exchange rate variables and using an error-correction specification and annual data for 1963–89. He reports partial elasticities of 1.9 and 1.6, depending on model specification. From a variety of sources, samples, estimation procedures and precise measures of the variables concerned, the evidence appears very strongly to substantiate the existence of a strong and statistically significant relationship between changes in the level of world industrial production and changes in the prices of primary commodities.[16]

Table 10.3 *Changes in world industrial production and changes in commodity prices*

Study	*Period*	*Constant (t ratio)*	*Coefficient (t ratio)*	$\bar{R}^2$	*DW*	*Chow test using all subsequent obs'ns*
Sylos-Labini	1958–71	−5.1	0.9			
Sylos-Labini	1972–80	9.1	2.4			
Author	1961–71	−0.02 (−0.80)	0.6 (1.50)	0.19	2.28	$F(2, 24) = 3.84$
Author	1972–80	0.04 (0.76)	2.35 (2.40)	0.46	1.68	$F(2, 13) = 1.29$
Author	1972–88	−0.01 (−0.20)	2.46 (3.2)	0.41	1.32	n.a.
Author	1961–88	−0.08 (−1.35)	1.88 (3.10)	0.28	1.21	n.a.

Sources: Sylos-Labini (1982); all author's data: *International Financial Statistics*.

C Changes in Macroeconomic Synchronisation and their Effect on World Industrial Production and Commodity Prices

World industrial production is heavily dominated by a few key countries. The seven most significant producers of industrial products, the so-called G7 countries, are the United States, Japan, West Germany, the United Kingdom, France, Italy and Canada. Between them these countries account for over 85 per cent of industrial production of OECD countries. Various weightings for the main countries and country groupings are given in Table 10.4, which includes all countries whose share of OECD industrial production exceeds 1 per cent.

Clearly, if all industrial countries were to expand at the same time, the growth in world industrial production would be at its strongest and the pressure on commodity prices would be at its greatest. We seek to examine the extent to which the major economies have been synchronised and the extent to which the degree of synchronisation has changed over the periods 1960–71 and 1972–88 and then to examine any relationship between any changing degree of synchronisation and cycles in world industrial production and commodity prices.

Table 10.4 Percentage weight in calculation of OECD industrial production, 1985

United States	37.5
Japan	17.2
Germany	9.5
France	5.9
United Kingdom	6.7
Italy	6.4
Canada	3.6
Spain	3.2
Netherlands	1.7
Belgium	1.1
Australia	1.9
Total G7	86.7
Total EEC	35.8
Total OECD	100

Note: The relative importance of the different countries has, of course, changed over the period. Figures for 1985 are chosen since this is the base year used in calculating the OECD index of industrial production.

Source: OECD, *Main Economic Indicators*, August 1990.

The degree of synchronisation is examined in two ways. First, at a superficial level, time series of growth rates of industrial production are compared for various groups of countries. Second, trend growth rates are computed separately for the two sub-periods, 1960–71 and 1972–88. *A priori* the two periods were chosen to reflect the different world exchange rate regimes. Subsequently, the logarithm of world industrial production was regressed against time for the period as a whole and for the two sub-periods. A Chow test confirmed a structural break between the two periods. The trend growth rates for each country having been calculated, the sign of the residual was taken as an indication of whether the country was above or below trend for each year. The results are given in Table 10.5. Where two or more countries have a positive sign then they are both growing at a rate above their trend growth rates and for the purposes of this analysis are considered to be synchronised. Similarly, if a number of countries share a negative sign, they are all growing at a rate below their trend growth rate and are also considered to be synchronised or 'in phase' with each other. It should be noted that for two countries to be synchronised in this respect does not mean that they are necessarily in the same phase of their business cycle as conventionally defined. However, since our interest is focused on the pressure of demand for primary inputs to the industrial sector, this two-way classification is adequate. Pressure of demand for primary products can be considered high when a significant proportion of large countries show a positive sign. To try to compress this information into a single summary measure, we compute the average number of countries 'in phase' for each of the two sub-periods.

Changing degrees of synchronisation are examined at three levels. The group of three big economies (G3) of the United States, Japan and Germany, together comprising 64.2 per cent of total OECD industrial output, are considered first. We then consider the G5 countries, comprising the big 3 plus France and the United Kingdom, followed by a look at G7. The reasons for this presentation should become clear as the analysis unfolds.

i The big three

Figure 10.4 shows growth rates of industrial production for the United States, Germany and Japan. It is apparent that at some time around 1971 the cycles became more synchronised. Figures 10.5 and 10.6 show deviations from trend, again based on the assumption that the trend growth rate was different for each country for the two periods, an assumption borne out by the data. Referring to the information in Table 10.5, in only one out of the first twelve years were the three economies simultaneously above their trend (1969) and only once were they simultaneously below trend (1963). In eleven of the seventeen years 1972 to 1988 the three were simultaneously in phase. The boom periods

Table 10.5 **Deviations from trend, main industrial countries**

	All industrial countries	*USA*	*Canada*	*Japan*	*UK*	*France*	*Germany*	*Italy*	*Netherlands*	*Belgium*	*Sweden*	*No. of big 3 in phase*	*Av. of same sign*	*No. of G5 in phase*	*Av. same sign*	*No. of G7 in phase*	*Av. same sign*
1960	−	−	−	+	+	−	−	−	+	−	−	2		3		5	
1961	−	−	−	+	−	−	+	−	−	−	−	2		3		5	
1962	−	−	−	+	−	−	+	+	−	−	+	2		3		4	
1963	−	−	−	−	−	−	−	+	−	+	−	3		5		6	
1964	+	−	+	+	+	+	+	+	+	+	+	2		4		6	
1965	+	+	+	−	+	−	+	−	+	+	+	2	2.2	3	3.5	4	4.8
1966	+	+	+	−	+	−	−	+	+	−	+	2		3		4	
1967	+	+	+	−	−	−	−	+	−	−	−	2		4		4	
1968	+	+	+	+	+	−	−	+	−	−	−	2		3		5	
1969	+	+	+	+	+	+	+	−	−	+	+	3		5		6	
1970	−	−	−	+	−	+	+	+	+	+	+	2		3		4	
1971	−	−	−	−	−	+	+	−	+	−	−	2		3		5	
1972	−	+	−	+	−	−	−	−	−	−	−	2		3		5	
1973	+	+	+	+	+	+	+	+	−	+	+	3		5		7	
1974	+	+	+	+	+	+	+	+	+	+	+	3		5		7	
1975	−	−	−	−	−	−	−	−	−	−	+	3		5		7	
1976	−	−	−	−	−	+	−	+	+	+	+	3		4		5	
1977	−	+	−	−	+	+	−	−	+	−	−	2		3		4	
1978	+	+	+	−	+	+	+	+	+	+	−	2		4		6	
1979	+	+	+	+	+	+	+	+	+	+	−	3		5		7	
1980	+	+	+	+	−	+	+	+	+	+	−	3	2.7	4	4.1	6	5.8
1981	+	+	+	+	−	+	+	+	−	−	−	3		4		6	
1982	−	−	−	−	−	−	−	+	−	−	−	3		5		6	
1983	−	−	−	−	−	−	−	−	−	−	−	3		5		7	
1984	−	+	−	+	−	−	−	−	−	−	+	2		3		5	
1985	+	+	+	+	+	−	+	−	+	−	+	3		4		5	
1986	−	−	+	−	+	−	+	−	+	−	+	2		3		4	
1987	+	+	+	−	+	−	+	−	+	+	+	2		3		4	
1988	+	+	+	+	+	+	+	+	−	+	+	3		5		7	
												max = 3 min = 2		max = 5 min = 3		max = 7 min = 4	

Note: Trend growth rates were calculated separately for the periods 1960–71 and 1972–88.

were 1973–4, 1979–81, 1985 and 1988. The average number of countries in phase for the first period was 2.2, which increased to 2.7 for the second period. Paradoxically, the period following the breakdown of the Bretton Woods regime is associated with a far greater degree of synchronisation between these three major industrial economies.

Figure 10.4 Growth in industrial production, US, Japan, Germany (%)

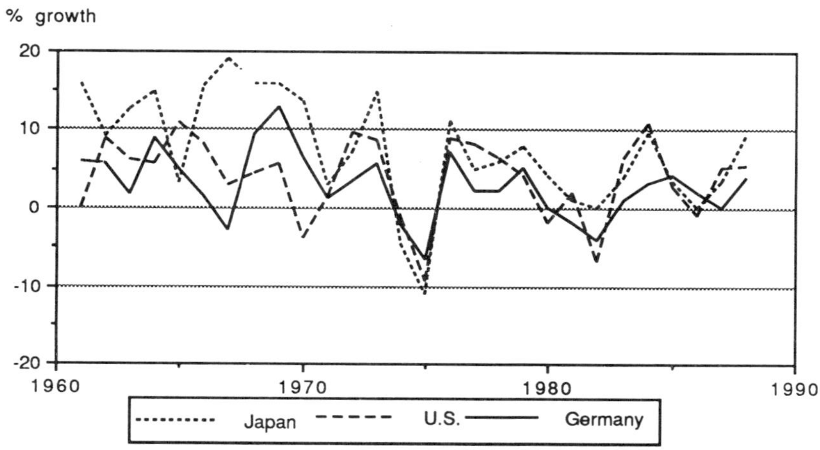

Figure 10.5 Deviations from trend of industrial production, US, Japan, Germany (I)

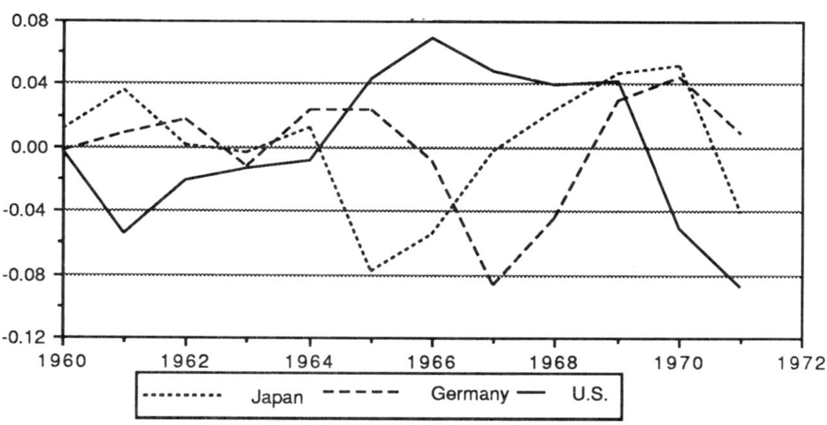

Figure 10.6 Deviations from trend of industrial production, US, Japan, Germany (II)

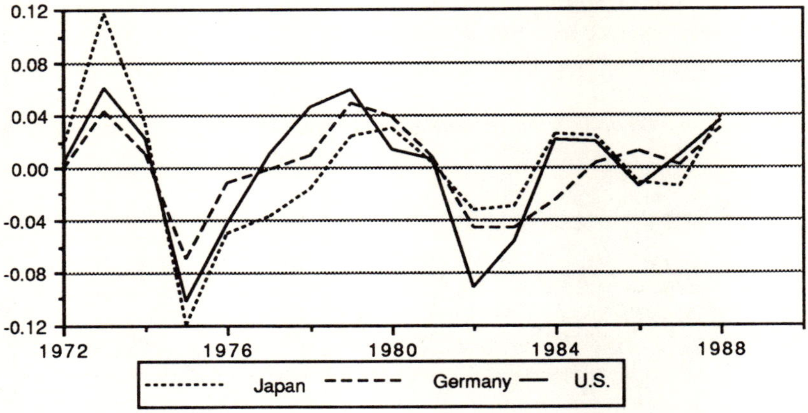

ii The group of five

Figure 10.7 plots growth in industrial production for France and the UK against industrial production for all industrial countries. Interestingly, any change in pattern before and after 1971 is much less pronounced. A similar story is told by examining deviations from trend, shown in Figures 10.8 and 10.9, with Germany included for comparison.

Figure 10.7 Growth in industrial production, world, UK, France (%)

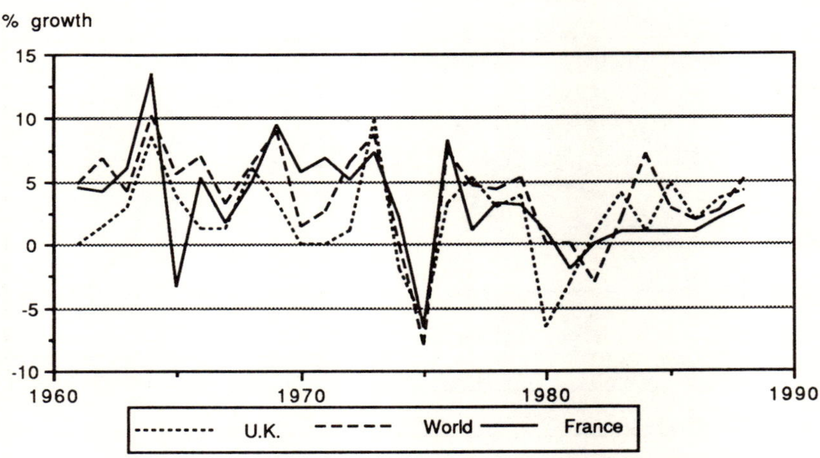

Figure 10.8 Deviations from trend of industrial production, UK, France, Germany (I)

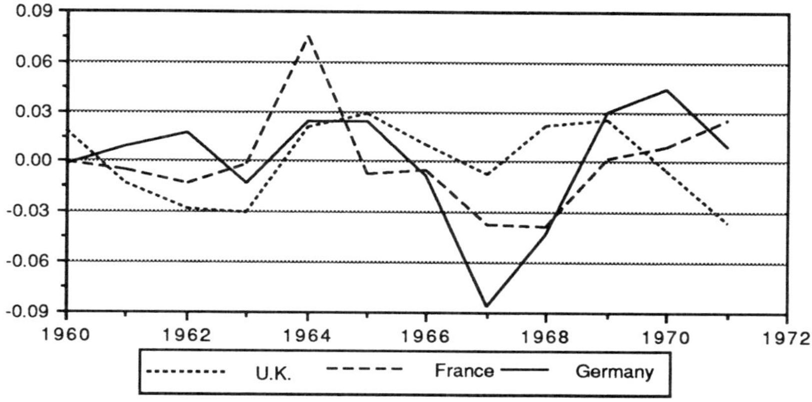

Figure 10.9 Deviations from trend of industrial production, UK, France, Germany (II)

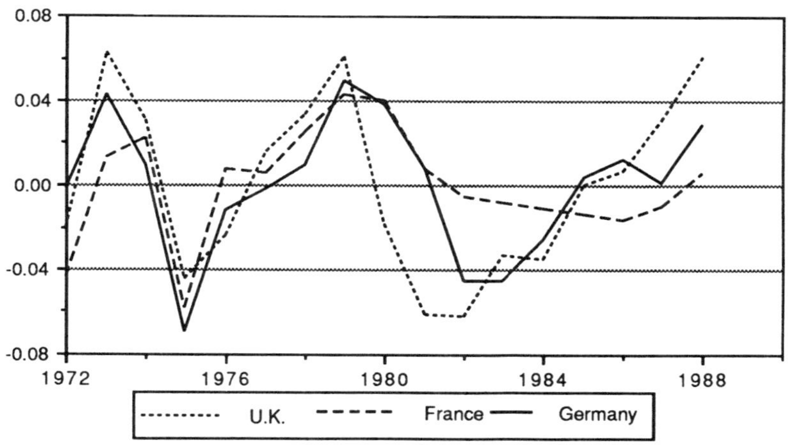

However, closer examination suggests that the three countries were more or less in phase with each other until about 1982, with France enduring a much more prolonged recession in the mid-1980s. Taking the G5 countries as a whole, it is again instructive to return to Table 10.5. With five countries, the number of countries 'in phase' must always be either 3, 4 or 5. Prior to 1971 the average over the twelve years was 3.5. The average for the latter 17 years was 4.1. Prior to 1971, complete synchronisation did occur in the trough of 1963 and the boom of 1969, though there were only two other instances, 1964 and 1967, when even four countries were in phase. In eight of the twelve years the minimum degree of synchronisation occurred. After 1972, once again, synchronisation was greatest during the boom of 1973–4 and the following trough and then from the peak of 1979 until 1983. The only country to move out of line was the UK, which plunged much more deeply into recession after 1979, being below trend during 1980–1 while the rest of G5 was still above trend. Universal expansion occurred again in 1987, with all countries above trend in 1988. In only five of the seventeen years did the minimum degree of synchronisation occur, whereas all five moved together on seven occasions.

iii The group of seven

In examining the G7 countries, the relationship between the US and Canadian economies is important. These two economies are so interlinked that they were out of phase only once in the first period, when the US was a little slower at expanding in 1964, and on only three occasions in the second period, each time being when Canada was a little slower than the US in recovering from a recession. Since these two economies together account for over 41 per cent of OECD industrial output, the US business cycle alone has a very big impact on the pressure of demand for primary products. Taken together, the G7 countries were never all in phase in the first period, yet all seven economies were synchronised on six occasions since 1972. These included the two consecutive boom years of 1973 and 1974, corresponding to the biggest-ever commodity price boom; the recession of 1975, again corresponding to the largest recorded depression in commodity prices and the boom period of 1979, again a boom period for commodity prices. Although all seven economies were not synchronised again until 1983, six of the seven were in phase over the next three years, including the recession of 1982. Full synchronisation occurred again in 1988, along with a commodities prices boom. The average number of G7 countries in phase in the first period was 4.8, increasing to 5.8 in the second period. Thus the major industrial economies, accounting between them for 86.7 per cent of OECD industrial output, showed a marked increase in propensity to move together in the second period. From the above analysis, it is difficult to escape the conclusion that the increase in the volatility of world commodity prices appears to be associated with an increased propensity for the major economies to move together.

iv General conclusions on synchronisation

Taking all of the results together, it appears to be the case that the major industrial economies have moved more in phase with each other during the second period than the first period. This greater degree of synchronisation in the rates of industrial expansion achieved by the major industrial powers has been associated with increased volatility in commodity prices, with feedback effects that have tended to increase the magnitude of cyclical fluctuations in industrial demand and production.

V CONCLUSIONS AND IMPLICATIONS

The theoretical case for policy co-ordination must be made in the context of a model which captures the most important international linkages and policy spillovers. Interaction between the industrial and primary producing sectors may have received insufficient attention in this regard. Consideration of these linkages leads to the view that any proposal for international policy co-ordination that is to have a chance of avoiding the instabilities of the last two decades must go beyond just the stabilising of exchange rates and ensure that aggregate world industrial demand grows at a rate consistent with supply conditions in the primary sector.

Periods of alternating synchronised expansion and contraction by the main industrial powers most certainly do not lead to increased stability. They can only serve to aggravate the inherent tendency towards inflation and recession in the world economy.

NOTES

* This chapter derives from work on the implications of European monetary policy co-ordination for commodity input prices, partially supported by a grant from the European Commission and initially planned in conjunction with Hassan Hakimian of Wye College, University of London. A very early version was presented at the annual conference of the Association of Polytechnic Teachers in Economics (Glasgow 1990) and I am grateful to conference participants for some valuable comments. I also wish to thank Victoria Chick and Philip Arestis for detailed comments on an earlier draft. Remaining shortcomings are mine alone.

1. Also quoted by Currie (1990: 125).
2. An alternative definition might be 'the reduction in discord and increase in harmony among national policies. It is a process by which the policies of each state are adjusted to reduce the adverse consequences, or reinforce the positive effects, as the participants define them, for the policies of other states' (Henning 1987: x).
3. For other expositions, see Currie (1990), Frankel and Rockett (1988), Artis and Ostry (1986), Cooper (1985) and Oudiz and Sachs (1984).

4. The Stackelberg solution is the analogue of the duopoly price-leadership model.
5. See, for example, Frankel and Rockett (1988).
6. *JMK* XXVII. Also see Gilbert (1987).
7. Though Ghosh and Masson (1988) argue that if policy–makers explicitly take account of such uncertainty, the case for co-ordination may be slightly stronger than that indicated by Frankel and Rockett – though under quite restrictive assumptions concerning the allocation of probabilities to each model.
8. Lee (1990), for example, reminds us of the work of Gardner Means in this respect. For further references see Reynolds (1987).
9. The behaviour of a service sector is not crucial for our purposes. It is suggested that part of this sector be allocated to each of the other two sectors, depending on the institutional conditions surrounding each constituent service.
10. See Thirlwall (1989) for further discussion of such models.
11. For further discussion see Reynolds (1987, 1990).
12. For a thorough exposition of such a model, including further references to the literature on small-menu costs, see Hall (1986).
13. Key studies include Eckstein and Fromm (1968), who found that cost factors were more important than demand factors in explaining changes in manufacturing prices in the US economy; and Coutts, Godley and Nordhaus, who examined how industrial prices in the UK responded to short-run changes in demand by testing the hypothesis that 'the firm calculates the level of costs at a normal level of output, and sets prices as a mark-up on normal costs without reference to temporary variations in demand' (1978: 1–2). Their results were interpreted as strongly favouring this hypothesis (*ibid*.: 67). Sawyer (1983) includes results from a fairly comprehensive study based on a sample of 40 UK manufacturing industries for the period 1963–75. In only nine of the 40 industries studied do changes in output have a positive and significant effect on price changes. Sylos-Labini (1979) found similar results in a study of the effects on the aggregate price level of changes in demand and costs for the period 1954–73 for Italy, the United States, the United Kingdom, West Germany and Argentina. A further particularly interesting feature of this study is that the effects of raw-material costs and wage costs were considered separately and that changes in raw-material costs were found to be completely and symmetrically passed on as price changes. Similar but more recent results for the UK, using quarterly data for the period 1965–84 are reported by Arestis (1986).
14. Kaldor's 'ratchet effect' has not gone uncontested. Goldstein (1977) tested for asymmetry in the effect of import price changes on domestic prices for five industrial countries, using a variety of models, and found no evidence of it. Macbean and Nguyen (1987) suggest that this casts doubt on the importance of Kaldor's argument. In fact, the particular asymmetry emphasised by Kaldor concerned the effects of import price changes on wage claims; he argued that real-wage resistance applied more to erosion than to enhancement of workers' income. Furthermore, Sylos-Labini (1979), adopting a post-Keynesian pricing model, provides empirical evidence which concurs with the view that changes in import prices are passed on symmetrically (and completely) whereas changes in wages are passed on asymmetrically and only partially. This would tend to support the view that it is the indirect effects of changes in the terms of trade – via their effect on wages – that are responsible for the ratchet effect suggested by Kaldor.
15. See, for example, Cooper and Lawrence (1975), Sylos-Labini (1982), van Wijnbergen (1985).
16. For references to other empirical studies, see Gilbert (1989, 1990). Also see van Wijnbergen (1985), who finds that OECD unemployment has a statistically significant effect on real commodity prices.

REFERENCES

Arestis, P., 1986, 'Wages and Prices in the UK: The Post-Keynesian View', *Journal of Post Keynesian Economics*, 8, 339–58.

Arestis, P. and Y. Kitromilides, eds, 1990, *Theory and Policy in Political Economy*, Edward Elgar, Aldershot.

Artis, M. and S. Ostry, 1986, *International Economic Policy Coordination*, Royal Institute of Economic Affairs, Chatham House Papers, 30, Routledge & Kegan Paul, London.

Beckerman, W., 1985, 'How the Battle Against Inflation was Really Won', *Lloyds Bank Review*, 155, 1–12.

Beckerman, W. and T. Jenkinson, 1986, 'What Stopped the Inflation? Unemployment or Commodity Prices?' *Economic Journal*, 96, 39–54.

Cooper, R.N., 1985, 'Economic Interdependence and Coordination of Economic Policies', in R. Jones and P.B. Kenen, eds, *Handbook in International Economics*, vol. II, North Holland, Amsterdam.

Cooper, R.N. and R.Z. Lawrence, 1975, 'The 1972–75 Commodity Boom', *Brookings Papers on Economic Activity*, 3.

Coutts, K., W. Godley and W. Nordhaus, 1978, *Industrial Pricing in the United Kingdom*, Cambridge University Press, Cambridge.

Cowling, K. and M. Waterson, 1976, 'Price–Cost Margins and Market Structure', *Economica*, 43, 267–74.

Currie, D., 1990, 'International Policy Coordination', in D.T. Llewellyn and C. Milner, eds, *Current Issues in International Monetary Economics*, Macmillan, London.

Eckstein, O. and G. Fromm, 1968, 'The Price Equation', *American Economic Review*, 58, 1159–83.

Eichner, A.S., 1973, 'A Theory of the Determination of the Mark-up Under Oligopoly', *Economic Journal*, 83, 1184–1200.

Eichner, A.S., 1976, *The Megacorp and Oligopoly*, Cambridge University Press, Cambridge.

Frankel, J.A. and K.E. Rockett, 1988, 'International Macroeconomic Policy Coordination when Policymakers Do Not Agree on the True Model', *American Economic Review*, 78, 318–40.

Ghosh, A.R. and P. Masson, 1988, 'International Policy Coordination in a World with Model Uncertainty', *IMF Staff Papers*, 35, 230–58.

Gilbert, C., 1987, 'International Commodity Agreements: Design and Performance', *World Development*, 15, 591–616.

Gilbert, C., 1989, 'The Impact of Exchange Rates and Developing Country Debt on Commodity Prices', *Economic Journal*, 99, 773–84.

Gilbert, C., 1990, 'Primary Commodity Prices and Inflation', *Oxford Review of Economic Policy*, 6, 77–99.

Goldstein, M., 1977, 'Downward Price Inflexibility, Ratchet Effects, and the Inflationary Impact on Import Price Changes: Some Empirical Evidence', *IMF Staff Papers*, 24, 569–612.

Group of 30, 1988, *International Macroeconomic Policy Coordination*, London.

Grubb, D., 1986, 'Topics in the OECD Phillips Curve', *Economic Journal*, 96, 55–79.

Hall, R., 1986, 'Market Structure and Macroeconomic Fluctuations', *Brookings Papers on Economic Activity*, 2, 285–338.

Hamada, K., 1974, 'Alternative Exchange Rate Systems and the Interdependence of Monetary Policies', in R.Z. Aliber, ed., *National Monetary Policies and the International Financial System*, University of Chicago Press, Chicago.

Hamada, K., 1985, *The Political Economy of International Monetary Interdependence*, MIT Press, Cambridge, Mass.

Henning, C.R., 1987, *Macroeconomic Diplomacy in the 1980s*, The Atlantic Institute for International Affairs, Atlantic paper no. 65, Croom Helm, London.

Hughes-Hallett, A., 1989, 'Macroeconomic Interdependence and the Coordination of Economic Policy', in D. Greenaway, ed., *Current Issues in Macroeconomics*, Macmillan, London.

International Monetary Fund, *International Financial Statistics*, various issues.

Kaldor, N., 1976, 'Inflation and Recession in the World Economy', *Economic Journal*, 86, 703–14.

Kaldor, N., 1983, 'The Role of Commodity Prices in Economic Recovery', *Lloyds Bank Review*, 149, 21–34.

Kalecki, M., 1943, *Studies in Economic Dynamics*, Allen & Unwin, London.

Kalecki, M., 1954, *Theory of Economic Dynamics*, Allen & Unwin, London.

Kalecki, M., 1971, *Selected Essays on the Dynamics of the Capitalist Economy*, Cambridge University Press, Cambridge.

Keynes, J.M., 1980, *The Collected Writings of John Maynard Keynes, Vol. XXVII*, ed. D.E. Moggridge, Macmillan, London.

Lee, F.S., 1990, 'G.C. Means's Doctrine of Administered Prices', in Arestis and Kitromilides, eds (1990).

Macbean, A. and D.T. Nguyen, 1987, 'International Commodity Agreements: Shadow and Substance', *World Development*, 15, 575–90.

OECD, 1990, *Main Economic Indicators*, August.

Oudiz, G. and J. Sachs, 1984, 'Macroeconomic Policy Coordination Among the Industrialised Economies', *Brookings Papers on Economic Activity*, 1, 1–75.

Reynolds, P.J., 1987, *Political Economy: A Synthesis of Kaleckian and Post Keynesian Economics*, Wheatsheaf Books, Brighton.

Reynolds, P.J., 1990, 'Kaleckian and Post Keynesian Theories of Pricing: Some Extensions and Implications', in Arestis and Kitromilides, eds (1990).

Sawyer, M.C., 1983, *Business Pricing and Inflation*, Macmillan, London.

Sylos-Labini, P., 1979, 'Prices and Income Distribution in Manufacturing Industry', *Journal of Post Keynesian Economics*, 2, 3–25.

Sylos-Labini, P., 1982, 'Rigid Prices, Flexible Prices and Inflation', *Banca Nazionale del Lavoro Quarterly Review*, 140, 37–68.

Thirlwall, A.P., 1989, *Growth and Development*, 4th edn, Macmillan, London.

van Wijnbergen, S., 1985, 'Interdependence Revisited: A Developing Countries Perspective on Macroeconomic Management and Trade Policy in the Industrial World', *Economic Policy*, 1, 82–137.

Wallich, H.C., 1984, 'Institutional Cooperation in the World Economy, in J.A. Frenkel and M.L. Mussa, eds, *The World Economic System: Performance and Prospects*, Auburn House, Dover, Mass.

Wood, A., 1975, *A Theory of Profits*, Cambridge University Press, Cambridge.

Name Index

Subject Index